ONE MAN'S WORD

'Better a man with a past, than a man with a future.'
Matthew Parris

ONE MAN'S WORD

The Untold Story of the Cash-for-Questions Affair

IAN GREER

ANDRE DEUTSCH

To Clive Ferreira

And to our parents and families, whose love and
prayers have seen us through.

First published in 1997 by
André Deutsch
a subsidiary of VCI plc
106 Great Russell Street
London WC1B 3LJ

A CIP record for this title is available
from the British Library

ISBN 0 233 99166 2

Typeset by Derek Doyle & Associates
Mold, Flintshire.
Printed and bound by Mackays of Chatham plc.

CONTENTS

ACKNOWLEDGEMENTS

My grateful thanks to David Prosser for his outstanding research and invaluable help.

Particular thanks to my editor, Louise Dixon, my agent, Mary Pachnos, and Gillon Aitken of Aitken and Stone, Mark Stephens of Stephens Innocent, and, for their encouragement and personal support, Michael Dobbs and Matthew Parris.

I would also like to thank all those who have worked at IGA over the past fifteen years for the many kindnesses that they have shown to me and for the part that they played in the success of IGA. In particular those who remained loyal until the bitter end – Sara Bell, Susan Child, Denise Donovan, Patrick Ferreira, Ivo Ilic, Perry Miller, Jeremy Sweeney and Liz Swindin.

For the advice and support of my non-executive directors, I am indebted to Ian Mablin of Wilson Wright, Andrew Stone of Lewis Silkin and the Baroness Turner of Camden.

Of those in the industry, the kindness of Steve Atack, Sir Tim Bell, David Boddy, Michael Burrell, Nick Gibbon, Lord Gillford, Lord Gummer, Tony Knox and Lord Saatchi, has been much appreciated.

I am very grateful to the many parliamentarians, in both Houses and on both sides of the political divide, who have been particularly kind over these past traumatic months, especially David Amess, Sir Graham Bright, John Bowis OBE, Alan Duncan, the Hon Mrs Gwyneth Dunwoody, Rt Hon Tristan Garel-Jones, Rt Hon Jeremy Hanley, Doug Hoyle, Hon Bernard Jenkin, Rt Hon Norman Lamont, Hon Tom Sackville and Sir Michael Thornton.

To the many friends and former clients, whose loyalty to the company and whose personal friendship means so much, thank you. My special thanks to: Stephen Allcock, QC, Mr Dave Allen OBE and Mrs Allen, John Ayre, Rosemary Barker, Mike Beard, Henry Becket, Sheila Black, OBE, Edward Blair, CBE, Mr and Mrs Ray Bowden, Cedric Brown, Brendan Bruce, Marcia Bryce-Cousens, Barbara Burgess, Dominic Cadbury, Lucas Campos, Rachael Canon, Anthony Cardew, Robin Cardozo, Scottie Childs, Robert Clark, David Clark, Tim Clement Jones, Jack Criswell, Phyllis Cunningham, Michael Davidson, Kenrick Davis, Peter Davis, Mr and Mrs Mark Deller, Nicholas Drake, Mr Bert Farrimond, CBE and Mrs Farrimond, Roger Firth, Mr and Mrs Clifford Fisher, Lady Finsberg, Anthony Fry, Sir Edward and Lady Gardner, Mr and Mrs Stephen Gardner, Mr and Mrs Michael Gibbs, Gilly Godfrey, Richard Gordon, Isobel Greenwood, Claes Hall, David Hall, Tony Hardwell, Robert Hayward, OBE, Mr and Mrs Hardy Henniger, Mr and Mrs Michael Hoffman, David Holmes, CB, Gerald Howarth, Peter Ibbotson, Sharon Johnson, Alistair Kendrick, Richard Kramer, Luis Marques, Alistair Michie, Sarah Mindham, Terry Moore, Sir Geoffrey Mulcahy, Philip Naylor, Archie Norman, Mr and Mrs Derek Oakley, Martha Olson, Colin Parsons, Howard Paver, Ann Pettifor, Stephen Pomeroy, Michael Reidy, CBE, Peter Reiser, Charles Richardson, Jeff Richardson, John Roberts, Victoria Schofield, Brett Schneider, Roger Scrutton, John Simmonds, Mary Snowden, Christopher Stainforth, Bradley Stephen, David Stephen, Graeme Strang, Roy Swainson, Belinda Taylor, Tom Thorpe, Mr and Mrs Derek Thrower, Robert Venables, QC, Gloria Walker, Sandy Walkington, Ed Wallis, John Walters, Gary Watson, Mr and Mrs Peter Welch, Francesca Welbore-Ker, Oliver Whitehead, Michael Whittaker, Nigel Whittaker, Mick Williams and Mr and Mrs Jeremy Wyatt.

INTRODUCTION

Politics has been my life. I recall that at the age of twelve, I stood as the Conservative candidate at my school's mock elections. Although I lost the vote heavily, it did not deter me or dampen my enthusiasm for the hustings.

In later life I was to join the Conservative Party as a full-time professional, in an attempt to develop a career within the party organisation. I then believed that I did not have the necessary talents to become a Member of Parliament, but as long as I was in the political fray, I was content. Over the years, however, my view has changed: I think that I would perhaps have succeeded on the parliamentary benches as well as many. An overriding necessity at the time I had to make my decision as to whether or not to follow a parliamentary career was the need to have a sound bank balance. This was something that I did not possess.

I was born in London in 1933. My parents were and are Salvation Army officers. To use today's phrase, they could be described as 'born-again Christians', although my father, like his father before him, concentrated his energies and talents on the Army's business side. My grandfather had been the general manager of the Salvation Army Assurance Society, a large, efficiently run organisation, the profits of which were used to assist with the Army's work both at home and abroad. My father's brother was the society's company secretary and my father held a number of senior positions within the organisation.

Although my father's position within the society was that of a businessman, his commitment was that of a parson: births, marriages, deaths and preaching were interwoven into my parents' lives. My mother devoted herself to social work in whatever town or city we were posted to.

My parents' work in London, Liverpool, Newcastle and Glasgow was, above all, aimed at providing Christian care for those less fortunate than themselves. They were, and remain, able to speak from experience, unlike modern-day lefties, only a few of whom have spent the night looking after those on the streets.

My upbringing was, understandably, influenced by my parents' strong Christian beliefs – grace before meals, the reading of the family Bible and prayers were all an integral part of my childhood. However, my father also had strong political convictions and was a committed Conservative. He believed in prayer, in the helping hand, but also in the individual's ability to make his or her own way in life. Spongers – of whom there were many – shocked my parents, but those in genuine need received the utmost compassion.

My parents were posted to Scotland, where I set foot for the first time at the age of fourteen. My father became manager of the Assurance Society's Scottish office, and we were fortunate to live in a rather old and lovely apartment in the Broomhill area of Glasgow, which I later found out to be in the Hillhead constituency. It was here that I was to join the Young Unionists in time to play an active part in the 1950 and 1951 general elections. It was a great experience and, although I didn't know it at the time, it was to be my first step in what was to become a life dominated by politics.

I was born, my mother tells me, weighing 2lb 12oz (a surprise to those who know me now!), with a grand head of brown hair. As a child, I spent long periods in hospital and this, together with the war and parental moves around the country, might account for my undistinguished academic performance.

On leaving school, I joined a business training college. My ambition then was to become a newspaper journalist. My first job, however, was a temporary one, with the Scottish electricity authority. My short spell there was memorable in one particular respect: I won the 'best speaker' competition for Scotland. Shortly after that, the family was back on the move again, to London this time, and for me it was into real politics. Initially, I was a constituency campaign organiser for the Conservative Party, paid £6 per week. Later I was to work at Central Office, and was eventually appointed the party's youngest agent. It was enormously hard work, great fun and very exciting.

During the thirteen years I spent working for the Conservative Party, I met many people who were later to become Members of Parliament, Cabinet Ministers, party leaders and also firm friends. It was a splendid grounding for later life and taught me a tremendous amount about people, their ambitions and the lengths to which they would go to fulfil them.

In 1965, aged 32, towards the end of my career at Central Office I harboured ambitions of standing as a Conservative candidate and subsequently put my name forward. My application was rejected. I asked to be given the opportunity to see Richard Sharples, a former government minister and the then Deputy Chairman of the Conservative Party, responsible for candidate selection. I wanted to know why my application had been rejected. The interview with Mr Sharples was rather short – he huffed and puffed, seemed anxious and yet reluctant to give me the reasons. He found it difficult to use the word 'homosexual' (gay was not a word that had been coined at that time). Although it seemed unlikely that I would be the first such person who had ever walked through the Members' entrance, it was sufficient to put a black mark against me, and it put an end to my parliamentary ambitions. I was disappointed, but not terribly surprised. I was not destined to become an 'honourable Member'.

At about this time, I decided to confront the issue of my sexuality with my parents. It was difficult. Homosexuality was still illegal. My parents were active, committed Christians, working very publicly within the Salvation Army. I plucked up the courage to speak to them both one Saturday evening. I believe that it is fair to say that they had suspected what I had known all along, but they had hoped against hope that they were wrong. When I had finished explaining my position, I remember well that my father put both his hands on my shoulders and said, 'Son, you are what God made you. It does not matter what or who you are. What matters is how you live your life. All we ask is that you keep your faith and ensure that you care for others.'

We have always been a close family. Being an only child carries with it the advantage of being the apple of one's parents' eyes and, later, shouldering the responsibility for their care. The joy of my life has been the fact that I have been able to talk to them about every aspect of it. They have been and remain, above all else, good friends. Their faith has helped to sustain not only them, but me too, in what has been a devastating period.

I left the Conservative Party in 1966 to take a position as national director of the Mental Health Trust (MHT), a cause that appealed to me enormously. The MHT was an organisation, created by the good and the great, with two clear objectives. The first was to remove the public stigma of mental illness by establishing a nationwide organisation to campaign for a new understanding for sufferers and their families. The statistics of those affected by mental illness were horrific, and, by and large, their care was undertaken in underfunded institutions. The second objective was to raise money in order to allow progress to be made. The Trust's president was the former Conservative Deputy Prime Minister, Lord (Rab) Butler, a Master of Trinity, Cambridge, whom I had known for many years. On my first day, the Trust's chairman, Evelyn de Rothschild, entertained me to lunch at Claridges, a rather formidable experience. Other colourful characters, such as Jocelyn Stevens (now Sir Jocelyn, Chairman of English Heritage), played an important role in the furtherance of the Trust's aims.

My experience in politics was good training for charity work. Party battles – be they at a constituency or a national level – are nothing compared to charity warfare.

My experiences at the MHT demonstrated to me the opportunities that existed to lobby the government on a whole host of issues – social, commercial, financial and good causes. So, after two years, I decided to establish a professional lobbying company, aimed at ensuring a better understanding between government and those who felt it was out of touch with their interests. I studied the system in the United States, where lobbyists were playing an increasingly important role in the formulation of administration and government policy on a whole raft of state and national issues.

In 1970, together with a close personal friend, John Russell, I launched Russell Greer, one of the country's first political lobbying companies. John and I had known each other for many years. He had graduated from Oxford and was working at the large and successful insurance brokers Sedgwick Collins, prior to launching the company with me. He was bright, charming and able.

Sadly, we were ahead of our time. Belief in the old-boy network still prevailed. The friends and contacts I had established while working for the MHT, and whom I genuinely believed needed our help and advice in pursuing the government on issues relevant to their employees' and shareholders' interests, did not share my views: the occasional shoot with the constituency MP, or contact with a brother-in-law in the Lords continued to dominate their approach to the briefing of parliamentarians. This, together with the reading of the *Financial Times*, were considered sufficient to see a company through any matter that had political ramifications.

Russell Greer therefore struggled, and the bank inevitably pressed. The first client we were appointed by was the London Taxi Drivers' Association, at a fee of £250 (even in those days, a fee with which it was difficult to keep the wolf from the door). We had taken offices on the top floor of 13 Hill Street, London W1, the then new premises of surveyors Strutt and Parker. We furnished the offices rather well, which meant that we found it difficult to muster the financial resources to employ enough staff. Other clients did, however, follow: the Government of Zambia, MacDonald Douglas, Fisons, Midshires Building Society, Midland Bank, and the Unitary Tax Campaign were among our early successes. We were eventually able to move to Mount Street in Mayfair and the staff grew to about a dozen, although profits remained poor.

After twelve years I decided to make a break and, with a £5,000 bank loan, launched Ian Greer Associates (IGA). Four former employees of Russell Greer joined me in my new venture –

Wendy Donovan, my hard-working and efficient secretary; Rhys Manley-Sale, a highly intelligent and breathtakingly flamboyant Canadian; Charles Miller, who now runs his own successful lobbying company and is Secretary of the Association of Professional Political Consultants; and, the youngest of the team, John Roberts, who had just given up a career at the Foreign Office. It was a team that lacked experience but knew the importance of hard work. John Roberts, particularly, was not only outstandingly talented and able, but also proved – in both good and bad times – to have a maturity beyond his years and, more importantly, a loyalty and commitment that have remained true.

The company grew at a phenomenal rate and staff numbers increased. Three more people joined the company at an early stage: Andrew Smith, a young, bright, enthusiastic ex-Ministry of Agriculture, Fisheries and Food employee; Brian Baxter, a former junior Foreign Office official; and Stanley Godfrey, the former press secretary to the then Chancellor of the Exchequer.

IGA blossomed, moving into charming, well-appointed offices close to the Houses of Parliament and Whitehall. Its clients and staff were to multiply. Within twelve short years, offices were established in Brussels, Scotland and Ireland; associate offices were launched in Eastern Europe and the United States. It had, at its peak, fifty employees and the longest list of blue-chip clients of any political consultancy in London and Brussels, including British Airways, Midland Bank, Coca-Cola, Philips and Drew, Cadbury Schweppes, Whitbread, Prudential, Philip Morris, Thames Water, Kingfisher, Asda, British Gas, Short Brothers, Plessey, Calor, the Royal Ordnance Company, Trafalgar House, and the governments of Canada, Malaysia, Pakistan, Kuwait and Taiwan. It was also involved in campaigns to save the Royal Marsden, Brompton and St Mary's hospitals, the campaign for heads of household passports for Hong Kong residents, and that for leasehold reform. The company was regularly called upon to play its part in mergers and acquisitions where there was a political aspect, along with privatisations.

Our success allowed us to provide a free service to the charity ActionAid and, later, to the London and Brussels bureaux of the African National Congress. I was particularly delighted to be able to assist the ANC. I had always abhorred apartheid, and strongly believe that irrespective of race, religion or creed, all men and women are equal. I was a member of the Anti-Apartheid League during my time as a Conservative Party agent, something which, at the time, would have raised a few eyebrows in the party. The opportunity to play a small part in helping the ANC in preparation for democratic government delighted me. Over the years, there were others, however, who sought our advice and support to whom, out of conscience, we said no, such as the apartheid government of South Africa, the pro-whaling and fur-trapping campaigns and a Scandinavian government which wanted to continue their practice of seal culling.

I have never found any easy rule of thumb for accepting – or declining – work on grounds of like or dislike for the cause. The simplest position – easily argued in a newspaper column – is to accept no brief with which one is not in full-hearted personal accord, but no barrister (indeed no builder, publisher or dry-cleaner) could live by that, and it is arguable that all who believe they have a case should be able to take advice on presenting it. To say otherwise may be to condemn unfashionable or minority interests to a sort of silent censorship – as struck me when I turned down an offer of work from the Libyan Government (it was subsequently taken up, I noted, by my competitors, GJW). But sometimes a brief does stick in the throat and one takes a personal decision not to touch it. This is a gut reaction and actually harder to justify than the professional advocate's moral neutrality.

In 1992 I was appointed by the Home Office to the Board of Visitors at Wormwood Scrubs. It was something that I had wanted to do for a long time. To say that I enjoyed it would be wrong, but being able to visit the prison at any time, being provided with the keys to open any door or enter any cell was an amazing experience, and one that I will not forget. The hopelessness of so many saddened me profoundly. The unpleasantness of a large number of them was frightening, as was the treatment by inmates of those of their fellow prisoners who were weak, black, or, like me, gay. The bureaucracy of the prison administration was overwhelming, making any change in the regime almost impossible. I resigned eighteen months later.

I turned down offers to sell IGA on half a dozen occasions because I was devoted to the staff and their excellence. They were young men and women to whom I wanted to hand over the business. Selling would not guarantee their futures, so I carried on, seeing the company's income grow to almost £4 million. Its reputation was second to none. Its ethos was to provide an un-rivalled expertise to clients – but above all to have fun doing so.

Re-reading my manuscript, I can almost predict the reviews before they are written. They will say we were blind, careless, self-serving: that this is a tale of greed. With hindsight I can understand that judgement. My account could have been a breast-beating lamentation from one era, over an era which has passed; or it could have been a litany of special pleading from a man still unable to understand the indignation with which the nineties views the habits of the eighties. I wanted it to be neither. I just wanted to record how it seemed at the time.

A repeated cry of 'mea culpa' may give satisfaction to the censorious, yet obscure real shifts in the mind-set of a political class and its commentators. I have preferred to describe the mind-set as it was. I must accept without complaint the indignation of readers who would have preferred to encounter a text laced with gasps of shame and horror; and reviewers who look for a chronicle of human aberration from the accepted norm may miss the sense of sin such a chronicle would convey. But to dismiss IGA's work as an aberration is exactly what today's lobbying industry and today's MPs, who were my colleagues and friends yesterday, would prefer. The sensationalist view is altogether too convenient.

1

'I WANT PROCESSIONS IN THE PARLIAMENTS'

'I an, I think I've got some business for you.' Lord King, the chairman of British Airways and one of Mrs Thatcher's favourite businessmen, was on the phone. 'I've met someone who could do with your help.' It was October 1985. Business had never been better. Within days of Lord King's introduction, another household name – the Knightsbridge store Harrods and its Egyptian owner, Mohamed Fayed (also known as Mohamed Al-Fayed) – would be added to my company's already growing list of clients.

My first fateful meeting with the ebullient Fayed was professional, businesslike – the histrionics were to come later. We shook hands one Monday evening at his elegant Park Lane apartment. It seemed a routine business deal. Little did I know that I had just set the scene for what was to become one of the biggest political scandals in decades. In the space of less than ten years, four government ministers would be forced to resign. The Prime Minister would take the unprecedented step of announcing to the House of Commons that he was not prepared to give in to blackmail. Lord Nolan would be asked to draw up a new parliamentary code for MPs, drastically curtailing their scope for outside earnings. Self-regulation would be lost. The reputation of the Palace of Westminster, the mother of all Parliaments, would be dragged through the mud and MPs would replace journalists and estate agents as the number-one social pariahs. And my multi-million-pound firm would collapse in ruins about me. Political lobbying would become the new swear word. The

1

name Ian Greer, thanks to the *Guardian* newspaper, would wrongly become synonymous with sleaze.

As you will read in these pages, many people were damaged by Fayed: Margaret Thatcher, her son Mark, Home Secretary Michael Howard, half a dozen ministers of the crown, and a string of little-known backbench MPs – all would get caught up in the so-called cash-for-questions affair. All these individuals appear in these pages. Some allegations will be heard for the first time, but the *Guardian* reader will be disappointed to learn at the outset that one essential allegation is untrue: I was asked to do a lot of things, but I was never given cash by Mohamed Fayed to pass to MPs to table questions or for any other reason. One MP, Tim Smith, admits he *was* paid directly as a consultant, some of it in cash. Another, Neil Hamilton, vigorously defends himself against the charge that he received any payment from Fayed, and, despite knowing him for many years, I have no information to offer to the contrary.

But it is still a story of greed, arrogance and excess involving MPs; of miscalculations and attempts to obscure the truth; and of mistakes, many my own. It is the story of a powerful businessman whose actions were to damage the reputation of a number of Her Majesty's ministers.

Members of the government will ask me why I, a committed Conservative supporter for forty years, must tell a story which can only embarrass them. My answer is simply the frustration of not having been able to tell my side of the story before. By abandoning my libel action against the *Guardian* (a mistake, I now realise) I gave the green light for anyone to say whatever they wanted about me. Faced by the resulting ferocious onslaught, I could not ask or expect my clients to stay with me. Journalists, who before had been sceptical of the allegations made against me, suddenly began to believe they might be true. To some it seemed as though I was admitting to the accusation of cash for questions, by refusing at the eleventh hour to fight my corner.

So here I am, a little late in the day, fighting my corner. I realise, if I am to be believed by you, the reader, I cannot deny you information which is relevant. Many confidences – and in forty years in politics, as you can imagine, I was privy to a great number of conversations – have been left out to protect the individuals who have played no part in this episode. But I have included many details on the conduct of MPs where they provide the context and understanding of the world we inhabited in the eighties.

The story begins midway through that decade with one of the bloodiest takeover battles in British corporate history. Lord King had met Ali Fayed, the brother of Mohamed Fayed, by chance, on a British Airways flight. The Egyptian poured his heart out to the BA chairman, who was one of my favourite clients. Ali and Mohamed had just spent £615 million in securing a controlling interest in the House of Fraser – a vast chain of department stores stretching from Scotland to Scandinavia and employing 23,000 people. Harrods was the jewel in its crown. But the Fayed brothers were unable to enjoy their new purchase, being subjected to a daily bombardment of damaging allegations and innuendo from the man they had beaten in the takeover battle, Tiny Rowland, chief executive of Lonrho, the UK-based mining and minerals group. Their feud was little other than a bitter public slanging match. Rowland used the editorial columns of the *Observer* newspaper, which Lonrho owned, to blacken the reputation of Mohamed Fayed, challenging his ancestry and his wealth. Sir Edward du Cann, kingmaker in the 1975 Tory leadership contest and chairman of Lonrho, championed Rowland's cause in the House of Commons.

I wish John King had been present at that first meeting with the Fayed brothers, as arranged, for it was here that I am supposed to have made my most memorable remark to date: that you have to 'rent an MP like you rent a London taxi'. With the meeting scheduled for 6.30 pm, Lord King pulled out at the last minute due to pressure of work and I made my own way to 60 Park Lane – Fayed's imposing six-storey apartment block next door to the Dorchester Hotel.

I found the entranceway protected by two sets of bullet-proof glass doors, which trapped me between them like a vacuum-packed meal while a security guard, inside the building, examined my image on a television monitor. 'An unusual security precaution,' I thought. I was used to such contraptions in some embassies, I was aware they were common for biological warfare establishments, but not private residences in fashionable Mayfair. Momentarily, I found myself wondering how much oxygen shared my eight foot by six container.

My calculations were interrupted. 'Mr Fayed is waiting for you on the fourth floor,' the security guard announced. I entered the building proper.

It may not have been the fourth floor. On every occasion I visited 60 Park Lane – and it must have been about twelve occasions in all – I was directed to a different floor. Sometimes I would meet Mohamed Fayed in small rooms the size of shoeboxes; at other times in vast suites with views across Hyde Park. Quite often, directed to a particular room, I would sit patiently waiting, when suddenly a bookcase in the wall would slide open, and he would appear with a flourish.

'Why,' I asked him one day, 'do you keep using different rooms?'

'Security, Ian. Security,' he muttered darkly. Over the next eight years I was to learn much of Mr Fayed's anxiety over security.

That evening I was entertained in one of the best rooms in the building. There was plenty of gold. Beautiful sofas and one or two original masters graced the gently lit room, creating an air of restrained opulence. The butler brought us drinks. Mohamed occupied a sofa on my right; Ali, one on the left. I took a chair between them. Facing me, large windows overlooked a rapidly darkening Hyde Park.

'You know, Mr Greer, how we are suffering,' Mohamed led. 'Lord King speaks very highly of you. What can you do for us?'

These were clearly high-powered businessmen. They were polite, charming even – but I could see it was straight down to business. Ali said very little, but Mohamed was keen to drop both the Prime Minister's and the Sultan of Brunei's names very early in the conversation. Mohamed had taken tea at Number 10 in January, when sterling was in desperate trouble on the foreign exchanges. He had invited along his 'close friend', the Sultan of Brunei. The Sultan, the richest man on earth, had granted Fayed power of attorney over his funds when buying the Dorchester Hotel next door. Joining forces with Mrs Thatcher, Mohamed Fayed had persuaded the Sultan, who had moved £5 billion out of sterling, to do Britain a good turn and move it back. The pound stabilised. If anything should have earned Fayed his longed-for British citizenship, it was his orchestration of this meeting. The Sultan, clearly impressed with Mrs Thatcher, followed it up with £½ billion of defence purchases from British firms.

Mohamed boasted about his hotline to Number 10. He was clearly in favour at the time and bragged about how he was 'accepted' by the Conservative Party. He mentioned his friend Lord Bramall, the former Chief of Defence Staff and currently Lord-Lieutenant of London – 'a close friend of mine, Mr Greer, as well as a close friend of Her Majesty the Queen'. He would later claim that Lord Bramall had signed his application for a British passport.

According to the *Sunday Telegraph* the Fayeds were 'one of Egypt's most distinguished families'; 'fabulous Pharaohs' living off 'fourth-generation Egypt money', said the *Financial Times*. 'Cotton millionaires for 100 years', echoed the *Daily Mail* and a host of other newspapers. City bankers Kleinwort Benson concurred: they were worth 'billions', with 'widespread international interests' including shipping, hotels, construction, oil, banking and property ranging from London's Park Lane to the Paris Ritz to New York's Rockefeller Center. In Scotland, the Fayeds own 32,000 acres at Easter Ross.

But now, the Fayeds having beaten Lonrho to the grand prize of Harrods, Tiny Rowland was attacking Mohamed's character and suggesting he had lied about his ancestry and his wealth. The *Observer* was claiming, rightly as it transpired, that Fayed had adopted the 'al', suggesting noble birth, in his name in the late seventies. Rather than being the inheritor of old money, Fayed's wealth originated from the far more recent Middle East oil boom. In every meeting, every telephone conversation, in every single encounter I had with Fayed, four words would keep cropping up time and again: 'honour', 'dignity', 'pride' and 'family'. He became obsessed with Tiny Rowland's assaults and thought about how to stop, or avenge, them every moment of the day.

Mohamed Fayed explained that he already paid one MP, the recently knighted Sir Peter Hordern, to act as a parliamentary adviser to the House of Fraser. As far as he was concerned, the fifty-six-year-old Hordern was a fine English gentleman, but not really suited to the kind of guerrilla-warfare tactics which would be required if they were to out-manoeuvre Lonrho. The Fayeds needed a champion in the House of Commons to match Sir Edward du Cann, whom they regarded as an effective advocate of Rowland's cause. Peter Hordern was an old-fashioned type of Tory, a little pompous, perhaps, but he was listened to by ministers. However, I could understand why a tough Middle-Eastern businessman like Fayed would feel he was not 'aggressive' enough for the battle ahead. Hordern boasted to me once that in all the years he had worked for House of Fraser he had never asked one parliamentary question on Fayed's behalf. I believe that partly explains the Egyptian's subsequent obsession with parliamentary questions – a device which, I have always felt, was of limited value.

I explained what I could do for them. Firstly – as for all clients – provide political intelligence, ensuring they would not be out-witted by any sudden legislative changes. Secondly, keep them abreast of what the other side – the Rowlands and the du Canns – might be up to in the House. Thirdly, ensure ministers, special advisers, MPs, civil servants and peers on both sides of the House were briefed on Fayed's concerns: hardly difficult, I thought, Mohamed was certainly favoured in government circles over Rowland. The Lonrho boss was, in Ted Heath's phrase, 'the unacceptable face of capitalism'.

I put to Fayed the idea that we should try to mobilise a well-briefed group of MPs to counter the Lonrho influence in the House. We agreed a fee for my company of £25,000 per annum, and I left after about forty-five minutes, thinking I had done rather well. In the flurry of excitement which always follows the signing of a new client, I did not heed the words of my good friend the Labour MP Doug Hoyle, 'Don't get involved with these men,' he cautioned.

Over the next eight years, Fayed demanded everything from parliamentary questions and Early Day Motions to processions through Parliament. Often I would take his calls after lunch – he was usually a bit more aggressive at these times. He would use the same phrase over and over again: 'Ian,' he would shout, 'they are shitting on me from a great height.' It became a standing joke in the office. I would return from lunch to be told: 'Big Mo's been on the phone. It's falling on him yet again.'

'They' were invariably Rowland, du Cann, a group of hostile Labour MPs and the media. Momentarily I would allow my mind to wander, visualising the image, as he regaled me with the latest insults to which he had been subjected. 'Please, Ian, I beg of you,' he would plead in his heavily accented voice. 'Your friends must do more. I want action. I want it now. I want processions in the Parliaments.' It was always 'parliaments' in the plural.

The idea that I could persuade Peter Hordern and the others to march through Central Lobby chanting Fayed's name aloud in a public show of support was ludicrous, but seriously suggested. The only procession I have ever seen through the Commons is at the Queen's Speech. Even given Fayed's delusions of grandeur, and the Royal Warrants bestowed on Harrods, I had to break the news gently: he did not have the same pulling power as Her Majesty.

I doubt that even 'processions in the Parliaments' would have satisfied Mohamed Fayed – unless of course they had been led by Black Rod bearing Tiny Rowland's head aloft. Neil Hamilton notes how Mohamed was always very insistent on the telephone. I would go further and say he became close to a bully: to me, his staff and our band of supportive MPs. Often, in a desire to please him, MPs tabled questions at times when I felt that silence would have served us better. Only questions would keep Mohamed happy as they provided opportunities for publicity.

Despite his outrageous demands and his temperamental outbursts, I liked him. At our meetings, I watched nervously as he would clench his fist and bring it down heavily on the table, narrowly avoiding the bone china teapot. The cups would rattle and the cake would come dangerously close to slipping off on to the floor. But he rarely got angry with me – his apparent violent intent was directed at his enemies. I feared more for the carpet.

2

AWKWARD QUESTIONS

Back in 1958 I was asked by Peter Walker, the parliamentary candidate for Dartford, to be his agent – much to the annoyance of Central Office. I left Willesden East, where I had been the agent for two years, and went to join Peter. Once there, I teamed up with his young personal assistant, Michael Grylls, who was later to enter Parliament himself, become an influential backbencher, and play such an important part in this story.

During the general election campaign of 1959, the previous (and unsuccessful) Tory candidate came to the constituency to speak for Peter Walker. She had put up a good fight in 1955 and been selected for a much safer seat in a North London suburb. Her name was Margaret Thatcher. I gave her a lift back to London and she joked about how she was glad to be selected for Finchley, leaving behind the Dartford Conservative Association and particularly its chairman, Penny Everard, JP, who, we agreed, was a woman consumed by her own self-importance and the hat she would wear on the magistrates' bench.

After Dartford I became the agent for Billericay and remained friends with the constituency's MP, Sir Edward Gardner, long after leaving Essex. One evening in 1980, I called at his Gray's Inn flat, and together we headed out to dinner, where he introduced me to a bright and affable young MP who had just been elected to represent Huntingdonshire. I was meeting many people in those days, but I must admit that it did not occur to me that either Margaret Thatcher or John Major would be future prime ministers.

When I launched IGA in 1982 I had little money, but many

friends. I probably knew personally half the Cabinet, half the junior ministers and half the parliamentary party from my time working at Central Office, when I would have met them as young candidates. Mrs Thatcher was installed in Downing Street and the market revolution was under way. The total defeat of the unions after the miners' strike had destroyed, once and for all, the Conservative Party's 'corporatist tendency'. There would be no more beer and sandwiches for union bosses at Number 10. Large-scale privatisations were planned and the business community began to sit up and take note. I had hit the market at the right time. In just the same way as companies hired professional advisers such as solicitors, accountants, management consultants and PR men, so too were they beginning to realise they needed professional advice to protect and promote them in the world of politics. I was not the only one to see the new opportunities. From the outset, I had competition. Within weeks of IGA's launch we were appointed by a whole raft of clients. But by far the most important account we gained in the early days was British Airways.

John King telephoned my friend Michael Grylls virtually in despair one day. Such a call was not unusual. Michael, as chairman of the Conservative Backbench Trade and Industry Committee, was on good terms with many leading British industrialists. Although never enjoying ministerial office himself, he was rightly regarded as having the ear of ministers on important trade and industry matters. He was often sounded out as he represented Conservative backbench opinion, which was far more enthusiastic about privatisation than parts of Whitehall. Lord King was growing frustrated by the lack of government support for his ambitions for British Airways.

'I will shoot myself shortly. I'm getting nowhere with the Department of Transport!' he exclaimed. 'I've got some public affairs people called Shandwick, but they are not getting anywhere.'

'Why don't you meet a chap I know called Ian Greer? He's good,' Grylls suggested.

And so a meeting was arranged. Within days I met with the

British Airways chairman and proposed a series of briefings of backbench Tory MPs to kick-start a parliamentary campaign to pressurise the government. Lord King was impressed by the approach. However, just as IGA was about to be appointed, *Private Eye* ran a story about me.

It was not a particularly malicious swipe, but potentially quite damaging. The piece stated that all the boys at Ian Greer Associates were very attractive. The implication was clear: Ian Greer must be gay, but the magazine did not have the guts to say so. It was the first of a decade of articles from timorous journalists who could not bring themselves to use the word 'homosexual', but would make great play of the fact that I was a bachelor, had never married, and that I lived with another man, who was described as my 'personal assistant'. Clive Ferreira, whom I met in 1982, is a barrister and a director of the company, and much more besides. He has been my great strength during the past three years. Few people I met in business or politics cared two hoots about our relationship. Of those that did, most showed us the respect they would have shown any couple – which is why I grew angry with the constant references in the press to my 'personal circumstances' and the insinuation that there was something wrong.

We had received a tip-off about the first *Private Eye* article. We knew it would be out the following morning. Of all days, Nigel Lawson, the Chancellor of the Exchequer, had agreed to lunch at the Connaught Hotel with the chairmen of twenty British companies, who were my clients. What the hell was I going to do, I wondered.

I rose early the next morning and went to a newsagent. I stood in the shop staring at the small article, absolutely horrified. My company had been in business for nearly two years. This was a vital occasion for me. I knew that Lawson's officials would be tut-tutting over a copy of *Private Eye* and saying, 'Really, Chancellor, I don't think you ought to keep this engagement.' If Nigel Lawson cancels lunch, I am dead, I thought.

I raked over the contacts book I carry around in my head. A good friend of mine, Sheila Black, worked on the *Financial Times*.

I knew she was great friends with Nigel Lawson, who had been on the paper with her in the late fifties. 'Sheila, I'm in a mess,' I pleaded with her. 'Can you have a word with Nigel Lawson and ensure that he doesn't cancel lunch?'

Sheila rang the Chancellor and, much to my relief, he came. I sat opposite him. It was an excellent lunch. He spoke well. As I was seeing the Chancellor out, I said, 'Nigel, thank you for coming today. There must have been some doubts in your mind.'

'Don't mention it,' he replied. I should not have feared. He was too big a man to be embarrassed by a story in *Private Eye*.

Our contract with British Airways was put on hold.

Several months later, however, in July 1984, Nicholas Ridley, Secretary of State for Trade and Industry, brought out a consultation paper in which the Civil Aviation Authority proposed that, as British Caledonian wasn't doing very well, British Airways should give up many of their most profitable routes and hand them to British Caledonian. Lord King hit the roof, as you might imagine. Ian Greer Associates was appointed within the hour. The House of Commons was about to rise for the summer recess but we launched an enormous campaign which developed extraordinary backbench Tory support. The campaign made Nicholas Ridley's life hell, but it was a great success and as a result, BA gained a reversal of the policy. Although BA lost its lucrative Gulf routes, it won South America in return. (The Gulf routes were reacquired when BA took over British Caledonian in 1987.) Through that campaign I developed a friendship with Lord King, who became one of IGA's greatest supporters.

On the back of our success we would gain many new clients. Besides privatisations, the eighties saw a great number of takeover battles. The electronics giant Plessey hired us to help stave off a hostile takeover bid from GEC. Midland Bank reappointed IGA when threatened by Lloyds. After a major battle, Midland were saved when the Hongkong & Shanghai Bank made a friendly bid. During a takeover battle I would join the company's bankers, accountants and solicitors at morning meetings with the chairman and chief executive. We would be mobilising parliamentary and ministerial support, highlighting, for instance, the impact on jobs for various Members' constituencies if the takeover went ahead.

From having ignored Westminster and Whitehall through the seventies, it became recognisably necessary for companies to hire lobbyists during the eighties. Later, they began to set up teams in-house. Some would drop companies like IGA. Many would keep them.

Reading the newspapers these past couple of years one would think lobbying was the most thoroughly wicked of professions and we wielded unwarranted influence on government. Some have the impression we spent all our time wining and dining, whilst having 'quiet words' in a minister's ear. What is forgotten is that politicians are anxious to be well informed. Good, confidential briefing helps them understand a company's problems and ensures better legislation.

At IGA we had a full-time Research and Information Unit scrutinising every page of *Hansard*, every newspaper and every published government white paper. We had a three-person Policy Unit which would do nothing other than analyse Government and Opposition policy and pore over think-tank reports. We had account executives who were steeped in the client's business.

Clients were impressed to receive a call at 10.30 on a Sunday morning at home to be told by an IGA executive, 'I've been going through this morning's papers. I see there is a piece in the *Telegraph* which is unhelpful to our case. Here are the options . . .' Our system was to have a duty roster with someone going through all the papers from 6.30 am. The directors would know by 7.30 if there was anything they should draw their clients' attention to. Often I would get called in the car if there was an important development and would pick up the phone to a client there and then. That was if a company chairman, such as Lord King, had not already phoned me. He would begin his day around 6.30 – even earlier as we neared the last leg of privatisation. It became a race to see whether I could get in and out of the bath before Lord King telephoned.

13

At our zenith, IGA would be orchestrating two or three lunches each day and possibly a dinner most evenings where our clients would brief ministers, MPs or peers. We quickly realised that Members appreciated three things: taxis, good briefings and discipline. I rarely trusted MPs to find their own way to IGA's or the client's offices for lunch. Navigating London's streets in search of the Savoy or Howard Hotel – other favourite luncheon spots – could prove too much for some Members, so I would station an IGA member of staff at the Members' entrance of the Palace of Westminster. Armed with a list of who was expected where, he would direct the right MP into the right taxi. Each MP would receive a further copy of the two-page briefing note they had been sent earlier, setting out the controversy to date together with recent developments (BA's drive for privatisation, or the *Observer*'s attacks on House of Fraser, for instance), and brief biographies on whom the MP was about to meet.

Meanwhile, I would be putting my client through his or her paces, rehearsing exactly what he or she planned to say. Invariably, at the end of a lunch or dinner, as an MP relaxed over coffee he would turn to his host and say, 'Thank you for lunch, now tell me, what action would you like me to take?' It was fatal if my client answered, 'Well, I'm not really sure.' They would know in advance how to answer.

Lunch would finish promptly at 2.15 pm. It was important that clients demonstrated that they were busy people. A taxi would be waiting to ferry each MP back to the House of Commons. We would breathe a collective sigh of relief, sit back and assess the success – or otherwise – of the occasion. Promises given to supply additional information or draft questions would be given further consideration.

IGA also organised several lunches a year with the chairmen of client companies. They were normally held at the Connaught or Berkeley Hotels, and were off-the-record briefings which were appreciated by all. Company guests for such occasions included the Prime Minister, the Rt Hon. John Major, Nigel Lawson, Norman Lamont, Gillian Shephard, Norman Tebbit and

Leon Brittan. Labour parliamentarians were also happy to accept IGA invitations to meet captains of industry – Tony Blair, Margaret Beckett and Chris Smith amongst them.

Many evening functions took place elsewhere. I would go back to the office after a Commons reception to pick something up on my way home. It would be ten, eleven, even twelve at night, and I would find the place buzzing. I adored my staff – their professionalism and their enthusiasm – but I would worry for them too. They repaid me with an intense loyalty. There was hardly any turnover of staff. Until the end, that is, when all fifty lost their jobs.

In the autumn of 1985 Mohamed Fayed's battle with Lonrho was receiving regular national press coverage. The House of Fraser, although not our most lucrative contract (it was about one-third the size of British Airways), was nevertheless a high-profile campaign. With Margaret Thatcher and Norman Tebbit the main butt of the *Observer*'s attacks, it was a campaign in which I knew it would not be difficult to interest a number of MPs.

In 1981 the Monopolies and Mergers Commission had rejected Lonrho's bid for the House of Fraser. For Neil Hamilton, a young tax barrister at the time, the decision – based on guidelines inherited from the previous Labour Government – demonstrated everything that was wrong with old-style government control. The MMC thought Lonrho lacked experience in retailing, plus the company's fifteen top executives were ageing and they felt 'overstrain' could set in. Hamilton believed this kind of interference was absurd. It was not the role of government to second-guess boardroom decisions.

In 1984, with a hundred-seat majority in the House, the Conservative Government caught up with the market-driven radicalism of some of the younger members of their party. The Trade and Industry Secretary, Norman Tebbit, announced that, in future, planned mergers or takeovers would only be halted if they were likely to have an adverse effect on competition. The 'Tebbit Doctrine', as it was known, came at a crucial moment in the fortunes of the House of Fraser. After their 1981 knock-back,

Lonrho believed that they were out of the running for the control of House of Fraser and, on 2 November 1984, decided to dispose – temporarily they thought – of their 29.9 per cent holding in the group to Mohamed Fayed (a Lonrho board member at the time), while the MMC took three months to look once again at Lonhro's offer for the company. With Tebbit's sudden announcement, the Fayed brothers were allowed a clear run in their takeover ambitions. Suddenly, the brothers produced £615 million in cash and on one feverish day bought every House of Fraser share they could lay their hands on through their Liechtenstein-registered company, Alfayed Investment and Trust (UK) Limited (AIT). Three days later, Lonrho's Tiny Rowland won permission to make a counter-bid. But it was too late: AIT were in control, and not willing to sell.

The Fayeds' takeover still had to be approved by the DTI. The Egyptian brothers had produced a lot of money, but Norman Tebbit found it was vouchsafed by an impeccable source: John MacArthur, a director of Kleinwort Benson, who went on television to say the Fayeds' 'net worth, from what I know, is several billion dollars'. The merchant bank produced a prospectus – a document which would in later years reduce the bank to 'speechless shame' according to Rowland – which stated 'the al-Fayed family is an old established Egyptian family, which has interests in the USA, Europe and the Middle East which include, in particular, shipping, construction, oil, banking and property. The shipping companies are based in Genoa, Piraeus, London, Dubai and Egypt'. An impressed Norman Tebbit waved the bid through in ten days.

Tiny Rowland smelt a rat. Sixty-six years old, and over six feet tall – hence 'Tiny' – Rowland was born R W Fuhrhop, in India, the son of a German father and a British mother. Just before the Second World War, he dropped his father's name, but spent part of the war as an alien living on the Isle of Man. After the war, aged thirty, he made a fresh start in Africa, turning a run-down Rhodesian mining and ranching firm, London-Rhodesia (or Lonrho), into an industrial giant. When he joined, in 1961, annual profits were just £200,000. Fifteen years later, his acquisitive company was making annual profits of £92 million, and he enjoyed a salary of £1 million and a personal fortune of some £250 million. But despite his business success, Rowland remained out of favour with the British Establishment. In 1978 Ted Heath slammed the company as the 'unacceptable face of capitalism' after an enquiry revealed that Lonrho had deposited large payments to directors – including a former Cabinet minister – at banks in tax havens.

Now, Rowland embarked on a £12 million campaign to oust the Fayed brothers from the top floor at Harrods. From the outset he alleged that the money they had used to buy House of Fraser could not possibly have belonged to the Fayeds. He claimed they had lied about their origins and their wealth. Through his newspaper, the *Observer*, he tried to drag in the Sultan of Brunei, with the sensational claim that Mark Thatcher, the Prime Minister's son, had helped solicit money from the Sultan. Mohamed had enjoyed temporary power of attorney over the Sultan's funds when helping him buy the Dorchester Hotel. At the height of the affair, it was alleged Mark Thatcher flew to Brunei with Fayed in his private jet – no evidence was ever produced of the truth of this story. The Sultan's Downing Street meeting with the PM in January 1985, orchestrated by Fayed, the Sultan's subsequent friendly gestures to Britain over sterling and defence purchases, Fayed's attendance at a Downing Street reception for the Egyptian President just hours before the government speedily approved his purchase of House of Fraser – all these were cited as evidence of a conspiracy to shut Lonrho out of the bidding.

Lonrho's 1981 bid for the *Observer* had only been approved after the appointment of five independent directors to guarantee the paper's editorial independence. In mounting his campaign against Fayed, Rowland did not need to tear up that guarantee. Forceful and persuasive, he convinced the paper's dreary editor, Donald Trelford, of the injustice he, Rowland, had suffered. Five years later Roy Jenkins remarked, 'One of the things that Mr Rowland and the Fayed brothers appear to have in common is a capacity to fill those working close to them with a kind of spontaneous fury of battle.'

It is true. Just as we sought to convince the world of the rightness of the Fayeds' acquisition, Tiny Rowland, Trelford and myriad advisers attached to Lonrho set out to do the exact opposite. The five independent directors appointed after the Lonrho takeover were powerless to intervene as there was no conflict between the paper's editor and its proprietor. Admittedly there were moments when Trelford seemed embarrassed by the front-page coverage he was giving to a boardroom feud of limited public interest. But the same compliance spread to the lower ranks of the staff. 'Without any overt pressure being applied, there had developed a tendency to anticipate Mr Rowland's wishes and to cater for his interests,' the *Observer*'s deputy editor Anthony Howard told the *Independent* years later.

Almost immediately after the Harrods takeover, Lonrho's lobbying efforts were prompting questions in the House. The SDP Trade and Industry spokesman, Ian Wrigglesworth, had gained an admission from the Prime Minister that she knew of Fayed's links with the Sultan of Brunei. Norman Tebbit would not be drawn on what sources, other than Kleinwort Benson and the Fayeds, he had consulted before agreeing the takeover. Such information was 'confidential', he said. But the question had hit the target. As was later revealed, Tebbit had consulted no other sources.

We were hired by Fayed just as the new session of Parliament was about to start. I had to plan a counter-attack. We could not brief all 651 Members of Parliament. We had to identify those it would be valuable to have on side. There was an obvious starting point: Michael Grylls, Neil Hamilton, Jeremy Hanley and Tim Smith were the four officers of the Conservative Backbench Trade and Industry Commitee. The House of Fraser battle was a trade and industry matter. They met with the Secretary of State at least once a week.

Royal Naval College-educated Michael Grylls had been a friend since Peter Walker's Dartford campaign in 1959. A former lieutenant in the Royal Marines, Grylls had been a hard-working constituency MP for the safe seat of North West Surrey since 1974. During his time as chairman of the Trade and Industry Committee, he had built up an impressive portfolio of outside interests, with a raft of consultancies and directorships in business. One of these was as a £10,000 per year paid adviser to the Unitary Tax Campaign, which brought him into regular contact with IGA.

Neil Hamilton was a witty and enthusiastic backbencher with strong libertarian instincts. The son of an engineer, he grew up in the Welsh valleys. I had first got to know him in the late seventies when he was a tax barrister, and courting Christine Holman, Michael Grylls' House of Commons secretary. They had married just before Neil's election in 1983 to the safe seat of Tatton in Cheshire. A rising star in the Tory Party, Neil became the committee's joint vice-chairman a year later.

Tim Smith was a chartered accountant whom I hardly knew. The committee's secretary, he seemed rather dull, but worthy. He had enjoyed a brief spell in the Commons from 1977 to 1979 after winning the Ashford by-election during the time of the Labour Government. He was returned for the Beaconsfield seat in May 1982, and held it until his resignation in March 1997.

They all agreed to be briefed over lunch with my new client. Jeremy Hanley, the new MP for Richmond and Barnes, and joint vice-chairman of the committee, was approached, but did not accept the invitation. The MP for Horsham, Sir Peter Hordern, an adviser to the House of Fraser, was also present.

I had my blueprint for the perfect client lunch, however, from the outset, I realised Mohamed Fayed was not going to follow the blueprint either at lunch or at any other time. (Far too gregarious a character to be constrained by me, he would constantly pick up the phone to MPs to whom I had introduced him, and invite them to lunch, or even a weekend on his 32,000-acre Scottish estate.) That day on the top floor of Harrods, the food was superb and the wine excellent. Big Mo was charming, but did not wait to be asked what his guests could do for him. Instead, he launched into a lengthy monologue charting his troubles with Rowland, with Lonrho and with the *Observer* newspaper – and their attacks against his honour, his dignity, his pride and his family.

Neil Hamilton hit it off with him straight away. Hamilton had lunched at Harrods a year earlier, as a guest of Professor Rowland Smith, the then chairman, at the height of the takeover, although this was the first time he had met Fayed. He can therefore reasonably claim a prior interest in the affairs of the company. The two men had a lot in common: Hamilton is an outspoken free-marketeer; Mohamed Fayed is a successful international businessman. Both competed in their adoration of Mrs Thatcher.

From the very outset Hamilton did not need to be paid to ask questions helpful to Fayed. A convinced supporter, he just needed to be briefed on the key issues. Indeed, he had already asked parliamentary questions prior to meeting Fayed. Michael Grylls, while not asking parliamentary questions, assisted by writing letters and as a member of several delegations, on Fayed's behalf, to ministers. But this was less the result of ideological differences than the fact that the relatively newly elected Neil Hamilton was a far more enthusiastic backbencher than Grylls, who had sat in the House for over fifteen years.

Around 45,000 parliamentary questions are tabled in a parliamentary session. The cash-for-questions affair has exaggerated their importance. One is unlikely to learn anything that the civil service does not wish to be known. But questions were important for Mohamed. They were a visible sign that action was being taken. Virtually every question would be drafted, or the information supplied by Royston Webb, Fayed's in-house legal adviser. Whatever motivation the MPs had, Fayed wanted questions designed to discredit Tiny Rowland or Lonrho in some way. At the outset, I would ask a Member if he would be prepared to table such a question – it was his judgement and decision as to whether or not to do so. In later years Royston would often pick up the phone to an MP himself.

Between them, Rowland and Fayed had bought up most of the high-fee professional advisers in London. Fayed had the former BBC TV court correspondent Michael Cole as his press spokesman. He had Gordon Reece – the man who is credited with lowering Margaret Thatcher's voice and raising her hair – as his image consultant. I remember Reece as a rather remote figure in the background, on both the House of Fraser and the Plessey accounts. A consultant rather than a doer, very cleverly Reece did not have a large staff, just a part-time secretary, working out of an office at the Dorchester. He had enough charisma, ability and contacts to turn up to meetings, hear a concern, nod to the chairman and say, 'Hmm, let me ponder that.' He would come back a few days later with valuable, if seemingly effortless advice, whereas I would have agreed to take on the task of fifty parliamentary initiatives.

Mohamed also retained Brian Basham, the PR guru, and there were regular conversations between his office and ours because many of the parliamentary questions were asked purely for publicity purposes. If Members asked a question or gained an answer unhelpful to Lonrho, Basham would seek to place it in the press. Whilst Mohamed was happy to read of the successful efforts of his own team, he was just as likely to read a news report which was critical of himself or Harrods, as Rowland's team were also active within Parliament and the media.

Michael Palmer of Palmer-Cowan was one of Fayed's solicitors. On the very first day of our contract with House of Fraser, 5 November 1985, he faxed over three suggested PQs about the *Observer*. I talked them over with Royston Webb, honed them down to two and rang and later saw Neil Hamilton, who had no hesitation in agreeing to table them. Hamilton has described how he was very keen to 'lob a grenade' in the direction of the *Observer*, a newspaper which he says, 'had been conducting a campaign against Margaret Thatcher and the government which I supported'.

It was a regular exercise for us to draft questions on behalf of our clients for Members of Parliament to consider tabling. Indeed, on occasions, government departments sought our assistance in the drafting of replies to questions on other issues.

Within days of the *Guardian*'s cash-for-questions allegations in October 1994, the Labour MP for Neath, Peter Hain, came to the IGA office for lunch with DHL International. Peter is a former research officer for the Union of Communication Workers, and we wanted his support over the privatisation of the Post Office (to which he would naturally be hostile). His parting words to John Fraser, a company account executive, were, 'Could you draft me some questions?' This will not come as any surprise to the media. Over the years, newspapermen have become as skilled as lobbyists in the drafting of PQs, and in ensuring that they are tabled to assist them in writing news stories.

Neil Hamilton's first question asked the Secretary of State for Trade and Industry if he was 'satisfied that the independent directors appointed to the board of The *Observer* Ltd., in accordance with the conditions recommended by the Monopolies and Mergers Commission in 1981, can effectively exercise the role ascribed to them'. A week later, the Corporate Affairs Minister, Michael Howard, answered that he was and that he had received 'no representations from the independent directors that they are unable to exercise the functions ascribed to them'.

Hamilton's second question asked if the Secretary of State was 'satisfied that all the conditions recommended by the Monopolies and Mergers Commission in 1981 for the transfer of The *Observer* Ltd., to Lonrho are being met in full; and if he will make a statement'. Howard again answered that he was satisfied that the conditions had been met.

The asking of these two questions have been used by the *Guardian* to suggest that they were tabled for financial gain, but, as you can see, the answers are barely worth recording. But it was the first week of our contract with House of Fraser, Basham could let his contacts know that questions about the *Observer*'s independence were being asked in the House and it signalled to Rowland that the counter-attack had begun.

In January 1986, the *Observer* ran a front-page article under the headline 'Mark Thatcher's Mystery Trip To See Sultan'. It alleged that Fayed's acquisition of House of Fraser was smoothed through the DTI as a reward for introducing the Sultan of Brunei to the Thatcher family. Fayed successfully sued on the article. The award-winning journalist David Leigh, associate editor of the *Observer* and co-author of a book on Fayed's most recent allegations, privately admitted the article was 'journalistically unacceptable. It reads as though not only the information within it, but also the very wording of it, had been dictated by the proprietor.' Later most of the people quoted in the story were to sign affidavits denying the words put into their mouths. But it was seized on by Labour, who launched a four-pronged attack against the government. Tony Banks, Dennis Skinner, Dale Campbell-Savours and Brian Sedgemore probed Downing Street dinners, visits by the Sultan of Brunei and the government's approval for the House of Fraser takeover.

They gained the first formal admission that Fayed had dined at Number 10 the day before the takeover was approved. What these Labour MPs did not realise was that my client was still attending meetings at Downing Street. As recently as 7 January he had been to Number 10 to discuss arrangements for a forthcoming meeting between the PM and the Sultan of Brunei.

The parliamentary onslaught continued with Campbell-Savours, in questions favourable to Lonrho, asking why the company had been shut out of the bidding for the House of Fraser by a three-month delay on the part of the Monopolies and Mergers Commission. Michael Howard replied it was usual practice to grant extensions to MMC decisions.

We were racing to keep up. Not only could Lonrho rely on the support of a number of Labour MPs who were keen to embarrass the government, but they held in reserve a well-briefed group of MPs on the Conservative benches led by Sir Edward du Cann.

Throughout most of 1986 Neil Hamilton was consumed with his libel action against BBC TV for the *Panorama* programme 'Maggie's Militant Tendency', which claimed that he was an extreme right-winger. Hamilton went on to win the case. However, despite his enthusiasm for the cause, he could not be the sole champion Mohamed sought in Parliament. I organised for Fayed to write to a group of fourteen Conservative MPs arguing the injustice of the *Observer* campaign. We drew up two lists: MPs who had spoken up in the 1981 debate about the paper, and others who had an interest in trade and industry matters. One of them was the Thanet North MP, Roger Gale. Unfortunately, we did not make it clear enough which list he should have been placed on. The exchange of letters which took place is illuminating. Gale wrote to Fayed on 20 January 1986, thanking him for the letter which Fayed had sent to him as one of the MPs who spoke in the *Observer* debate in 1981: 'As I was not elected to Parliament until June 1983, I can only hope that the rest of the comments contained in your letter are based upon a rather greater degree of accuracy!' he sneered.

Mohamed was furious, but before calling me, sent back a characteristic reply: 'I am sorry you have seen fit to reply in such a flippant manner as I feel the attacks on my family, the Prime Minister, a member of her family and members of the Government are extremely serious and should be treated accordingly.'

After raging incoherently down the phone at me for fifteen minutes, Mohamed wrote to me about the 'extremely rude' letter he had received from Roger Gale. He reminded me that he was a 'very busy man', and continued, 'I trusted you implicitly ... It was my understanding that all these gentlemen were personally known to you ... I did not expect you to instruct my secretary to send these [letters] out in the fashion of a "mail order catalogue" ... As a result so far I have received several letters of sympathy, which are totally useless to me, and numerous telephone calls from people merely wishing to talk to me ... I would like to hear from you as to what concrete results you feel have been achieved by this exercise.'

I stayed in my office until late drafting my reply.

Strictly Private and Confidential

23rd January 1986

Dear Mohamed,

Thank you for your letter of January 23rd enclosing a copy of the letter that you sent to Roger Gale. I fully understand the reasons why you feel his letter to be both arrogant and rude.

I must take responsibility for the mistake which was made by my office when we sent to your Secretary the list of Members to whom we felt it was important for you to write. The necessary research had most certainly been undertaken. The mistake we made was in not making clear those who had a trade and industry interest and those who had spoken favourably in the original debate. Hence Roger Gale received the wrong letter. There was no reason for him to behave in a petty and unpleasant way.

I think it is important for you to take stock of the position. At the time of the *Observer* article two weeks ago there was an urgent need to communicate with a carefully selected group of Members of Parliament, the purpose being to ensure that your position in relation to the allegations being made about Mark Thatcher and the Sultan, along with the continuing saga of the House of Fraser, was clearly understood by potentially sympathetic Members. I gave a lot of thought, before submitting the list to you, as to whom you should write . . . Roger Gale is the Secretary of the Media Committee and therefore there was every reason why we should have included him.

The letter has been well received by all the Members of Parliament we have written to, with the exception of Mr. Gale.

I personally delivered the letters to the House of Commons and within a matter of 48 hours had seen, spoken to or arranged to see and brief each and every Member concerned. You have in fact received a considerable success. The replies you have received indicate genuine interest in the issue, support for your position and a willingness to be helpful if a way can be found. Two Members of Parliament have already made contact with the Secretary of State's office in an endeavour to get him to once again look at the role of the independent directors. In my view, you should feel very satisfied with the results to date. . . .

We want to build up in Parliament a group of Fayed supporters so that as and when it is necessary for us to defend our position or take an initiative they are in place . . .

With kind regards,

Yours sincerely,

IAN B GREER

Lord King of British Airways helped me out, pouring oil on troubled waters. He wrote to Mohamed suggesting he should 'not expect a crusade to commence' in the House of Commons because he had sent off a few letters. Roger Gale was 'clearly a rather touchy sort of fellow and would enjoy prodding the proprietor of the House of Fraser'.

All this was taking place against the backdrop of Leon Brittan's resignation from the DTI over the Westland affair. Although we saw strategic long-term advantages in his replacement by Paul Channon, Mohamed's frustration – and desire for immediate action – was ever-present.

One of the most sympathetic responses Mohammed had received was from Tim Smith, who agreed to push his case with his fellow officers on the Trade and Industry Committee. Over the coming months, I set about successfully persuading Tim to go for an adjournment debate on the *Observer*. The timing was apposite.

On the 15 June the *Observer* went in for the kill with a hard-hitting full-page article in their business section entitled 'In Search Of The Fabulous Pharaohs: The history of the Egyptian Al-Fayed family, owner of Harrods, is traced back, through the shifting desert sands.' The journalist who wrote the piece, Peter Wickman, a former correspondent for the German magazine *Stern*, had been assigned to Egypt 'in search of the Fayed dynasty'. He could not find it. Instead of a family mansion he found a small office in Salah Salam Street with 'Fayed and

Castro Agency' handwritten on the window. At the cotton exchange no one had heard of the one-hundred-year-old Fayed dynasty. Mohamed's father turned out not to be a shipping magnate but a humble schoolteacher.

We released a letter from the Egyptian Ambassador, who had written to Mohamed saying he was 'shocked' to read the article. For the *Observer* 'to portray you and your family in such a manner is really surprising and unbecoming', he wrote. The Fayed family 'who have for years been successful and have accomplished many economic and financial achievements, not only in the United Kingdom but in Egypt and all over the world, are highly regarded by all Egyptians. To try to defame the Fayeds in such a way is not only absurd, it is also an affront to all of us.' These were strong and soothing words from the ambassador and were very helpful to Fayed's PR counter-offensive. It won't surprise you then, to hear that the ambassador was known to be a good friend of Fayed.

Inevitably, questions were raised over the origin of the £615 million in cash which the Fayeds had used to buy House of Fraser, but the government continued to resist calls for a new enquiry into the takeover. Like me, senior ministers believed the allegations to be false – part of a vicious personal campaign waged by Tiny Rowland. We urged the government to call off the *Observer* dogs.

On 18 June Tim Smith stood up in an almost deserted House of Commons to raise the subject in an adjournment debate. Even before he opened his mouth, what we called the 'gang of three' – the Labour MPs Brian Sedgemore, Dennis Skinner and Dale Campbell-Savours – had tabled an Early Day Motion 'deploring' his conduct in trying to silence the *Observer*. Dale Campbell-Savours told the Commons it was 'an attempt by Conservative backbenchers, along with government ministers, to silence the *Observer* over the whole issue of the takeover of Harrods'. Undeterred, Tim took Rowland to task for pursuing a 'personal vendetta', stating that the 1981 safeguards at the time of the *Observer* sale had proved to be inadequate. Responding, the Minister for Information Technology, Geoffrey Pattie, suggested some of the individuals named in the most recent *Observer* report should sue but ruled out government intervention. It is easy to assume that one of the reasons why Mohamed did not sue was that the central allegation, that he had lied about his family background and his wealth, was true, as was later disclosed in the DTI report.

One other weapon in our parliamentary armour was the Early Day Motion. Theoretically, these are motions to be debated at an early date. In practice, none ever is, but they allow MPs to express an opinion, and test out the feelings in the House or allow allegations to be made under parliamentary privilege. An MP gives the wording to the clerks in the Table Office and it is then printed in the daily Order Paper. Other MPs can then add their names. It will appear on the Order Paper every day a new signature is added. By the end of each session, there are well over a thousand. One of the most pathetic EDMs of all time had been placed the previous May by the Conservative MP for Dudley, John Blackburn, a former detective sergeant with Liverpool police:

> That this House extends its congratulations to the Chairman, directors, management, staff and players of Everton Football Club on the brilliant performances which have resulted in the club winning the Football League Championship, together with the excellent conduct and behaviour of their supporters which have made them excellent ambassadors of the national game.

Only ten members signed it, but it gained them valuable local press coverage.

In July, the *Observer* was forced to admit in the High Court that it could not justify the allegations made in its January article – that the Sultan of Brunei, rather than the Fayeds, was the true owner of the House of Fraser. The Sultan issued a formal statement that he had never invested in any Fayed business. Rowland then moved on to assert that the Fayed brothers had borrowed the money to buy House of Fraser. He began openly calling the Kleinwort Benson prospectus produced for Fayed the previous year a 'fraud', inviting the merchant bank to sue him.

There was little rest throughout the summer. We heard late in July that Lonrho planned to double its 36 per cent shareholding in News UK Ltd – the owner of *Today* newspaper – and organised another letter-writing blitz for Mohamed, urging Members to contact Paul Channon, the Trade and Industry Secretary, to block the move. Again, Hamilton could not be of help. Eddy Shah, the proprietor of *Today* who was looking to sell, was a constituent of his. Rather than commit himself to paper, Hamilton asked that one of my staff explain this to Fayed. But Sir Peter Hordern, Graham Bright, Andrew Bowden and Sir Geoffrey Finsberg did write to Channon expressing their concern. Michael Grylls called for an Office of Fair Trading enquiry. There was little the DTI could do. Michael Howard explained that under the rules, Lonrho were already considered a proprietor because they owned more than 25 per cent of the company. Their acquisition of more shares could not be halted.

With hindsight, it is clear the net was closing in on Mohamed. In the autumn the *Observer* claimed his ownership of Harrods had led to a £20-million loss to the Treasury. With the purchase funded by borrowing, the group which had once contributed some £20 million to the Inland Revenue was now offsetting profits against interest on borrowing.

By December 1986, Lonrho had accumulated a dossier of evidence which, they claimed, proved that Fayed could not have been a billionaire at the time he bought Harrods. Triumphantly, Rowland handed these documents over to the DTI. They pointed to 'one conclusion', he said. 'Fayed used the aura of the money of the Sultan of Brunei, over which he had some temporary control, to have himself introduced into Number 10 Downing Street.' Rowland was convinced that the introduction was made by Gordon Reece, and went on to claim that an impressed Mrs Thatcher and Norman Tebbit had 'flung aside the rules for a cheat'.

(Gordon Reece has refused to take the credit for Fayed's late insertion on to the guest list for a crucial Downing Street reception with President Mubarak of Egypt in March 1985.)

Lonrho's delivery of the evidence against Fayed was immediately followed by a rush of pro-Lonrho questions from MPs calling for prompt action by the DTI. Teddy Taylor thought the information 'startling' and called for the takeover to be referred back to the Monopolies and Mergers Commission. In February, the Conservative MP for Christchurch, Robert Adley, pressurised the Trade and Industry Secretary. For Labour, Campbell-Savours called the apparent loss of tax revenues to the Treasury a 'disgrace'. Paul Channon felt it wisest not to comment.

Rowland continued to threaten the government. 'If it were not for the involvement of the Prime Minister, Mrs Thatcher, and Mr Norman Tebbit, one tenth of the papers supplied to you would have precipitated an immediate enquiry,' he wrote to Paul Channon on 4 February. 'The central problem faced by the Fayeds and to which the Ministry should have immediately addressed itself when the takeover of the House of Fraser was proposed by the Fayeds, is the absolute lack of documentation for the astonishing fortune of the Fayeds prior to April, 1984.' Time and again, he repeated the same point in public.

In the circumstances, it was important for us to try and fight back. I arranged for two key parliamentary private secretaries to lunch at Harrods on 20 January 1987, David Atkinson and Rob Hayward, whose respective bosses, Paul Channon, Trade and Industry Secretary, and Michael Howard, Corporate Affairs Minister, were at that moment poring over the Lonrho documents. Sir Peter Hordern, Tim Smith and Michael Grylls were there too. Both PPSs undertook to raise the matter with their ministerial bosses, and Mohamed followed this up at drinks with the two of them at Park Lane two weeks later.

Still searching for his parliamentary champion, Mohamed wanted me to sound out potential recruits who would act as paid advisers to the House of Fraser, in addition to Sir Peter Hordern. I spoke to Tim Smith on 4 February shortly before he left on a trip to Oman. I wrote back to Mohamed the next day:

Tim is extremely sympathetic to you and your position and has promised to do everything he can to help . . . he has asked me to draft some questions that could be tabled which he will look at on his return. I think it is unlikely that he will accept the position of paid adviser to the House of Fraser before the general election is over . . . I am lunching on Monday with another Conservative Member of Parliament, whom I think might be helpful to you. I will talk to Royston [Webb] and Michael [Cole] about their ideas for parliamentary questions and get in touch.

My lunch was with Andrew Bowden on 9 February. I had known the Brighton Kemptown MP for over thirty years. A former personnel consultant for ICI, Andrew is a slightly morbid man. Crushing mortality seems to be a constant feature of his conversation and although we had known each other since the sixties – he had been chairman of the Young Conservatives – I would not call us close friends, though we did share a love of dogs. I recall a hilarious conversation we had once when he came to see me.

'How are things going?' asked Andrew Bowden.

'Very well, Andrew,' I answered.

'Making lots of money?'

'I don't know about that . . .'

'Because, Ian, there's something I've been meaning to ask you. Have you at any time given thought to including me in your will?'

Slightly rocked, I stuttered, 'No, Andrew, I haven't!'

Without hesitation he asked, 'Would you be prepared to consider leaving a note with your trustees to bear me very much in mind when the sad event occurs?'

I *think* it was a joke. All I could think of saying was that not foreseeing the event with any great imminence, I had not made plans to quite that level of detail. But despite his eccentricities, I was impressed by Bowden's ability to take an independent line in the House. There were two reasons why I thought he would be good for the campaign. Firstly, he was a good friend of the chairman of Lonrho, Edward du Cann. Secondly, he had told me that the deputy chairman of his constituency association, Michael Land, was a former Lonrho executive who had fallen

out with Rowland. I thought he might be useful to Royston
Webb.

Bowden agreed to look over the Fayed file with a view to taking on the job as a paid parliamentary consultant to the House of
Fraser, which I have no doubt he would have declared. I was
confident he would say yes and faxed a note to Mohamed on my
return to the office: 'At last we have a campaigner! . . . I have
known Andrew for twenty years and can depend on him. He is
without doubt the right person, we can use Tim Smith in other
ways.'

However, I had been over-optimistic. Bowden said no to the
role of paid adviser, although he introduced Michael Land to the
campaign. Land struck a financial deal with Royston Webb at a
meeting I did not attend. Their arrangement ran for about three
months and during this time Bowden remained on-side and
asked a series of questions. But the relationship between Webb
and Land was to end unhappily. Webb told me that the former
Lonrho employee was not producing the sort of information that
the House of Fraser required. Worse, Webb wanted me to relay
the message to Land via Bowden. Land has subsequently
claimed he was paid a total of £800 in a brown envelope for his
services. After the 1987 general election, I went to see Bowden in
his office. When I told him Webb wanted to end the arrangement
with Land, Bowden was furious. I imagine he felt deeply embarrassed by the slight to his constituent. From that day on, my relationship with him was strained. His support for the Fayed campaign came to an immediate halt.

Meanwhile, trouble was brewing on the Harrods shop floor.
On 10 February we heard that Labour MP Clare Short was planning an EDM about Harrods' treatment of its staff. It condemned
'the attempts being made at Harrods since the Al Fayad [sic]
takeover to undermine staff conditions despite a 50 per cent
increase in turnover in the past two years' and called on the
management to restore traditional negotiating procedures with
the union USDAW.

USDAW, which represented only 800 out of 4,000 staff
members, was resisting a move to keep the store open an extra

hour until 6 pm. At a poorly attended union meeting, a majority had voted to take industrial action. It seemed a storm in a teacup. Harrods bosses had said any staff member who wanted to continue to finish at 5 pm could still do so. The EDM had made no mention of this and had attracted sixty-three Labour MPs on the first day, and had been released to the press. The London *Evening Standard* and the *Daily Telegraph* carried the story.

When the staff settled with the Harrods management on 19 February we sought to amend the EDM condemning 'party political moves by certain honourable Members to undermine negotiating procedures' and congratulating 'the government on its decision to allow the purchase of Harrods by AIT (UK) plc especially in view of the enormous investment by the owners'. When Clare Short got wind of our plans, she suddenly withdrew her motion. The next day, 20 February, I faxed Mohamed the good news: 'We now intend to table our motion this morning. A double victory I think.'

Knowing Neil Hamilton's strong views on labour relations, it seemed an ideal opportunity to bring him back into the fold. He was now freed up after winning his libel action against the BBC. He tabled an Early Day Motion on 10 March applauding the agreement Harrods had come to with its staff and criticising Clare Short for raising the matter under the cloak of parliamentary privilege.

It seemed a classic case of successful lobbying on our part, but in truth it was just a satisfying side-show. We continued to protest Fayed's innocence to the DTI. Webb launched a string of counter-accusations against Rowland. All the time Fayed was growing more and more agitated at the apparent lack of progress in the substantive task of convincing the DTI to rule against any enquiry. He wrongly felt that parliamentary questions would put pressure on the minister. His solicitor, Michael Palmer, wrote to me on 12 February saying, 'As you know, Mohamed is extremely keen to progress questions in Parliament.' By this time, Mohamed had begun picking up the phone to individual MPs he had wined and dined. The fact that he was beginning to take the initiative is evident from a letter I wrote to Tim Smith on 6 March 1987.

Dear Tim,

I have heard from Mohamed that you are going to put down another question. Can I pop down and see you for five minutes if you are free on Monday? Sorry to be a pain.

With kind regards,

Yours sincerely,

IAN B GREER

March was a busy month. On the 10th Lonrho, frustrated by the DTI's inaction – they had now been looking at the Lonrho documents for three months – launched a multi-million-pound damages claim against the Fayeds, House of Fraser, John MacArthur and Kleinwort Benson, claiming they conspired to mislead public bodies over the wealth of the Fayeds at the time of the takeover.

In Parliament, Tim Smith, working on the advice of Royston Webb, hit back the following day, calling for the prosecution of Lonrho executives based on the 1976 DTI enquiry into the company. A week later he asked about possible breaches of company law by Lonrho subsidiaries in Zimbabwe and South Africa. The *Financial Times* picked up the story. Lonrho dismissed the question as 'another Mohamed plant'.

Smith asked another question on 23 March about Lonrho's purchase of ten whisky brands from Guinness plc. He was told it was under investigation. He was working hard. He declared a couple of Harrods teddy bears in the Members' Interests Register.

Meanwhile, Andrew Bowden was asking questions based on some information Royston Webb had unearthed about a retired police officer. Chief Superintendent Kenneth Etheridge had led a fraud squad investigation of Lonrho which cleared the company of criminality. The police officer had then resigned and accepted a £50,000 a year job as Lonrho's security adviser. Bowden called on the Home Secretary, Douglas Hurd, to investigate. The Home Office was not having any of it: Etheridge had retired at the end of August 1977, they said, and his subsequent employment was a matter for the individual concerned.

These were highly specific, detailed and partisan requests. It would have been clear to the minister that their preparation required the involvement of outside commercial interests. Although civil servants were weary of preparing answers to such questions, it was important for ministers to take them seriously, as their objective was to root out wrongdoing on the part of either company.

Battle ensued in their Lordships' House too, during March 1987. According to Lord Mackie of Ardbrecknish, Tiny Rowland was 'showering' peers with letters. The Treasury was being robbed of tax revenues, peers were told. Lord Avebury thought it was a matter for the police rather than the DTI. A weary Lord Nugent appealed for an end to 'the appearance of this unseemly personal vendetta on the Order Paper'.

Keeping the leash on Mohamed was difficult. For every letter Rowland sent to MPs or peers, Fayed would want to send two. I tried to explain that a dignified silence would serve our purpose better. As we approached the Easter recess, Fayed announced he would like to show his appreciation to the MPs who had been fighting his corner in the House. He asked me to organise a trip to Paris to visit the Duchess of Windsor's villa and stay at the Ritz. Fayed had recently completed the restoration of the villa in the Bois de Boulogne, and no expense had been spared on restoring the Ritz to its Edwardian splendour. Prime Minister Jacques Chirac had given Fayed the Legion d'Honneur for his efforts. He was obviously keen to show the two buildings off, and anxious to demonstrate his interest in keeping British heritage intact.

There were obvious Members to invite. Peter Hordern, House of Fraser's paid adviser; Michael Grylls, chairman of the Backbench Trade and Industry Committee, and Sir William Clark, chairman of the Backbench Finance Committee – both men who were working on Fayed's behalf behind the scenes;

Andrew Bowden, who was still on-side at this time; Tim Smith and Neil Hamilton – who had both stuck their heads over the parapet. All six MPs were invited, together with their wives. The plan was to fly from Heathrow in one of Mohamed's private jets and meet him over there. I was wondering how I could get Clive invited along too – but knew it would not be easy. My letter said:

> As I am sure you know, last year Mohamed Al-Fayed bought the Duchess of Windsor's home in the Bois de Boulogne, Paris. Mohamed thought that you and [your wife] may like to join him for a weekend in Paris, staying at the Ritz and visiting the Bois de Boulogne. I said I thought that you and one or two of your parliamentary colleagues would be delighted to accept his very kind offer. I am sure you will appreciate that this is in every way a private invitation and I would therefore be grateful for it being kept as such.

I suggested two weekends over the Easter recess: 25/26 April or 9/10 May.

On 7 April, as the Easter recess approached, I wrote to Fayed about the current state of play. Bowden had agreed to table more PQs about the *Observer*. I explained I was trying to persuade Grylls, Hamilton and Smith – the officers of the Trade and Industry Committee – to write to Paul Channon at the DTI, and that I planned to have tabled a series of motions about the letters Lonrho was showering on Members of Parliament and peers.

I was planning for Royston Webb to update some of the MPs at a 3 pm meeting on 9 April in Room W3 at the House of Commons, which Andrew Bowden had agreed to chair. Within hours of our meeting, we heard that Michael Howard and the Secretary of State, Paul Channon, had given in to the Lonrho onslaught and ordered a DTI enquiry.

The Paris trip was planned for two weeks hence. The following morning I hurriedly penned a note to the six MPs I had written to the previous week:

In the light of yesterday's announcement by the Secretary of State for Trade and Industry concerning the enquiry into the House of Fraser, I think it would be inappropriate for the visit to Paris planned for the weekend of 25/26 April to go ahead. I am sure you will agree. Hopefully, when the enquiry has been completed, we will be able to look once again at Mohamed's kind suggestion.

I felt tremendously relieved that we still had time to call the trip off. Imagine the headlines had the DTI announced a major fraud investigation into the business dealings of our host, whilst we were in Paris drinking his champagne! And in the light of recent events, who knows how this visit would subsequently have been construed? I should have read the warning signs better – there was every possibility an enquiry might be called, but we had been expecting its announcement for so long that we had grown immune to its significance. In any case, I have no recollection of any MPs in the proposed party objecting to the invitation or considering it improper. Even then, as the inspectors – Philip Heslop, QC, and Hugh Adlous, FCA – took up their posts, we all expected Fayed to be exonerated. We were wrong.

Neil Hamilton (*Rex Features*)

Tim Smith (*Rex Features*)

Sir Andrew Bowden (*Rex Features*)

Sir Michael Grylls (*Universal Pictorial Press*)

3

FROM THE CAMPAIGN
TRAIL TO THE RITZ

T he furious activity in the weeks leading up to the
announcement of the DTI enquiry meant I was in almost
daily contact with Mohamed Fayed or his staff. A month
later, on 11 May 1987, a general election was called.

On the day Parliament was dissolved I went to see Mohamed
and detailed my plans for the election campaign. It had been my
custom in previous elections, I informed him, to help a few
Conservative candidates in order to ensure that they had sufficient funds available for their campaigns. He was not inclined to
help at first. He explained that in the previous few months Lord
McAlpine, the Conservative Party Treasurer, had extracted
£250,000 from him. He was annoyed that the party which took
his money should see fit to launch an enquiry into his business
practices.

I tried to explain that the huge donation he had made, valuable as it was, would quickly disappear into Central Office cof-
fers. From my experience, the candidate fighting the front-line
marginal seat would be unlikely to benefit – and it was those I
wanted to help. Reluctantly, he wrote me a cheque for £12,000. I
had already solicited an £11,250 donation from DHL
International, in addition to the large contribution the company
had made to central party funds. The boss of DHL and
Mohamed were both committed, Tory-supporting individuals
whom I knew well enough to approach directly. The chairman of
DHL International, Dave Allen, has been a friend for many years
and is one of the country's foremost entrepreneurs, combining

personal kindness with great business skill. He is a man of conviction and was a great Thatcherite.

A number of MPs had already contacted me for help. When I looked at the list of those I wanted to help, it became clear £23,250 would not be enough. I tried to contact Mohamed but he was unavailable, so I spoke to his brother Ali. He agreed to send me a further £6,000. I sent him a note, a copy of which I have kept, which said that I wanted to help out 'one or two' additional Conservatives during the election. All donations were made by cheque, each one made out to the candidate's Election Fighting Fund.

Neither Tim Smith nor Neil Hamilton benefited as neither was fighting a marginal seat.

There were twenty-six constituency associations which benefited from the monies raised by me in 1987. None of them were told where the money came from. The relevant candidates were:

Norman Tebbit: I had known Norman and Margaret for a substantial number of years. I had developed a great deal of admiration for him. In addition, I knew Dave Allen of DHL was very fond of Tebbit's right-wing, Euro-sceptic views. The £500 donation I made to his Chingford campaign was not solicited.

Michael Portillo: I first met him when he was a speech-writer for John King at British Airways. I helped him when his own parliamentary ambitions took him on to fight the Enfield Southgate by-election. Although his was not exactly a marginal seat, I was very happy to support this bright, enthusiastic Whip with £500.

Gerry Malone: Gerry, an assistant Whip, had stepped in to fight Iain Sproat's marginal seat of Aberdeen South after Iain had moved to the Borders. Having previously helped Iain in 1983, it seemed natural to help the constituency in 1987 as well. His association received £1,000.

Lynda Chalker: Lynda had been a personal friend for many years, and an able Transport Minister, fighting an extremely tight campaign. I put staff there to help her in 1987 and 1992. A donation of about £2,000 was made to her association. There is a rumour that I single-handedly brought Wallasey into the computer age, but the truth is more mundane. DHL had offered a number of computers which I suggested they earmark for various Tory marginals. Lynda's was one of them. Most of my own donation was used to erect iron bars around the Conservative offices to protect their new computer.

Norman Lamont: Norman, my constituency MP, received £2,000. I felt able to give him a larger amount, although without consultation, because DHL had one of their offices in Kingston. Norman was not top of my list, but as with a number of others I wrote to him saying I was raising funds, but presumed the association had no financial needs. I thought Kingston was a wealthy enough area not to need my help. The letter was delivered by hand to the Treasury. Lamont, the Financial Secretary at the time, called back within the hour. 'Help,' he said. 'My association is really much more desperate than you think. Can we have a cheque today?'

David Mellor: Putney was my former constituency. Mellor, a Home Office minister at the time, has since said he would not have taken the £500 had he known it came from a pot to which Fayed had contributed.

Sir Michael Hirst: The chairman of the Scottish Conservatives lost his Strathkelvin and Bearsden seat despite my £500 donation.

John Moore: I had known Moore, the Transport Secretary, for a long time. We gave him a cheque and also helped him with some of his graphic design work for election addresses in his Croydon constituency, which is why the donation amounted to £1,367.

Colin Moynihan: Colin was a friend at the Department of Energy at the time, fighting the hyper-marginal seat of Lewisham. I sent him just over £900, arranged a couple of fund-raising dinners with businessmen at the Carlton Club, and provided him with staff. Sadly, since the *Guardian* published their big story I have heard nothing from him.

Robert Atkins: The larger-than-life South Ribble MP was friendly with Peter Holden, an IGA director and former Conservative agent. Robert asked me if I would release Peter to go and work for him during the campaign, which I agreed to do, and to donate £500 to his campaign.

Andrew Bowden: Andrew was always worried that he was about to lose his seat – which he considered the most marginal in the country. It wasn't. But his rather lacklustre Conservative Association in Brighton Kemptown had very dated office systems. They desperately needed a photocopier and other equipment which his association priced at £5,319.90. He and his constituency association were very appreciative at the time.

Sir Anthony Durant: Having known him since Young Conservative days, I sent £500 to Reading West for the 1987 election campaign. When we informed Tony this donation might become public, he collared me at a drinks party at Home Office Minister Tom Sackville's home. He told me somebody had written from my office saying IGA had donated to his campaign, which he said was not true. I told him it was me who had written, he had received the money and I would put a photocopy of the cheque in the post to him to prove it. Which I duly did. I have never heard from him since.

Gerry Bowden: I met Gerry, MP for Dulwich, in Hatchards bookshop one Saturday morning shortly before the election. As had others, he asked if there was anything I could do to help him. I sent him a cheque for £500.

Nirj Deva: The request to help Deva came via a keen Hammersmith Tory who was working at IGA at the time. His campaign got £750.

Sir Malcolm Thornton: The Crosby MP had not expected his £500 donation, but wrote a super letter back to us saying he was very grateful and hoped that IGA would be able to help out in the next election!

Other constituency associations which received help were: David Shaw's – the Dover MP, a good friend of the DHL chairman, received a £500 donation; Gerry Vaughan's in Reading East, Ken Warren's in Hastings and Rye, Richard Holme's in Cheltenham, John Lee's in Pendle, and Neil Thorne's in Ilford South, all of which received £500; David Trippier's association in Rossendale received £1,000.

In 1995, in advance of what we thought would be the publication of this list by the *Guardian*, we wrote warning all the former candidates. They had done nothing wrong and I wanted them to be prepared for the journalists' question: 'Ian Greer "claims" you had money for election expenses. What was it really for?'

It was midnight on a Sunday evening and I was fast asleep when the phone rang. It was Norman Lamont, who had just returned from a weekend abroad to find our letter on his doormat. 'What's all this about?' he asked anxiously. I tried to calm him down, explaining that the donation made through me was at the request of a constituency company.

'I presume there will be a lot of publicity about it?' he said.

I said I didn't know, but there might well be.

'Obviously I am the most senior person in the government that you gave money to,' he said.

'No,' I replied.

'What do you mean "no"? Someone more senior than me got money?'

'Well, sort of equal,' I replied, thinking of Norman Tebbit.

'But I was number three in the government!'

Norman couldn't believe that he would be pushed off the front page by a more heavyweight figure.

In 1987 I realised IGA could not be seen to be an exclusively Tory outfit. My old friend Doug Hoyle, the recent chairman of the

Parliamentary Labour Party, used to write a newsletter for me after he lost Nelson and Colne in 1979. As the 1987 campaign got under way he rang me from Warrington. 'My general management committee are asking whether that nice friend of mine in London can send us some money for the election,' he asked in his blunt northern tones. I sent £500 to help his Warrington campaign, as we subsequently did in 1992.

Another Labour MP who benefited was Stanley Crowther in Rotherham, who got £250. The Liberals' Alan Beith, whom I knew and liked, received £500 for Berwick-upon-Tweed, and Ian Wrigglesworth of the SDP got £500 for Stockton South. All were unsolicited.

The *Guardian*'s case was that Fayed handed over two cheques in 1987 to enable me to pay Neil Hamilton and Tim Smith for their parliamentary work. Fayed maintained that these two cheques were not paid to Ian Greer to pay to Conservative candidates in the 1987 general election. It was on this central allegation that the libel action would have been fought. However, when the *Guardian* published details of the twenty-six constituency associations that had been helped, immediately after the collapse of the trial, on 2 October 1996, Fayed's spokesman Michael Cole told ITN's *News at Ten*:

> Mr Greer approached Mr al-Fayed and said he needed money for some of the MPs who were going to be fighting the 1986–7 general election. Mr al-Fayed agreed to give him money. He gave him two cheques, one for £12,000, one for £6,000 drawn on his personal account.

I sat there astonished, staring at the television screen. Cole was now saying what I had maintained all along.

The donations I was making from funds raised were well known and openly discussed at Tory Central Office. After the whole affair came to light I received an amusing letter from a member of the public who said, 'I hear you give out money and ask for nothing in return. Can you add me to your list?'

But I did not consider my small donations to a few friends

bought me influence over them and did not ask for any favours. If my £500 to Norman Tebbit's campaign bought me influence, how much more influence would the late Matthew Harding's £1 million have bought him with the Labour Party? Why is one donation seen as corrupt, and the other not? My own view is that neither should be presumed so. I do not believe that Mr Blair would have used his influence in Mr Harding's favour, or that Norman Tebbit supposed I expected anything of the kind.

Once the election campaign is under way, there are no parliamentarians in Westminster and the task of a lobbyist effectively ceases. My staff were all political animals – I would not have employed them if they weren't. They were itching to get out on the campaign trail to help friends who were candidates. I encouraged them to go. The alternative was to give them a three-week holiday. Andrew Smith, my deputy, headed north to Wallasey in aid of Lynda Chalker. John Roberts went to work for Doug Hoyle in Warrington.

Sending my staff out to get a taste of real politics on an election campaign seemed a natural and sensible decision to take in 1987 and 1992. Now, of course, there is a terrible controversy about the practice. My staff made contacts and, yes, it is true people like Andrew Smith found it easier to get a meeting with Lynda Chalker having worked on her campaign. But it was common practice amongst lobbying companies and there was nothing wrong with it.

Offering staff to help someone's campaign was not a contribution which needed to be declared. In any case, were they going as IGA personnel or individuals? I learned recently that only financial contributions over 25 per cent of the total cost of a constituency campaign need to be registered, but how does one quantify an individual's time? We must remember that at any by-election each party can easily pour in up to sixty full-time agents and headquarters' staff to help a local candidate. These are never costed and declared.

Meanwhile, I remained in London. I had a paid contract worth £10,000 to fulfil for Conservative Central Office. 'Businessmen For Britain' was a campaign I had been talking to

Smith Square about for eighteen months. The plan was to identify and brief a select group of around twenty Tory-leaning captains of industry. At every opportunity, whether it was on television's *Question Time* or at a CBI gathering, they would trumpet the same message: that industry was thriving and the Tory Government should be returned. Michael Dobbs, Tebbit's Chief of Staff, was very keen on the idea. But, with the election looming, Central Office was distracted and, despite Dobbs' efforts, he was never able to get the final go-ahead. Peter Morrison, the MP for Chester and deputy chairman of the party, approached the campaign in the most relaxed manner. When I asked who he saw as chairman of the 'Businessmen For Britain' campaign, he picked up a copy of *Who's Who* and began peering through the entries.

When the election was called, Peter Morrison disappeared off to fight his seat and David Young, a peer with no pre-election worries, was drafted in to take his place. He told me he was shocked at the lack of preparation for the election at Central Office, being particularly critical about the party's failure to finalise the manifesto. He immediately agreed a contract with IGA.

Within a few days I had made contact with most of the big industrialists – such as Lord King, chairman of British Airways, Mark Weinberg, chairman of Allied Dunbar Assurance, George Jefferson at BT and Sir Ronnie Halstead, deputy chairman of British Steel. In addition, Lord Hanson was one of the most impressive operators. I went to see him one morning at his office at Hyde Park Corner, which is little more than a ten-minute taxi ride from IGA. He agreed to contact half a dozen businessmen for me. To my amazement, by the time I had returned to my office, there was a message from him saying he had spoken to all six, got the whole thing organised and wanted to know what next to do.

'Businessmen For Britain' made its own small contribution to the Conservative election victory, but, coming so late in the day, it was admittedly less effective than it might have been.

During the 1987 campaign, I was in almost daily contact with my staff out on the hustings. Some of the local intelligence I received I passed on to Michael Dobbs or David Young at Central Office to supplement their own network.

The Tories won the election with a huge majority. The days immediately afterwards were a tender time at the office. After three weeks slogging it out on the hustings, the Tories among my staff bounced back, jubilant. The Labour supporters arrived, despondent, a day later. John Roberts, a founder of IGA, was bitterly disappointed and found it difficult to come to terms with the party's defeat. I took the winning camp into one corner and implored them not to crow about their victory.

With Margaret Thatcher safely returned to Number 10, lobbying recommenced. On the Harrods account, just before the election Sir Peter Hordern had led a delegation to see Paul Channon at the DTI. Grylls, Smith and Hamilton accompanied him and pressed for an early end to the enquiry. They failed to persuade Channon to reopen investigations into Lonrho or the appointment of the ex-policeman, Etheridge, as security adviser for the company. But they succeeded in pressing for the replacement of one of the inspectors, Philip Heslop, QC, who was representing Guinness tycoon Ernest Saunders. Lonrho had recently bought some whisky brands from Guinness. The DTI agreed there was a possible conflict of interest and Heslop was persuaded to stand down. It momentarily cheered Mohamed up. Henry Brooke, QC, who was chairman of the Bar's Professional Standards Committee, took Heslop's place.

It was now more than two years since Mohamed had bought Harrods. In June, as the DTI team picked over the old bones on the takeover battlefield, we submitted to the Stock Exchange a report prepared by the accountants Arthur Young, which claimed that Lonrho had understated the true earnings and underlying trading performance of the group. Lonrho has always disputed its findings. And the Stock Exchange took no action.

On the other hand, Rowland's campaign against us, which reportedly ended up costing £12 million, showed no sign of abating – its 'unremitting vehemence historically is seen only in wars of religion', suggested one commentator. Off his own bat, Neil Hamilton tabled an EDM in July 1988, condemning the barrage of Lonrho propaganda which MPs and others in public life were receiving by post every week. Peter Hordern was unhappy with it as it provided an opportunity for Lonrho supporters and/or left-wing MPs to put down critical amendments, which, fortunately, they did not.

It was around this time that Fayed alleges he started making direct payments to Hamilton. It is true that the two men began seeing rather more of each other, but neither ever mentioned payments to me. Had Mohamed done so I would have told him he was not only acting wrongly but wasting his money – MPs are used to tabling questions on issues of concern and there was no need to pay them.

Fayed alleged in our subsequent libel case that he handed over three separate bundles of £2,500 in £50 notes on 2 and 18 June and 8 July at face-to-face meetings with the MP. Each time no one else was present. Whilst Hamilton has lost his diaries for this period, he rightly suggests that 2 June is an unlikely date for a meeting, as this was little more than a week before the general election. It is doubtful that he would have travelled from Cheshire to London at a critical time for any candidate to leave his or her constituency.

It strikes me as odd that Fayed should claim that he handed over so much money for so little work in such a short space of time. Hamilton had asked two PQs at the beginning of IGA's contract back in November 1985. He had tabled one EDM shortly before the 1987 election. He had attended one delegation to see the Trade and Industry Secretary.

What did occur at one of these meetings was that Fayed invited Hamilton and his wife to stay at the Ritz Hotel in Paris. Neil had mentioned to Fayed that Christine and he were heading to France in September, where they planned to visit an old family friend in Normandy, before driving on to Strasbourg. According to Hamilton, Mohamed was 'enthusiastic' about them stopping off in Paris, staying at the Ritz and visiting the Duchess of Windsor's villa.

Neil recalls he said 'something such as not wanting to cause problems if the hotel was busy', but Mohamed insisted, saying there would be no problem as he maintained rooms in the hotel for his personal guests. The couple could use these if the public rooms were full and stay for as long as they wanted. Mohamed's memory of the conversation is somewhat different. He claims Neil asked to stay at the Ritz and there are no private rooms in the hotel. Guests of his visiting Paris stay at apartments he owns on the Champs-Elysées.

The *Guardian* has wrongly alleged that I arranged BA flights for the couple. I did not. They drove to France, as they had always intended, little knowing that they had set the timer on a device which would explode in their faces seven years later.

On arrival at the Ritz they were met by the manager, Mr Klein, who asked how long they would be staying. They said they would stay for five nights – although it turned out to be six.

'That's fine,' Mr Klein said. 'The hotel is not full. You can take Apartment 356.' Upstairs was a welcome letter from the manager and a bottle of Ritz own-label champagne. A valet garaged their car for them. They relaxed over cocktails in their room, made a few phone calls and put some clothes out for dry-cleaning before dressing for dinner in the elegant Espadon restaurant.

Neil said later:

> We enjoyed the relaxation of a luxury hotel. We usually left the hotel after a light breakfast. We never have a cooked breakfast and prefer fruit juices, soft fruits, and the usual continental type of fare. We spent the days out but dined in the hotel restaurant, which was magnificent, in the evening. Sometimes Christine came back to the hotel at teatime. She has a back complaint which for years has needed regular visits to the chiropractor and there is a limit to how much footslogging she can do . . . So it was very pleasant, after a tiring day, to go up to our room for a soak, then go downstairs for a leisurely dinner and then go

back upstairs to bed . . .

It has been made to appear that we ran up especially large bills, but I do not recall that we ordered any dishes which were more expensive than the average in the hotel. We certainly never ordered bottles of wine costing £200.

While the Hamiltons were there, Mr Klein arranged for them to visit the Duchess of Windsor's villa. Perplexed by the reports of chauffeur-driven limousines, Neil says a car arrived automatically. The couple were shown around by Sidney Johnson, who had been the valet to the Duke of Windsor from the age of sixteen.

The total bill came to £1,482 for the room, plus £2,120 extras – a grand total of £3,602.

The Hamiltons were 'full of their experiences' on their return. 'We delighted in telling people what a splendid time we had had,' Neil recalls. Some colleagues in the House were less delighted. The Hamiltons were, by this time, famous for their tales of glamorous trips.

Allow yourself, for one moment, to look at this from the Hamiltons' point of view. You have been invited to stay for as long as you want at a hotel wholly owned by an extremely generous and wealthy friend. Money is not a problem to him. The prices printed on the rate-card look expensive, but you know these are marked-up costs, not real costs. They are not the amounts coming out of your friend's pocket. You do not for one moment consider that your bill will, some years later, appear on the front page of every national newspaper. What do you do? The Hamiltons response was to take Fayed's offer at face-value. They accepted his generosity. Neil took pleasure in saying that they had eaten every night at the Ritz, free. It was probably bad judgement on their part. Most people, I think, would have been embarrassed to stay there that long. In the eyes of many, they were greedy. But that does not mean they were corrupt. Corrupt politicians tend not to brag about their gains.

It did not occur to Hamilton to declare his stay in the Register of Members' Interests. A gift or benefit at the time needed to be registered if it could affect an MP's 'actions, speeches or vote in Parliament'. Neil felt it would not. He was already emotionally and ideologically committed to the Fayed cause long before the trip. When their six-night stay at the hotel was finally investigated by the Members' Interests Committee after a formal complaint from Alex Carlile in 1994, the committee decided that Hamilton should have registered it, but also expressed 'some sympathy with Mr Hamilton's impression that the requirements of the Register with respect to gifts and hospitality were not as explicit as they have since become and it was more difficult for Members to establish their exact coverage from the written material available to them'. Hamilton says he 'may have been mistaken in taking the view that I did, but I was not corrupt or dishonest'.

Fayed often claims no MP has ever thanked him for his generosity. He forgets that when the Hamiltons returned they gave him a House of Commons Wedgwood coffee service. A small gift in Fayed's terms, but it was a genuine gesture of thanks.

After the Ritz trip, Neil Hamilton continued to see Fayed and help with the campaign, but he was by no means the most active MP on behalf of the Harrods boss. He wrote to the new Trade and Industry Secretary, Lord Young of Graffham, in November, but missed a meeting with the minister the following month. Neil had been appointed to the Treasury Select Committee and one of their early meetings clashed. The delegation was led by Peter Hordern, with Tim Smith and Michael Grylls in attendance. Neil Hamilton did, however, send Mohamed a note, apologising and restating his enthusiasm for the campaign. He wrote to Lord Young in January 1988 urging the DTI to take action about a Lonrho subsidiary which, according to reports in the *Sunday Times*, had been withholding information from its shareholders. However, no action was taken. Neil repeatedly invited Mohamed to dine at the House of Commons – an invitation the Harrods boss always refused. For Christmas the MP gave him a bottle of House of Commons VSOP cognac.

But during all this time, although Hamilton was an important footsoldier in the parliamentary battle against Rowland, other MPs such as Tim Smith and Peter Hordern were leading the cavalry charge – which is why the allegation that Hamilton was being bankrolled by Fayed all through 1988 came as such a surprise to me.

Over two and a half years, Mohamed claims to have handed Hamilton at face-to-face meetings a total of £28,000. Tim Smith now admits to receiving between £18,000 and £25,000. Mohamed claims that I knew this, but it makes no logical sense. During this time, when Hamilton was supposedly receiving up to £10,000 per year, why did he engage in so little activity? In the 1987–8 session alone, Tim Smith asked fourteen questions. Hamilton asked two and put down one EDM. If both were being paid, why was Hamilton paid so much more for so much less work?

Throughout the world Mohamed Fayed is recognised as a ruthless entrepreneur, but he seems a very poor businessman in his dealings with MPs. He claims he gave Neil Hamilton money both directly and through me, free shopping and free Harrods gift vouchers (for which the store kept no records). All this would have added up to some of the most expensive questions ever asked. For IGA too – if it was true that I was paying Neil Hamilton £2,000 per question, why would I pay him when there are other MPs who would happily ask questions for free? At the same time, why did Fayed continue to pay Sir Peter Hordern, his parliamentary adviser, when Peter was asking no questions?

Fayed claims he handed over another £2,500 in £50 notes to Hamilton in February 1988. But it wasn't until June that the MP asked a question, when he queried the cost and the delay of the DTI investigation into the House of Fraser takeover – a thoroughly legitimate enquiry about the use of taxpayers' money. I could have persuaded a dozen MPs with an interest in the public finances to have asked it; particularly as the Minister's answer was £1,032,747 (and rising) with no end in sight.

Tim Smith, with his training in accountancy, was far more useful to the Fayed team during this time. The parliamentary questions Royston Webb was framing, all designed to discredit Rowland in some way, were of a technical financial nature. Smith was the right man for the job. He was jokingly referred to as the Member for Price Waterhouse, on account of the number of parliamentary questions he raised relating to accountancy matters.

Rowland was under no illusions about Tim's actions. In July 1988, following reports in the *Sunday Times*, Smith had urged government action over allegations that shareholders in two Lonrho mining companies overseas had been denied financial information. Lonrho responded with a press release attacking Tim Smith.

PARLIAMENTARY LOBBYISTS – TIM SMITH

Mr Tim Smith, an MP for Beaconsfield, has recently put several questions in the House of Commons which publicly implied, in the national forum, that two small subsidiaries of Lonrho, dealing in amethysts some twenty years ago, were guilty of unspecified financial wrongdoing during their trading life . . .

It has become clear that Mr Tim Smith is an associate of the Public Relations expert and Parliamentary Lobbyist, Mr Ian Greer, who in turn is connected with Mohamed Fayed.

I had wanted Tim to go for another adjournment debate. He was impressed by the information Royston Webb had been supplying about Lonrho. My conversations indicated he was willing to say a lot more about Rowland under the cloak of parliamentary privilege. But Lonrho's press release suggested that they would mount a personal campaign against him, questioning his motives, in any debate. I put the idea on hold.

Unbeknown to me, Tim Smith had by this time taken a paid consultancy with Fayed. He told the Cabinet Secretary, Sir Robin Butler, in 1994 that he received payments from Fayed between

1987 and 1989. He registered the interest only at the end of this period, and for only fourteen days, and this is why he resigned after the allegations in the *Guardian* broke. Although I had sought him out as a possible consultant before the 1987 election, I took no further part in negotiations. I did not know Tim was being paid. During this time he was regularly seeing Mohamed and Royston Webb without me present.

Meanwhile, with the enquiry dragging, Mohamed was getting depressed, but we all still believed he would be exonerated of any wrongdoing. At the end of January, 1988, Royston Webb and I agreed that after publication Mohamed should 'take a deep long breath, put everything behind him, concentrate on running Harrods and forging new relationships with government'. I reported my conversation to Tim Smith the next day, adding that Royston was, however, 'fearful that we may not persuade Mohamed to do that'.

To us, at the time firmly entrenched in Fayed's camp, the conduct of the enquiry did seem unfair. I was regularly on the receiving end of Mohamed's explosions. He thought the inspectors had set off with an agenda – the Rowland agenda. Lonrho's lawyers had led the inspectors by the hand to the evidence they had accumulated against the Egyptian. In March, Royston fired off a lengthy *aide-mémoire* to our team of parliamentary defenders. Eleven months into the enquiry, it said, Messrs Brooke and Aldous had unearthed not one single piece of evidence that the Harrods bid was financed by anyone other than the Fayed brothers. The majority of time was spent enquiring into 'the Fayeds' childhood, the birth dates of them and their father and a whole host of genealogical issues which were not even entertained by the Secretary of State [Norman Tebbit] when he made his decision [to allow the takeover to go ahead in March 1985]'. It was 'not easy for inspectors brought up in a rather narrow, privileged English manner to appreciate the cunning and ruthlessness of a man like Rowland', whom the DTI in previous enquiries had repeatedly exposed as a 'liar' and a 'criminal'. Rowland had 'attacked the Fayeds in communications to their own staff, he had vilified the Prime Minister and her family, he had denigrated Secretaries of State and civil servants, he had sought to upset the Fayeds' commercial relationships and more, all in pursuit of his spiteful vendetta'.

The report was completed in July 1988. Its conclusions were so serious that, unbeknown to us, Lord Young immediately sent it to the DPP and Serious Fraud Office. There is evidence that despite Fayed's protestations that the enquiry was unfair, his own team had not been entirely helpful to Brooke and Aldous. Only a week before the report was completed Fayed's solicitors handed over four volumes of papers, which they claimed was their first detailed submission on the subject. But by this time the inspectors had seen enough. Apart from two questions there was no other response from them. I arranged for MPs who had been supportive of Fayed to challenge Lord Young on whether the enquiry team could have had time to fully take into account Fayed's submission.

On 29 July 1988, Hamilton wrote the minister a strong letter saying the enquiry had only been set up to silence Rowland. Once under way 'the issues which the Inspectors appear to have examined are wholly irrelevant to the legitimate public policy question of competition. There appears to be an obsession with the [Fayed] family background and source of their wealth – enquiries which would be relevant to an application for membership of a gentleman's club, but which do not seem to me to have any relevance whatever to the Government's interests in a merger or takeover.'

Tim Smith wrote a similar letter asking, 'what does it matter whether the money was inherited or whether it was made by this generation? I thought we rather approved of self-made men.'

We now entered a strange period. For a time we believed the report was still in the hands of the DTI. Rumours that the Serious Fraud Office were making enquiries were not confirmed until November 1988. Mohamed was extremely edgy. With hindsight, it is obvious that his rubbishing of the report in advance and his strong denunciations of the inspectors were his way of preparing us for what he knew we would one day be reading.

4

THE GREEDY EIGHTIES

A new code of morality, forced on a reluctant Parliament, owes everything to the allegations of one man. During the writing of this book I spoke to a well-known senior backbencher, a man very much of the Tory old guard. He was annoyed with Hamilton. 'If he hadn't got involved with this damn foreign chap, al-Fayed, we would have been able to keep all our consultancies.'

Throughout the eighties, Neil Hamilton was not the only Member of Parliament who enjoyed freebies and consultancies. There were dozens of them. Until Nolan put a stop to it, around twenty times a year I would be approached by Conservative MPs wanting consultancies or non-executive directorships in business. They would ask directly for my help, or the approach might come through a friend, as when the Sports Minister, Iain Sproat, put in a kindly word for a backbencher he was worried about. 'He's got kids at school, Ian. He's desperately in need of additional income. Is there anything you can do?' As very few backbenchers are skilled in fields other than giving political advice – and that was IGA's business – there were fewer and fewer opportunities available.

During the eighties, to take a consultancy or directorship was not greed on the part of an MP. Earning little over £30,000, and usually running two homes, for many it meant economic survival. What we would now consider to be outrageous perks were regarded by many at the time as little more than basic comforts.

During the boom decade, several MPs recommended IGA to companies with whom they had contact, companies that they knew required professional political advice. Some received a referral payment from IGA for so doing. There was nothing wrong in making such a payment – nor in receiving it. The problem was that the rules on registration of one-off payments were unclear at the time.

MPs regularly demanded that they fly first class on their economy ticket; in that very different decade, a night in a hotel at somebody else's expense was accepted for the sake of convenience, not corruption. Even Tony Blair thought nothing of a Concorde flight across the Atlantic – so little, in fact, that he failed to register the trip at all. I do not make this point to denigrate him, but to underline how much more 'relaxed' was the whole political culture of the day.

These were not corrupt acts. However, that does not mean that some MPs were not greedy.

My biggest client, British Airways, experienced enormous problems with MPs who repeatedly demanded free flights and upgrades. A significant number abused and embarrassed the system. Virtually none were ever declared. At one lunch we arranged at the Savoy, over a hundred Tory MPs heard Lord King give an impassioned plea for privatisation. They came out, agreed he was a great businessman and that the government was dragging its heels over the sell-off. But within weeks, many were making flight requests. Some Labour MPs were no better.

After privatisation, many of these MPs failed to realise that with BA in the private sector, the gravy train had come to a halt. One Tory member summed up the mood: 'Before privatisation I would just phone up and get an upgrade here or a free ticket there. Now, bugger it, they don't need me any more.'

A former Transport Minister, winging off on holiday, actually tried to arrange for himself, his wife and three relatives to be upgraded to business class from a ticket with every restriction under the sun. He was surprised when it didn't happen.

The Conservative MP for Christchurch, the late Robert Adley, who flew around the world as the director of an American hotel group, was forever asking for free flights. There was an enormous row once when he was heading to the Far East as part of a delegation, even though he wanted to use part of the trip to further his own business interests elsewhere. Planning to fly out early one Saturday morning from Manchester, the MP discovered he had to be in his Dorset constituency for a function the night before. He demanded BA send a car to take him 300 miles from Christchurch to the airport. BA sought my advice. I told them they must not give in to him. He missed the flight but held it against the airline for years after.

A Tory colleague was facing a three-line whip when lounging on a yacht in the French Mediterranean. He contacted BA, who agreed to fly him back for free. Two years later the Members' Interests Committee turned its attention to British Airways and the issue of free flights. In a panic he sent a cheque to BA, for the wrong amount, to cover the cost of the trip. The committee's deliberations failed to uncover the flight in question, which was only one among many the company had provided. The MP then wrote to BA asking if he could have his money back. They refused.

A Welsh Labour MP, having campaigned vigorously on class issues during the 1987 election, immediately afterwards demanded an upgrade – because he didn't want to 'sit with them back there'.

Only recently, one Tory backbencher found himself among a group of MPs on a parliamentary delegation to the USA. They were travelling economy. He appealed to BA for an upgrade which was refused. When he arrived (late) at the airport, his parliamentary colleagues were waiting for him in the departure hall. Complaining of a sore back, he headed for the ticket counter, where he bought himself a business-class upgrade. He immediately ran into problems with his disgruntled parliamentary colleagues, who thought he had been given the upgrade for free. The MPs eventually calmed down when he produced a receipt which stated he had used his own money to buy the uprgrade. His club-class seat and the New England sunshine did wonders for his health. By the time he was due to fly back to London his back had improved. On his return he wrote to British Airways thanking them for the excellent service he had received in business class. He informed them of the miraculous spinal recovery he had undergone, which meant that he had not really needed his club-class seat on the return trip. Could he claim the difference he had paid? The answer was no.

By the late eighties, MPs' appetites for upgrades and free flights were making life so difficult for my client that I arranged to see Cranley Onslow, chairman of the 1922 Committee. He listened to what I had to say.

'I think you'd better come and see the Chief Whip,' he said.

I found myself in David Waddington, the Government Chief Whip's office. 'Name the members,' he demanded.

I refused. I had been brought up to believe one does not sneak.

'I'm very unhappy with what you're telling me, but without the names, there is nothing I can do,' said Waddington, indicating that the meeting was over.

I was given twenty-four hours to return to the Chief Whip with the names, phone Cranley Onslow, or keep my counsel, which is what I did. Nowadays I ask myself, had I named members back then, what difference could it have made? Would an early dressing-down from the Chief Whip have prevented some of the abuses which later caused the downfall of some MPs?

There was a shamelessness in the actions of many MPs. In an era when City yuppies boasted of the size of their bonuses, in much the same way, parliamentarians shared tales of their freebies. Neil and Christine Hamilton were by no means the worst, but their summer holidays throughout the greedy eighties will keep coming back to haunt them. I do not tell this next story to embarrass them, although it undoubtedly will. But although he may have lacked judgement, I do not believe that the MP is corrupt.

A year after the Ritz trip, during the summer recess of 1988, Neil was due to go on a four-week 'Meet The American People' tour of the US, taking in the Republican Party convention in New Orleans. Although the trip was paid for by the American Government, the invitation did not include spouses. Three weeks before Neil left I received a call from Christine. She wanted to go too, but she couldn't afford the flight. 'Could you arrange a DHL courier flight?' she asked. I made a call and they agreed, and put her on a BA flight to Washington to join her husband three weeks hence.

I then received another call from Christine. Could she be upgraded? My patience was wearing a little thin, but sometimes it is easier to say yes than no. I called David Burnside of BA, a friend of the Hamiltons, and Christine got her upgrade.

The afternoon of the flight I received a third call from Christine. She was stranded at Heathrow airport in a terribly distressed state. Her BA flight had been merged with a TWA flight to Newark. She was worried she would lose her upgrade. I told her there was little David Burnside, or I, could do to help – I had no links with TWA. But, to keep her happy, I arranged for a car to pick her up from the airport and drive her into New York and to put her up for the night. She made her own way to Washington the next day.

The Hamiltons, like a number of MPs, took full advantage of British Airways, but it is quite wrong to suggest that either BA or the Hamiltons felt that they were under any obligation to each other as a result of the hospitality they enjoyed or provided.

The American trip led to further trouble for Neil Hamilton. At the Republican convention in New Orleans, Hamilton drove in Gerald Ford's cavalcade from the president's hotel to the conference centre, where he met the former American Secretary of State Henry Kissinger, who was a consultant adviser to US Tobacco.

US Tobacco was a large conglomerate with a factory in Scotland – built with the help of a £250,000 Scottish Office grant – which produced a chewing gum called Skoal Bandits. In 1988 the British Government was seeking to ban the product. UST were fighting a rearguard action to prevent this from happening.

The company's executives were pressed by one of their vice-presidents, Jack Afrik, an amazing cigar-smoking American whom they all held in great awe, to hire an MP as a consultant. He wanted the Tory chairman of the backbench Finance Committee, Sir William Clark, on board. The two had met somewhere and the MP was subsequently hired for £10,000 per year to advise on parliamentary procedure. My advice to companies, especially those dealing in controversial areas like tobacco, had always been *not* to hire an MP as a consultant. I felt it did their cause no good to have someone stand up in the House of Commons, declare their interest and then argue the company's case. And indeed UST grew unhappy as their concerns received scant attention in Sir William's busy parliamentary schedule.

The Tory MPs Neil Hamilton and Michael Brown, the latter a smoker, were both attracted to the tobacco lobby for libertarian reasons. Brown was also in the States that year. He addressed a UST conference, receiving a small honorarium from the company which he did not have to declare because it was below the amount stipulated by the House of Commons' rules. Hamilton attended the same conference and he was later put up for two nights in New York in a UST-owned apartment block, Essex House, overlooking Manhattan's Central Park. As with the Ritz trip a year earlier, Hamilton did not register the stay. And why should he? The press have attempted to make out his accommodation was worth £4,000, but in fact the actual cost to US Tobacco of putting him up in an otherwise empty flat was well below the registerable limit.

At the conference, the company's executives explained to Hamilton and Brown the difficulties they faced in the UK, their fear of an imminent Europe-wide ban on their product, and their concerns over the time Sir William Clark was able to devote to their interests. They wanted to hire a hard-hitting political lobbying outfit in London. The MPs mentioned IGA, and subsequently we were appointed to act as advisers to UST. I made a new-business referral payment to Michael Brown. It was unsolicited; he was surprised and grateful. I also made a referral payment to Neil Hamilton, which was one of two. The other, for £4,000, was for the introduction of his constituency firm, the National Nuclear Corporation. Hamilton considered both *ex gratia* payments, imposing no obligation on him of any kind and, he says, they were 'not received "in relation to my parliamentary duties"'. When the Select Committee on Members' Interests was to look at the matter of referral payments in 1990 (see Chapter 6), they were to decide that these were registerable. The one commission payment to Michael Brown for the introduction of US Tobacco is the only payment he has received from IGA.

Several years later, in 1996, when Neil Hamilton was the butt of the Fayed allegations, a former IGA staff member who worked on the UST account was to breach his contract of confidentiality when he told the *Sunday Times* of Hamilton's two-night stay at UST's Manhattan condominium, with the proviso that he remained an anonymous source. The *Sunday Times* published an article in February 1996 under the headline: 'Tory MP in row over free hotel stays'. This immediately led to a complaint by Labour Members against Hamilton. The newspaper tried to persuade its source to give evidence in public before the Commons' Standards and Privileges Commitee. He refused to do so and Sir Gordon Downey rightly concluded that the Commons Privileges Committee could not investigate unsubstantiated anonymous allegations. Natural justice demands that all witnesses are rigorously cross-examined. The story died.

One of the largest IGA contracts during the eighties was the Unitary Tax Campaign, a group of sixty leading UK companies, including ICI, BAT Industries, Barclays Bank and Cadbury Schweppes. They were fighting the punitive taxation policies of six American states. Fearful that multinational firms might avoid taxes by moving monies abroad, these states imposed an additional tax based on worldwide profits. Because a company was already being taxed on this worldwide profit elsewhere, they were effectively suffering double-taxation.

The Unitary Tax Campaign (UTC) hired IGA to exert pressure on the British Government to get tough with Washington. Attracting cross-party support, an Early Day Motion that was tabled on the subject gained well over 300 signatures, one of the highest number every recorded on any motion. The campaign ran for thirteen years, before we won an outright victory and it was wound up.

In June 1986 I organised an all-party delegation to visit Washington, DC, to lobby on behalf of the UTC. The campaign funded the trip in full. Michael Grylls, a hard-working paid consultant to the campaign since 1979, led the delegation. From the Liberal/SDP Alliance the obvious man to go was their Trade and Industry spokesman, Ian Wrigglesworth, and from Labour, a young up-and-coming Treasury spokesman, Tony Blair.

Our decision to fly the MPs on Concorde was due to the exigencies of a crazed timetable rather than any wish to give them a thrill. Working with the American lobbyists hired by the campaign, the British parliamentary delegation had a full schedule of press conferences, interviews and high-level meetings on Capitol Hill. Key appointments included the British Ambassador in Washington and the American Treasury Secretary. Gus O'Donnell, who was on attachment to the embassy and later became John Major's press secretary at Number 10, was seconded to the delegation.

The trip was painstakingly organised – we wanted to ensure the delegation was made to feel comfortable to enable them to make effective presentations on behalf of our clients. Each MP was properly briefed prior to departure. The hotel and transport arrangements had been booked with extreme care.

This three-man team was doing the right thing, on the other side of the Atlantic batting for British industry. And doing far more than the British Government, which, although it voiced its support, was dragging its heels and not putting sufficient pressure on Washington to bring the six recalcitrant American states into line.

Upon their return, Wrigglesworth registered the trip and Sir Michael Grylls had already declared UTC on the register. Tony Blair saw no requirement to do so, and he remained an enthusiastic supporter of the Unitary Tax Campaign. He tabled an Early Day Motion on the subject in June 1987.

When the story of Blair's undeclared Concorde trip broke in April 1995, the Labour leader dismissed it as a 'smear'. It was a 'quasi-official trip with no gain received or sought'. Tory members jumped on this. It wasn't, they argued, it was a trip paid for by a third party, the UTC, and organised by a lobbying firm. It was a junket, they crowed, worth £4,000. Labour were rattled.

Blair's private office was on the phone to us almost immediately. Blair's defence rested on his assertion that this had been a government-approved trip, but his office at the House of Commons no longer had any of the paperwork relating to the visit. Could IGA help? We were able to supply briefings and itineraries, but crucial correspondence from the Chancellor of the Exchequer had been destroyed by the Treasury. After four or five increasingly desperate calls, my deputy, Andrew Smith, talked to the Labour leader personally. Eventually, late at night, we tracked down a copy of a letter the Chancellor, Nigel Lawson, had written in 1986, which had been lodged with the Unitary Tax Campaign's Washington-based law firm.

Relieved, Tony Blair was able to respond confidently to the Registrar of Members' Interest. On 24 April 1995 he wrote:

> The visit was supported by the Treasury, the Inland Revenue and the British Embassy in Washington. The Chancellor, Nigel Lawson, wrote to the US Treasury Secretary, James Baker, to urge him to see the delegation and as a result a meeting was arranged. Michael Grylls, the leader of the delegation, met Norman Lamont, then Financial Secretary, for a briefing before the visit which he relayed to us, and we all saw Mr Lamont on our return. On arrival in Washington, the party was briefed by the Ambassador in Washington, Sir Oliver Wright, and by Gus O'Donnell, a Treasury official on attachment to the Embassy. The Ambassador and Mr O'Donnell accompanied us to our meeting with Mr Baker, and Mr O'Donnell accompanied us to other meetings.

The Tory MP David Shaw had by this time registered a formal complaint against Tony Blair. When the committee studied the complaint it found that the Labour leader should have registered his Washington visit: 'Our view is reinforced by the action of Mr Blair in tabling an Early Day Motion on this subject.' However their report went on to say, 'We recognise that there was some doubt among the members concerned about the status of the visit.' The committee concluded the affair was not sufficiently serious to warrant further action. David Shaw was furious with me. IGA, a supposedly rightward-leaning lobbying firm, had foiled a backbench plot to turn the spotlight on Labour sleaze. Despite the serious allegations that had been made against us, our oustanding libel action against the *Guardian*, and the fact that by this time Labour Members were signing hostile Early Day Motions about IGA itself, we had let the Labour leader off the hook. I had done this, not for party advantage, but because it was the right thing to do.

The kindness was not reciprocated. Shortly afterwards, at a Labour Party fund-raising dinner, to which IGA had invited a number of its clients, Jonathan Powell, Blair's chief of staff, had agreed to join IGA's guests. Without explanation or apology, we discovered, hours before the event, that Powell had chosen to dine at another table.

5

'NOT TO BE RELEASED UNDER ANY CIRCUMSTANCES'

Back in the corporate boxing ring, Lonrho launched a legal challenge to try to force Lord Young to publish the DTI report into the Harrods takeover, which had been completed in the summer of 1988. They lost the first round in January 1989 and appealed to the House of Lords. We expected Tiny Rowland to wait for the law to take its course. It was not to be.

That same month, Lonrho published a vituperative 199-page attack on Mohamed Fayed, printing over 80,000 copies of *A Hero From Zero* in English, French and Arabic. Rowland said it was 'prepared in anticipation that the present government would find it extremely uncomfortable to publish the inspector's report'.

A Hero From Zero purported to be an accumulation of the damaging anti-Fayed evidence Lonrho had supplied to the DTI inspectors. It claimed that Mohamed Fayed had lived an entire life of deception. It alleged that he had deceived the Sultan of Brunei into giving him power of attorney over vast Swiss bank accounts belonging to the monarch; that by concealed serial bank transfers, monies were moved to Fayed's sole control; and that the power of attorney he enjoyed over the Sultan's riches allowed him to manufacture a suitable background, including a rich industrial family and worldwide business interests. It claimed that in the twenty years until 1985, when he launched his bid for House of Fraser, he had been living luxuriously in

Britain off commission payments from British contractors working in Dubai. The book delved further into his past and discovered that, in 1965, he had absconded from the Port Authorities of Haiti with money he had allegedly stolen.

On 23 January 1989, Tim Smith stood up in the House to ask the Solicitor-General if he would be recommending *A Hero From Zero* for 'the Booker Prize for fiction'. These were matters outside his responsibilities, the Solicitor-General answered.

Within days, Tim received a letter from Tiny Rolwand challenging him to 'name the page, out of one hundred and ninety-nine pages, where you in your capacity as MP for Beaconsfield have discovered a fiction . . . How is it that you know so much about the Fayeds and can say *A Hero From Zero* is a work of fiction? . . . For some little time I have been puzzling over why you should want to make supportive remarks in Parliament about the Fayed brothers, and offensive ones about Lonrho, but I don't think I have to puzzle any longer. As usual with the Fayeds, it's just a case of how much, and in what way.'

Tim was rattled.

Tim made one more intervention in support of Fayed when he called for the replacement of the *Observer*'s independent directors. It stated that the only known occasion 'when the independent directors of the *Observer* intervened in a dispute between its editor and its proprietor, the response of its proprietor was to reduce the fees of the independent directors from £4,000 to £1,000, to describe them as "troglodytes" and to say that they served no useful purpose'.

After Tim received Rowland's letter, Mohamed began pressing me to find a new champion in Parliament – and this time he wanted one from the Opposition benches, as he believed there was now an opportunity to embarrass the government.

Two years earlier, Mohamed had received a letter from a woman, Francesca Pollard – who claimed to be a distant relative of the Corporate Affairs Minister, Michael Howard. She said she had been defrauded by a friend of Tiny Rowland's – a man by the name of Harold Landy.

Harry Landy was formerly a director and deputy chairman of

a major Lonrho subsidiary, London City and Westcliffe Properties. Six other members of the Landy family were share-holders in Lonrho. In 1979 Harry Landy was the principal defendant in an Old Bailey fraud trial described at the time as the largest and longest fraud case ever brought in the City of London. He was convicted and sentenced, but the conviction was later quashed. Rowland had visited Landy in jail and encouraged him to appeal. Sir Gordon Downey, Parliamentary Commissioner for Standards, recently concluded that, as a result, Landy owed 'a personal debt of gratitude' to Rowland.

Landy was well connected. He was the uncle, Pollard claimed, of Michael Howard, who was Corporate Affairs Minister between September 1985 and June 1987, at the time when the House of Fraser takeover bid was under consideration. During this period Howard answered a total of fourteen parliamentary questions on the subject. He did not declare his family interest. 'Michael Howard's family name was Landau,' she wrote. 'Howard is his middle name.'

Ms Pollard became a regular feature at Tory Party conferences during the eighties – she would march up and down outside the hall carrying placards denouncing the Lonrho boss. In her letter to Mohamed, she complained that she had already written to her constituency MP, Jeff Rooker, who was no help. Rooker, like a number of MPs, was calling for Fayed's prosecution after the publication of *A Hero From Zero*. Mohamed passed Ms Pollard's letter on to me with the message, 'Can you do your best to see if any questions can be raised as a result of this?'

She was provided with security by Fayed's men. She came into the IGA office to brief Tim Smith one day. I did not believe Howard's family connection to Landy would have played any part in his decision to mount an enquiry into Fayed, but I could recognise Fayed's belief that there was an opportunity to embarrass the government.

At the beginning of February I went to see the Labour front-bencher Allan Roberts. The late MP for Bootle was one of the House of Commons' most spirited and likeable survivors. Despite *News of the World* allegations in 1981 that he had donned a studded dog-collar and been whipped in a Berlin S&M club – Allan admitted to a 'drunken spree' – he had become a clever and respected Opposition spokesman on the environment.

I showed him Francesca Pollard's letter and asked if he would be prepared to assist. He promised to talk to his boss. A few days later, he reported back to me. The Labour leader, Neil Kinnock, was happy for the issue to be raised in the House, but did not want one of his frontbenchers so closely identified with one side of the Lonrho–House of Fraser struggle. Kinnock said he would sound out the prolific Sorbonne-educated Dale Campbell-Savours.

Campbell-Savours seemed an unlikely choice. He had been one of the original 'gang of three', as I called them, placing questions highly critical of Mohamed. In June 1986, he had rounded on Tim Smith for calling the adjournment debate on Rowland's abuse of the *Observer* – even to the extent of labelling Fayed an 'anti-Semite' and calling for a boycott of Harrods.

An Early Day Motion he signed on 23 June 1986 is worth recalling:

> This House deplores the attempt of the honourable Member for Beaconsfield to censor and silence the *Observer* in reporting the takeover of Harrods and 1109 prestigious stores formerly owned by the House of Fraser, now owned by AIT [Alfayed Investment and Trust (UK) Limited], a Liechtenstein company; advises the honourable Member not to be taken in by a public relations exercise being mounted by Mr Mohamed Al-Fayed, whose anti-semitic views have been authenticated on tape recordings; and calls on the honourable Member to join in a boycott of Harrods.

In January 1986, Campbell-Savours had called on Michael Howard, then Corporate Affairs Minister, to allow publication of recent correspondence between his department and Tiny Rowland. He had asked about discussions between the DTI and the Sultan of Brunei during the Harrods takeover (there were none). He had asked about the DTI's delay in allowing Lonrho to bid for the company. And he had asked about the sources of information available to the DTI on Fayed and the Sultan during their consideration of Fayed's cash bid for the company. All these were partisan requests useful to Lonrho in mounting a case against the Fayeds.

'Surely, having been so publicly identified with the anti-Fayed assault, Dale Campbell-Savours was not now going to forgo his principles and switch sides?' I said to Allan Roberts.

'Kinnock will have a word with him,' Allan explained. The invitation to join Fayed's team, he added, should come not from me, a Tory-identified lobbyist, but direct from Harrods. I reported back my conversation to Royston Webb.

As the records show, a miraculous transformation did take place in the activities of Dale Campbell-Savours. The man who, less than three years earlier, had 'deplored' Tim Smith's attempt to 'silence the *Observer*', set about doing the very same thing. He became the most active MP in the Fayed armoury – far more so than Tim Smith or Neil Hamilton had ever been.

In what remained of the parliamentary session – four months – he placed a total of forty-seven Early Day Motions – sometimes as many as four a day. Within days he was noting the family links between Michael Howard and Harry Landy. This was hotly followed by calls on the government to prosecute Tiny Rowland, for the Lonrho boss to divest himself of the *Observer* and, even, for the paper to apologise to Mark Thatcher. Others highlighted Lonrho's links to Dr Ashraf Marwan, an Egyptian business associate of Rowland, and attempts to bug Fayed. Another attempted to embarrass the Lonrho chairman, Sir Edward du Cann, over a bounced cheque.

Campbell-Savours was closely involved with Royston Webb. Webb told me that, at the outset, he would draft the EDMs with Campbell-Savours 'looking over my shoulder'. After a while, Royston was able to draft them himself to the satisfaction of the MP. I kept a close grip on events, faxing Mohamed on 11 April 1989:

Have been talking to Neil Hamilton – he and I are talking further tomorrow about the Questions/Motions that will be tabled in the House by Dale Campbell-Savours relating to Lonrho and ownership of the *Observer*. There will be several Motions over the course of the next two or three weeks . . . Questions relating to MH [Michael Howard] are also likely to be made public this week, again by Dale Campbell-Savours. Kinnock's personal attention has been drawn to the issues and he has expressed interest. We are keeping him up to date with information. This must be entirely confidential as it could be embarrassing if Conservative Members knew of our plans regarding MH [Michael Howard].

Questions have already been put down by Campbell-Savours relating to Harry Landy, British arms sales to Kenya, Tradewinds arms exports and Marwan's diplomatic status. It is important that we start now to get press coverage on these questions.

Royston Webb now says that Campbell-Savours' agenda in helping the Fayeds was to wrest the *Observer* from Tiny Rowland and make it an entirely independent newspaper. I imagine this is true, but the Early Day Motions placed by the MP go far wider than Rowland's ownership of the newspaper, suggesting he rapidly developed a great sympathy for Fayed's cause.

Many of his Early Day Motions attracted the enthusiastic support of Neil Hamilton. In April, Hamilton was signatory number 3 on Campbell-Savours' EDM 738, regarding alleged proprietorial interference at the *Observer*; the following month he was signatory number 5 on Campbell-Savours' EDM 801, regarding an allegedly fabricated story in the newspaper which served Lonrho's commercial interests; Hamilton was signatory number 3 – with Campbell-Savours pipping him to the number 2 slot – on Tim Smith's EDM 857, calling for the replacement of the independent directors of the *Observer*; in June, Hamilton was signatory number 2 on Campbell-Savours' EDM 992, criticising Lonrho's trading connections with Iran and an article in the *Observer* designed to give credence to the Islamic regime in that country; on the very same day Hamilton signed Campbell-Savours' EDM 993, criticising Lonrho's use of the *Observer* to publish an untrue story alleging Mark Thatcher and the Sultan of Brunei's involvement in the Harrods takeover. An impressive workload.

Dale Campbell-Savours now sits on the House of Commons Standards and Privileges Committee. The committee is judging Neil Hamilton's role, along with those of other MPs and myself in the Fayed/cash-for-questions affair. Even though he did nothing wrong, it seems extraordinary that he would wish to play a part in judgement, given his former close involvement.

During all this time IGA was still being paid a monthly fee of £2,083 by Fayed. After the publication of *A Hero From Zero* we were forced into fighting a rearguard action. Royston wrote to a large number of MPs on 10 March 1989 saying, 'We are conscious that you may be concerned that our lack of an equally public response [to Rowland over *A Hero From Zero*] might be tantamount to our accepting the accuracy of his allegations.' He reminded them that legal action had successfully been taken against the *Observer* over the allegations that Fayed had used the Sultan's cash to buy House of Fraser.

Neil Hamilton replied enthusiastically to this letter. He wrote to Mohamed noting how his own libel action against the BBC had run from January 1984 until October 1986. 'I have long felt that the length of time which libel actions are taking has given the wrong impression,' he wrote presciently. 'Silence should not be interpreted as acquiescence in the allegations.'

The *Sunday Telegraph* had reported on 5 March that Lonrho was seeking to block British arms sales to traditional pro-British countries. And Royston Webb claimed a link between a Lonrho subsidiary and Libya, at a time when relations with that country were at a particularly low ebb.

Shortly after the *Sunday Telegraph* story, Royston sent over a rough draft of a letter to Douglas Hurd, the Home Secretary. Having responded so enthusiastically to his previous missive, he thought Neil might be prepared to sign a letter. Royston's plan was to get Brian Basham, Fayed's PR supremo, to release it to the press.

We would occasionally draft letters for members to sign.

Admittedly, in this respect we were acting as an extension of an MP's own private office. In the present climate, there are some who will respond angrily that this relationship was too cosy and must have led to undue influence or pressure on an MP. At the time it seemed sensible. MPs are grossly underpaid and disgracefully ill-served in terms of the most basic secretarial and research support. If an MP had already agreed to send a letter on behalf of one of my clients but his secretary was snowed under, he might say, 'can you type it for me?'. Members are used to being lobbied. They are used to being asked to put down PQs. They are used to taking up cases. They responded to IGA's advances because they knew we would not waste their time. We had done our homework, we knew what a particular MP would be interested in and we understood parliamentary procedure.

Only this time we got it wrong – and paid the price. I was away. My deputy, Andrew Smith, was unable to get hold of Neil, but typed the letter on a blank sheet of House of Commons notepaper. Not entirely sure whether Neil would want to send it, Andrew took a copy and marked it: 'Not to be Released Under Any Circumstances Without the Permission of Ian Greer' and faxed this copy back to Royston. He took the original over to the House of Commons to discuss it with Neil.

It was an error. Neil, although agreeing to put down some questions on the subject, did not want to sign a letter to the Home Secretary which appeared to be designed purely for publicity purposes (as indeed it was). But by this time the unsigned copy of the letter, with the inscription at the top, had been faxed back to Royston Webb. Five years later it was handed to the *Guardian* by Fayed. It became the centrepiece of a *Guardian* front page, although the extract shown did not disclose the fact that the letter had never been signed. Clearly shown, however, was the instruction not to release the letter without my permission. This instruction was directed at Brian Basham's office. Out of context it seemed I was telling Neil Hamilton or even the Home Office what they should release and when.

As it turned out, the Fayed story about Marwan lacked substance. Marwan was not, nor ever had been, an accredited

NOT TO BE RELEASED UNDER
ANY CIRCUMSTANCES WITHOUT
THE PERMISSION OF IAN GREER

HOUSE OF COMMONS
LONDON SW1A 0AA

Rt. Hon. Douglas Hurd. CBE, MP,   21st March 1989
Home Secretary.
Home Office,
50 Queen Anne's Gate,
London SW1H 9AT.

I am deeply concerned by press reports referring to the
activities of Ahmed Gadafadam, until recently a board
member of the Aircraft Cargo Firm 'Tradewinds', a Lonrho
subsidiary. I understand that Ahmed Gadafadam is a cousin
of Colonel Gaddafi, and brother of Said Gadafadam, Head of
Libyan Intelligence. I believe that the Gadafadam link
with the Libyan regime and the press allegations of illicit
arms dealing must warrant the closest examination.

Egyptian diplomat – as we found out from PQs Neil subsequently tabled. But such details were of little value when trying
to explain the letter some years later.

Lonrho got hold of the unpublished DTI report on or about 23
March 1989. The editor of the *Observer*, Donald Trelford, was
recalled from a week's leave to mastermind 'Operation Sphinx',
a special Thursday edition of the Sunday paper. The publishing
operation was carried out in almost total secrecy. Only twelve
carefully selected journalists were told of the plan – even the
news editor did not know. One of the independent directors
went on record stating that the first he knew was when he heard

about it on the radio. Under the front-page headline 'Exposed – the Phoney Pharaoh', the midweek edition made interesting reading at the Grosvenor House Hotel, where Lonrho happened to be holding their AGM that day. Thousands of copies were distributed free.

'The Egyptian Fayed brothers obtained Harrods and the House of Fraser, the biggest stores group in Europe, by fraud and deceit,' it screamed. Tiny Rowland, a lone voice over the previous four years, was fully vindicated, it said, in claiming that the Fayeds could not have owned the money with which they bought Harrods.

In a lengthy front-page editorial under the headline 'Why we are publishing today', Trelford sought to justify the action. There was no war on. This was not Khrushchev's historic denunciation of Stalin, he admitted. But the DTI report on the House of Fraser Holdings plc threw into 'sharp relief the unsatisfactory procedures of the DTI itself and of the Office of Fair Trading, the chief regulatory body for the conduct of business in this country'. In March 1985, it went on, the Trade and Industry Secretary, Norman Tebbit, had been 'led up the garden path'. The paper claimed that Mr Tebbit had exercised his ministerial responsibility by 'ringing up the ill-informed chairman of an interested merchant bank'. The present Secretary of State, Lord Young, was guilty of a 'cover-up'.

The *Observer* called for urgent changes to the City Code and Companies Act. By letting the report see the light of day, the *Observer* had cleared its name against the charge that it had acted at the behest of its owners – a charge 'now surely and officially disposed of'. Virtually everyone, including the rest of Fleet Street and some senior journalists on the paper, thought this last boast completely bogus.

The *Observer* bore the entire cost of the operation – £25,000. Newsagents were allowed to keep all the 25p cover price – a legal wheeze which meant that once the *Observer* handed over the 285,000 copies to the wholesalers, they no longer legally owned them. 'So much for commercial good sense and editorial independence,' sniffed Lord Young.

The paper was on the streets shortly after 10 am. The DTI acted swiftly. In the courts, government lawyers argued that if charges were to be brought against anyone involved in the House of Fraser takeover, an uncontaminated jury, uninfluenced by press reporting of the issue, would have to be found. The *Observer*'s leak of the report placed in jeopardy the chances of a fair trial. Within two hours Lord Young had gained an injunction stopping the publication of any more copies, which also covered reporting by anyone else. Press officers from the DTI immediately phoned all national newspapers, alerting them to the injunction.

Sir Edward du Cann, MP, was in full flow on the rostrum at the Grosvenor House Hotel when a call came through from the DTI, at 11.50 am, notifying Lonrho of the injunction. Attempts to interrupt him were not heeded. He continued to read from the report which, he said, was leaked to him 'anonymously' and arrived unsolicited.

The injunction was a farce. Coming so soon after the government's attempts to suppress *Spycatcher*, the memoirs of the former MI5 agent Peter Wright, it looked like heavy-handed censorship by an embarrassed government. Copies of the *Observer* continued to be sold openly throughout most of Thursday and Friday. By the weekend, the paper had been read by anybody remotely interested in the affair.

Tiny Rowland spiced the proceedings by revealing that pirate copies of the DTI report were being printed in Switzerland, Germany and the USA. 'Lonrho has no association whatsoever with those involved,' he told reporters. 'But of course we are not discouraging them. After all, it promises to be a 752-page bestseller.' A deeply embarrassed Lord Young argued weakly that the Swiss, German and American public were unable to sit on English juries.

Margaret Thatcher was in Namibia and was told on the telephone of the *Observer*'s sensational coup. She was not due to return until the following Sunday morning. Furious, she ordered a meeting at Number 10 with Lord Young and Solicitor-General Sir Nicholas Lyell on her arrival in London. When news of the planned meeting leaked, and was portrayed in the press as a 'crisis summit', it was hurriedly cancelled: television pictures of two senior ministers being hauled into Number 10 on a weekend were thought unwise. Lord Young spoke to the Prime Minister on the phone instead. They agreed to tough it out.

On the following Monday, Lord Young launched into an attack on Sir Edward du Cann in a statement to the House of Lords, which returned from the Easter recess a day before the Commons. Du Cann, he said, had refused to return all the leaked copies of the report to Lord Young, his former ministerial boss, or to give a sworn affidavit of how a copy came into his hands in the first place. For a Privy Counsellor, 'this shows an extraordinary lack of respect for the due processes of law,' Lord Young said defiantly. 'Lonrho and the *Observer* will not be successful in their attempt to cast me in the role of the Duke of Wellington. I shall not publish and I shall not be damned.' He set up an enquiry to chase the departmental mole who had leaked the report.

His Labour opposite number, Lord Williams of Elvel, told the House of Lords the situation was 'absurd'. By now interested parties knew the report 'chapter and verse'. Lord Williams announced he planned to table amendments to the Companies Bill to strengthen takeover regulations along the lines of the inspectors' recommendations. 'If the noble Lord wishes to know how I know what these recommendations are, I would refer him and the other noble Lords who are interested to the library of this House, which, as I found this morning, has a copy of the special edition of the *Observer* of last Thursday.'

The 'Phoney Pharaoh', meanwhile, was not enjoying his latest bout of publicity. He was on the phone almost before the *Observer* hit the streets. This was shit from the greatest height ever. We advised him not to go public – let others speak for him. After two days of dignified silence, he blew it when he turned up to a charity tea with Girl Guides and Boy Scouts at the store.

'Mr Al Fayed will not be making any comment,' his press spokesman Michael Cole had warned at the outset. But, goaded by journalists' questions, Mohamed launched into a lengthy tirade against Rowland and du Cann. 'Only God' could prise him from Harrods, he declared. 'I am making plans to be buried on the top of the building. I will have the tomb on the roof.'

Four hundred Guides, Scouts, Cubs and Brownies munching ham handwiches blinked into the cameras as Cole made efforts to restrain a fifty-six-year-old Egyptian man who by this time had donned a ridiculously small Cub's cap. 'Rowland? Who is he? He is mad,' he told the crowd of reporters pursuing him around Harrods' toy department. 'I will never give up Harrods. He gave it to me. I paid cash. It was done correctly. My cheque never bounced.' Where did the money come from to buy Harrods, he was asked. 'Does anyone have any right to ask you where you get your money?' he retorted. 'If someone comes in here and asks for a diamond ring costing £100,000 they aren't asked where the money comes from.' Was he a worried man? 'Do I look worried? I am not a worried man. I have other people to worry about these things for me.'

Royston Webb, Michael Cole and I were worried. And, despite his bravado, so was Mohamed. Out of the blue, our team had been rocked by a stunning goal from the Lonrho camp. For the first time IGA began to doubt whether everything Mohamed had told us about his background and his wealth was true. But we still stuck by him. Lonrho's actions in leaking the report, and poisoning the air against Mohamed, had gone so far beyond the limits of acceptable behaviour, we felt some sympathy for him.

Mohamed remained surrounded by some of the best professional advisers in the business – lawyers, bankers, accountants, public relations consultants and lobbyists. And in Parliament he still had the highly respected parliamentarian Sir Peter Hordern, as a paid adviser.

We consoled ourselves with the knowledge that this was not yet an official government report. Tim Smith's sentiment that, even if Mohamed had exaggerated his background and wealth, he should be admired for being a self-made achiever was something to hold on to. But for us to do this, Mohamed would have to reinvent himself. He would have to eschew his aristocratic pretensions. And his pride, his dignity and his honour – which had suffered so much during this whole affair – could not stomach that.

As for Rowland, he had caused extreme embarrassment to the government and Fayed. The IGA team were forced to admit that Rowland had effectively played two masterstrokes in public relations terms – the first being the publication of *A Hero From Zero*, which had mocked Fayed, and the second being the much more serious publication of the leaked DTI report, which dramatically focused the spotlight on Fayed's credibility – although the *Observer*, once a respected newspaper, also saw its independence questioned.

Until the end of 1989, Neil Hamilton continued to see Mohamed and Dale Campbell-Savours continued to see Royston Webb. Both men pursued the leak of the DTI report. Webb had received information which suggested that the copy of the report which had been passed to the *Observer* had been entrusted to the police officers investigating the affair. Campbell-Savours tabled a succession of EDMs exposing alleged meetings that had taken place shortly before publication of the midweek *Observer*, meetings between senior police officers and the paper's editor.

Mohamed claims he saw Hamilton once in November, and now alleges that he handed him Harrods gift vouchers as well as cash – a claim the MP refutes. Neil did write to the new Home Secretary, David Waddington, on 6 December 1989, bringing to his attention the EDMs placed by his Labour ally, Dale Campbell-Savours. A bottle of House of Commons cognac which Neil gave Mohamed for Christmas signalled the end of Neil's involvement with the campaign.

With Fayed labelled a liar, albeit still unofficially, lobbying on his behalf effectively came to an end. Ostensibly, the Serious Fraud Office were still considering mounting a prosecution.

At this point Royston Webb raised the fact that IGA were being paid £25,000 and not doing very much work. He was directly briefing the last remaining active MP in the Commons, Dale Campbell-Savours. I had to agree with him and the fee IGA charged House of Fraser was reduced to £500 per month from 1

December 1989. This covered no more than our parliamentary monitoring service.

Royston explained this in a fax to Mohamed, a copy of which he sent to me: 'We would of course also use IGA for any special assignments as and when the need arose,' he told his boss. Which is precisely what happened a few weeks later when the DTI announced there would be no prosecutions and it would publish the long-awaited report. IGA received a project fee of £13,333 to cover additional work over a three-month period from 1 February to 30 April 1990. We set out to brief MPs on Mohamed's well-rehearsed criticisms of the report and its authors, and his desire to seek redress in the courts. We all thought this last proposal was a bad idea which would drag out the affair for years, causing more hurt – as indeed it has done.

That cheque for £13,333 in 1990 was, according to Mohamed, handed over to put me in funds to pay MPs. The suggestion is ludicrous. I am not sure which MPs would have been receiving money by this time. Andrew Bowden had ceased, in 1987, to be an active supporter of Fayed. Tim Smith had also ceased to provide active support to Fayed a year earlier. Michael Grylls, although a friend of Fayed, had not taken any active interest in the issue for an even longer period.

And Neil Hamilton? Well, Neil has recently admitted to Sir Gordon Downey that he approached Mohamed Fayed in July 1990 and asked if he and Christine could stay at the Paris Ritz once again, as they were due to attend a friend's wedding just outside the city. Fayed said no, but suggested that they stay for two nights in his private apartment on the Champs-Elysées. This was just weeks before Hamilton became a government Whip and shortly after the DTI report condemning Fayed had been published. This second trip was something that the Hamiltons failed to disclose throughout the two years we spent preparing for our libel trial – either to me, or, I believe, to our lawyers. I am very angry about this – and especially the manner in which Christine Hamilton dismissed its relevance when I raised the matter with her recently. However, by the time the £13,333 cheque was paid, in February 1990, Hamilton was, as far as I was concerned, no longer an active Fayed supporter in the House of Commons.

I suspect the *Guardian* asked Mohamed, in an attempt to substantiate his allegation that he paid MPs via me, to produce any evidence of payments to IGA outside the regular monthly fee. Mohamed's book-keepers could find only three such payments – two cheques before the 1987 general election, which even Mohamed's spokesman now says, as I had always stated, were for the 1987 election campaign, and the project fee at the time the report was published.

I returned from Hong Kong just before publication of the report and sent Mohamed a note: 'Many congratulations on "toughing it out". All your friends, I know, will be delighted.'

With the report published, and protected by privilege, Fleet Street had a field day. Two quotes will give the flavour: Fayed was responsible for 'lies, deceit, cock and bull stories'. Here was an individual who committed 'a very serious offence . . . the dishonest acquisition of one of our major stores groups'. Both these quotes appeared in an editorial in the *Guardian*.

6

IN THE DOCK

In the eighties, lobbying was an entirely new industry in the United Kingdom. There were no statutory controls guiding our behaviour. Over five separate Parliaments, the House of Commons examined our activities and failed to come up with either rules or guidelines as to how we should operate.

In October 1988, when I first appeared before the Select Committee on Members' Interests, IGA was riding high. Our advertising boasted that we were Europe's leading public affairs company. Our turnover had just broken through the million-pound barrier. I valued our independence. We were not part-owned by one of the large US public relations firms, nor were we exclusively tied to one political party. I had many friends in both Houses of Parliament, on all sides of the political divide, but no politicians on our board. None were employed by us, and none depended on us for any part of their income. I had provided a memo about IGA to the committee. Subsequently examined in person, my performance was upbeat. Facing a semicircle of MPs all scribbling notes, I was happy to ram home the point.

'You claim independence, which is not always claimed by some public relations companies,' the committee chairman, Geoffrey Johnson-Smith, reminded me. 'You do not retain any peers or Members of Parliament, or Members of the European Parliament or other, so-called, political advisers. You are completely disassociated from them?'

'That is correct,' I answered, confidently. I was proud of that fact. However, if IGA or, indeed, any lobbying company had chosen to have any Member as a director or consultant, we would have been properly entitled to do so. Indeed, it was a fast-growing practice within the industry. The fact of the matter was that IGA had not and did not.

'This is a conscious policy decision, or is it that you do not find anyone outside the world in which you inhabit worthy of being employed by you?' Johnson-Smith asked.

'No,' I replied. 'It is very much a conscious decision, Mr Chairman, taken when the company was formed, and it is something that we do not see any reason to change. We have a great number of friends in both Houses of Parliament and I think there is no reason for us to engage or retain any Members. It is not in any way something that we feel should be mistaken by Members, but it is something that we do not feel is necessary.'

I should have reflected on the meaning of the word 'association' – but did not. I should have explained the payments I had made to Michael Grylls, Neil Hamilton and Michael Brown for referral of business. As these were one-off payments, with no lasting obligations, I felt 'completely disassociated' from all three MPs. I answered the committee chairman honestly. For my part, one of the benefits of paying a fee for new-business introductions is it immediately ended any sense of a continuing obligation. I wanted to avoid a situation, where two years down the line, MP X could phone me up and say, 'Oi, Greer. I got you that huge six-figure account, now you do me a favour.'

The referral payments were based on between 5 and 10 per cent of the value of the first year's contract. It was usual practice for lobbyists to pay introductory fees to each other during the eighties – although our rivals have gone very mute on this point. If two tobacco companies or two airlines approached you, you could only have one as a client. A rival lobbying firm might find a new client keen to come on board but, due to a conflict of interest with another of their clients, be unable to act for them. They would then recommend the prospective new client to another lobbying firm, which would be expected to pay a tidy sum to the first firm for the referral. The practice was already well established by public relations companies, accountants and solicitors. As for paying commissions to MPs for introduction of business, although the practice has now stopped, I believe one other lobbying firm did it during the eighties.

I would not pay an MP if I felt he had not earned a commission payment. The former Conservative MP for Wirral South, the late Barry Porter, was persistent in claiming that I owed him a commission fee after we were hired by one of his constituency companies. At one point he harangued me on the House of Commons terrace, yelling, 'Where's my commission?' It is perfectly possible he had said very nice things about me to this company, but I did not feel he had done anything to earn himself a commission from IGA. In the end, it became so embarrassing that I bought him a case of champagne. I then faced the difficulty of where to send it, and in the end left it at the Westminster pub around the corner where Barry was a regular visitor.

Mohamed Fayed and House of Fraser were introduced to me by Lord King. He introduced a number of clients to IGA, but would have been grossly insulted if I had ever suggested making a payment for this. He is a man of great integrity and made recommendations solely on the basis that he believed that IGA would do a good job. Indeed, he was surprised to learn many years after the event that Michael Grylls had been paid £10,000 for introducing British Airways to IGA.

Neil Hamilton and Michael Brown, who were in receipt of commission payments from IGA, did not register them. Michael Grylls was later to be criticised by the Select Committee on Members' Interests for not making clear in the register payments received from IGA. I strongly felt then, and continue to feel, that the decision as to registration is, and must remain, one for Members of Parliament. The House of Commons jealously guarded its power to regulate itself – the last thing I felt I should be doing as an outside lobbyist was telling Members what they should and should not declare.

Back in the eighties there was less attention paid to the register and things were not as clear-cut as today. MPs could reasonably argue that there was no section in which to record one-off payments. And even so, how should they be recorded? When Grylls introduced British Airways, how should that have been registered? Under British Airways or IGA, when he was working for neither? There was only one other type of payment we made directly to one MP. Michael Grylls had been in the House for many years. He was by anyone's standards a hard-working Member of Parliament. Whilst he was a keen constituency Member, he had, in addition, an increasingly large portfolio of outside interests as consultant, adviser and director to numerous associations, trade bodies and companies. He was paid £10,000 a year by the Unitary Tax Campaign, and although IGA undertook a vast amount of the administrative and political work necessary to ensure the campaign's success, Michael led the charge in Parliament. He was a tireless worker on behalf of the campaign. From 1979, he had been battling with ministers, sponsoring Early Day Motions, tabling questions and leading all-party delegations. Any Member of Parliament has a limited amount of time and it soon became clear that the £10,000 which was all the UTC could afford was not sufficient to ensure that Michael stayed on board. The campaign was a good one for IGA. It was high-profile and, as a result of frequent trips to the States, we were developing a useful network for the future. When Michael approached me about how much additional work he was undertaking for the campaign I agreed to pay him £10,000 per year. This was solely relating to parliamentary work undertaken on behalf of the Unitary Tax Campaign. He did not become a director or a consultant for IGA, nor did he provide active support for IGA on behalf of any client.

Michael declared the payments, either as UTC or 'Adviser to Unitary Tax Campaign (I. Greer Associates)'. Perhaps he should have sought advice from the Clerk to the Members' Interests Register, but as the fee paid to him by me related specifically and solely to the UTC, which he declared in the Register for thirteen years, he did not think it necessary. My deputy, Andrew Smith, was often in the House helping Michael with his work on the campaign and he was given a House of Commons researcher's pass, for a short time, to ease access. This too was declared.

I was very aware that during the eighties lobbyists were operating in an unregulated market. In October 1988, I strongly urged the Select Committee on Members' Interests to set up a statutory register of lobbyists, but that it should include all those who lobby for Commercial gain. By this time, dozens of individual companies, particularly in the oil and tobacco industries, and dozens of trade associations and trade unions were employing their own teams of in-house lobbyists. Lobbyists for charities such as the World Wildlife Fund would also have to be included – the organisations they represented were not profit-making, but their lobbyists were paid operators who were just as keen to influence ministers and MPs as any professional lobbying outfit. Similarly, and more importantly, all commercial companies – from BA to ICI – would have to register their in-house political teams. The register would have to be comprehensive and compulsory, similar to that which operated in the United States. However, California has taken the idea to its extreme. Their statutory register includes every individual who lobbies: they have to make detailed quarterly declarations of their activities, who they have entertained and what expenditure they have incurred. The Californian lobbyist is under considerable constraints: he can spend a maximum of $25 entertaining a legislator or official.

I argued that all lobbyists on a Westminster register would have to abide by an agreed code of conduct – to be policed by Parliament. That, I maintained at the Select Committee, seemed the only workable solution. All payments to MPs, either one-off commission fees or on-going consultancies with lobbying firms, would be covered by this uniform code.

But the House of Commons Select Committee on Members' Interests, especially Dale Campbell-Savours, seemed keen to argue for a voluntary register and self-regulation by the lobbying industry. Following Nolan, it has been shown that Parliament is incapable of regulating itself. Why, I ask, should the lobbying industry be any better at it? Nevertheless, in 1988 I gave my assurance to the committee that if they decided to propose a voluntary rather than a statutory register, IGA would fully support it, and gave a personal undertaking that we would register all of our clients. Instead they chose to do nothing.

Just as I thought my examination by the Select Committee was coming to a close, Dale Campbell-Savours, who had not begun working directly with Royston Webb by this time, asked me another question:

> Can I ask you a question that requires a courageous answer? . . . Is there anything in your view in the relationship that may exist if a chairman of a Select Committee of the House of Commons is also a director or a shareholder of some lobbying company to cause unease? Do you think, without picking on any specific example, you would place a question mark over that kind of relationship? We are not talking about an ordinary Member of Parliament, but a chairman of a Select Committee?

The Tory members on the committee groaned. This was obviously a pet subject for the Labour Member and one of which they were growing tired. I realised immediately who he was talking about: Sir Marcus Fox, who headed the Committee of Selection, was more than just another Select Committee chairman. His committee was in charge of allocating Members to all Select Committees, which studied legislation as it passed through the Commons. Sir Marcus was also a director of a rival lobbying firm, Westminster Communications. Critics were concerned about the possibility of a conflict of interest when Sir Marcus had to choose which MP to place on which committee.

Labour's frontbench Home Affairs spokeswoman Ann Taylor, Liberal Democrat heavyweight Menzies Campbell and Sir Keith Speed, a former Tory minister, were also directors of Westminster Communications – all four were to give up these directorships when the cash-for-questions affair broke in 1994. I felt it was quite improper that Campbell-Savours was asking me to condemn a practice which was nothing to do with me. I tried to dodge the question.

'May I answer by saying, Mr Chairman, that my company would not find themselves in that position.' I looked directly at Geoffrey Johnson-Smith. Before he could save me, Campbell-Savours jumped in.

'I understand that and accept that,' he said. 'Is that your answer?'

'Yes,' I replied.

'I see,' he said, rolling the word over his tongue. 'You would not clearly, therefore, because you would be uneasy about this kind of relationship. That is why you advise against it?'

I hesitated. 'I would not allow it to happen,' I replied truthfully.

Campbell-Savours smiled. 'Thank you,' he said.

Hell, I thought. I had walked straight into his trap. Marcus would not be happy. A few days later I plucked up the courage to go to see him in his office at the House of Commons. He was more than unhappy, he was livid.

'You should bloody know that Dale Campbell-Savours is an unpleasant man,' he barked in his blunt Yorkshire tones. 'You should have realised that was a trick question.' Whilst Fox had in truth done nothing wrong, my response did him no favours.

I should have realised it was a trick question, but what could I do, other than apologise? Marcus Fox survived. He remained chairman of the Selection Committee until 1992, when he became chairman of the powerful 1922 Committee of Backbench Conservative MPs. He resigned his directorship at Westminster Communications in 1994, following the example of Dame Angela Rumbold, the Conservative Party vice-chairman, who had resigned from the lobbying firm Decision Makers, after Labour reported her to the Members' Interests Committee. Decision Makers had lobbied for the company which won a government contract to build the Channel Tunnel rail link station at Ebbsfleet, south of the Thames, in preference to Stratford, a Labour heartland in East London, with railway land to spare. It was claimed that Dame Angela had used her influence which resulted in this decision.

Apart from my error over Marcus Fox, my appearance before the Select Committee had gone well. IGA continued to expand. Although frustrated by the committee's inaction over laying down ground-rules, I was too busy doing my job to worry unduly. Until suddenly, a full year later, the left-wing former *Guardian* journalist Andrew Roth (a man to whom I had never warmed, but who had made his services on a freelance basis available to my previous company) alleged that I had misled the committee. With absolute horror, I read the 1989 edition of his *Parliamentary Profiles*, where he highlighted IGA's commission payments to Michael Grylls, claiming that I had deliberately withheld this information.

I immediately wrote to the committee and volunteered to appear before it again. The clerk wrote asking me if I still stood by my earlier remarks. I replied saying I did not wish to alter my statement, but wanted to add by way of expansion:

> That from time to time we were approached by third parties (including, occasionally, Members of Parliament) with an introduction to a potential client. In accordance with what I understand to be industry practice, a fee is paid to the introducing party should the introduction result in our acting for the client in question. By this I mean that we have no contractual arrangement with any third party under which the intention is that they should introduce business to us on a continuing basis ... no introducing party is 'retained' or 'engaged'.

As I expected, this was not enough to satisfy the committee. I was informed they would want to see me again.

The registrar sent a note to all MPs ordering them that 'single payments, such as commissions received for introductions or other services, should be registered (under the category most appropriate to the circumstances) where such payments relate in any way to Membership of the House'. He did not demand MPs to back-date any entry. In subsequent years, Michael Grylls registered IGA as a 'client'. MPs were not expected at this time to include the amount of any payment received. Neil Hamilton and Michael Brown – who had not referred any new business to the company since 1988 – did not inform the registrar about their previous payments. There was no requirement for them to do so.

Michael Brown had received £6,000 for the introduction of US Tobacco in 1988. Neil Hamilton had received the same amount, also for the introduction of US Tobacco. It was a joint introduction.

In addition Neil introduced the National Nuclear Corporation, a constituency company. He already had a consultancy with the firm, which he declared in December 1987. Because the workload was too great for him, he referred the company to IGA and received a £4,000 fee. Neil did not register his two payments to the Inland Revenue and planned to produce evidence in court from his accountant stating he did not need to – arguing that these payments were one-off gifts rather than income.

Neil received his payment – which totalled £10,000 – by cheque and 'in kind'. This was how he asked for it: I paid £700 to a Penzance antique shop in 1988 for pictures, £959.85 to John Lewis for garden furniture he and Christine had chosen, £1,594 for air fares for them to fly to New Orleans and then to Aspen, Colorado. He received a cheque for the balance of £6,746.05 in July 1989. It is now suggested that I was naïve in consenting to Neil's request that the referral payment was partly made in kind. It was of no consequence to me as long as it was fully recorded in IGA's books, which indeed it was.

After the Roth 'revelations', just before Christmas 1989, Dale Campbell-Savours phoned me as I was leaving the office to go to lunch. He was extremely charming. When I should have said, 'Mr Campbell-Savours, I think it would be wrong to enter into any discussion with you prior to my appearance before the Select Committee on which you serve,' I answered his questions as honestly as I could. I should have been alerted by my first encounter with him at the committee in 1988. On the telephone that lunchtime, he took me for a ride. He told me he agreed with me that there should be no need for a Member to register such one-off commission payments. He agreed he didn't know under what category such a payment would be registerable anyway. I told him I had made such payments to three MPs. I explained the process. Unbeknown to me, he was taking notes.

I was due to go before the committee again in April 1990, an experience I was not looking forward to. I was also unsure of what questions I would be asked – although I was sure that the issue of Members' declarations on the register would be high on the agenda. I firmly believed it was the MPs' responsibility and not mine. Westminster had a procedure for regulating the actions of its Members. I knew many MPs would take a very dim view of the fact that I, an outsider, had seen fit to make a declaration on a Members' behalf. I sought some friendly advice from a senior Government Whip, conscious of the fact that I had made commission payments to two Members in addition to Michael Grylls. 'What do I tell the committee?' I asked him.

'Leave it to me,' he replied. A few days later, he came back with the advice: 'Apologise profusely to the committee but do not give the names.' This fitted entirely with my own thoughts.

I did not ask where, or from how high, the Whip had sought this advice. David Willetts was forced to resign for seeking to give advice to Geoffrey Johnson-Smith, the chairman of the Members' Interests Committee, several years later.

Apologise and refuse to name names is exactly what I did. A member of my staff told me I had paid Michael Grylls three commission payments, Neil Hamilton two and Michael Brown one. I took his word for it. At that moment I was more concerned about how I was going to explain my reading of the word 'disassociated' (see page 83–4), which, in the light of Mr Roth's revelations, had suddenly taken on a whole new meaning.

My appearance before the committee this second time was a long and tiring affair. Dale Campbell-Savours, glancing from time to time at notes he had made when on the phone to me before Christmas, launched immediately into his interrogation. Weren't my previous answers to the committee inaccurate? No, I replied. How many MPs had I paid and how often had I paid them, he wanted to know, 'in the context of the conversation we had on the phone'.

This, I thought, was below the belt. It suggested I was going to say something different to the committee from what I had said to him on the phone. I was then put under intense pressure by the committee to disclose the names of any and all Members to whom I had paid commission. Following the friendly advice I had been given, and my own conscience, I refused to do this.

Under pressure from the Tory MP Peter Griffiths to explain my understanding of the word 'disassociated', I admitted: 'Perhaps it would have been helpful to say at that juncture during the committee proceedings, "I don't retain any Members as consultants or advisers but from time to time, yes, I have made a payment for the introduction of business" . . . I apologise to the chairman.'

'In the context of our telephone conversation,' Campbell-Savours asked, had I checked the register?

Yes, as I said 'in the context of our telephone conversation', I had, and had seen that these payments were not registered.

'I am not criticising you,' Campbell-Savours said. 'You have not done anything wrong in failing to require them to register, that is not your responsibility. You have entered into a commercial transaction.'

I admitted I was placing the committee in some difficulty. Without knowing who these Members were, they could take no action. I suggested they write to all 651 Members of Parliament asking them if they had received any money from Ian Greer a suggestion Neil Hamilton was later furious with me about, in case they did.

Eventually, Campbell-Savours suggested that I supply the committee with a list of the number of payments I had made and the date I had made them, but without giving names. Reluctantly, I agreed.

9 May 1990

Dear Mr Hastings,

The Committee requested that I provide a note of dates on which payments were made by IGA to individual Members of Parliament.

As you will recall, it was agreed that Members should be identified by a prefix and no amounts specified.
The note covers the period between my company's inception in January 1982 and my first appearance before the Select Committee in 1988. As stated in my recent evidence before the Committee, there were five payments and these are as follows:

Member	Year
A	1985
A	1986
B	1986
B	1988
C	1988

For the sake of completeness, I should mention that one other payment was made to Member A between my first and second appearance in 1990.

Yours sincerely,

IAN B. GREER

My evidence was published. Michael Grylls (Member A) – utterly charming, very much of the old school and terribly vague – had already registered a client relationship with me in a newly created category, specified by the committee to cover any one-off payments, such as business referrals. He was asked to verify the three payments I had referred to in my letter to the committee in May 1990. He looked at his paying-in books, found the three payments and wrote to the committee confirming the position. What we had all failed to notice was that there had been six referral payments, not three.

However, the principle was established. Campbell-Savours had said that I had done nothing wrong in making new-business referral payments. The committee had agreed. At this stage, it would not have made any difference if I had stated that there had been three or thirty-three payments. But I had, unwittingly, just set the ticking on my own incendiary device, which was to explode just before the libel trial was due to begin.

Commission payments to MPs were later outlawed by the industry, but looking back it angers me that the press were prepared to insinuate that I acted improperly in paying MPs, when the House of Commons had decided that the practice was acceptable as long as the payments were declared.

Eventually, in 1994, after a couple of false starts, IGA, together with four other large lobbying firms, founded the Association of Professional Political Consultants, with a code of practice and an annual report which required every member to register its clients. That list is circulated to the Cabinet Office and the House of Commons' library. Every Member of Parliament received a letter informing them of the association's existence.

There was little interest from other lobbying firms on the question of commission payments to MPs and peers for referral of business. Many had parliamentarians on their boards, and although Labour's frontbench spokesman in the Lords, Baroness Turner, had joined IGA's board as a non-executive director in 1990, we were still seen as more independent than most. At the association's first meeting I pushed hard for a rule one way or the other on com nission payments to parliamentarians. I did not much care which way the decision went, but I wanted it stated in black and white whether the practice was right or wrong. I must admit I was not displeased when the association ruled against any company making new-business referral payments, and further that no Member of the House of Commons could any longer serve in any capacity with any lobbying company: it meant that I would no longer be pressed by MPs seeking payments for referral of business.

Sadly, few MPs have taken an interest in the new association. A poll in the December 1996 edition of the *Public Affairs Newsletter* showed that 89 per cent of MPs would not take any notice of whether a consultancy is a member of the Association of Professional Political Consultants before dealing with them. The industry has followed the Select Committee's wishes, it has set up an organisation to regulate itself, it has informed MPs of its existence and two years down the line it learns that MPs do not really care. This reinforces my original plea to the Members' Interest Committee in 1988, that statutory controls are both desirable and necessary. Members of the now disbanded Select Committee on Members' Interests should realise and publicly accept that it failed to do its job adequately over some twelve years: it could have played a part in protecting Parliament from many of the allegations which were later to surface.

With my Father and Mother at IGA's tenth birthday party (*Barry Swaebe*)

With Rt Hon Norman Lamont (*Barry Swaebe*)

'Sir' Humphrey (*Studio Venosa*)

With Lord King of Wartnaby (*Barry Swaebe*)

7

ON THE TEAM

It was a Thursday morning in November 1990. Clive and I were on a British Airways flight to Brussels, where we had recently opened an IGA office. The stewardess had just handed us a glass of champagne, when the pilot made a special announcement. 'Ladies and gentlemen, it is with great sadness that I have to tell you that since we have been in the air, Mrs Thatcher has resigned as Prime Minister.'

It was the end of an era.

As soon as we landed in Brussels, we dashed to the office, made our apologies and immediately booked a return flight to London. The contest to choose Mrs Thatcher's successor was already under way. I had no formal part to play in the campaign, but I did not want to miss it.

I arrived home to find Westminster awash with gossip. My friend Tristan Garel-Jones had positioned himself as campaign manager for Douglas Hurd, but at sixty Hurd was, I thought probably too old for the job. Michael Heseltine, whose own leadership ambitions had brought about Mrs Thatcher's demise, did not appeal to me – too pro-European. The opening of the IGA office in Brussels was a recognition of modern political realities, but that didn't mean I was enamoured with the European dream.

The recently appointed Chancellor of the Exchequer, John Major, I already knew and admired. John's challenge for the leadership was to be co-ordinated by Norman Lamont, my own constituency MP. I rang him later that evening at home.

'I hear you're backing Major. Is there anything I can do?' I asked.

'God, yes. Alan Duncan's given over his house. Turn up tomorrow morning. It's all hands on deck.'

So I rolled up the following morning at Gayfere Street to find Alan Duncan's three-storey house – a short walk from the House of Commons – a hive of activity. Alan, a wealthy oil-broker and Conservative candidate, was making coffee for everyone when I arrived. Someone was battling with the instructions for a new fax machine and BT engineers were busy installing extra phone lines. At any one time, twenty or thirty members of the government or Parliament were crowded into Alan's basement or ground floor.

Through the pandemonium it was clear that Richard Ryder was slowly but surely taking responsibility for the nitty-gritty planning and implementation of the campaign strategy, to sell John Major to backbenchers and in some cases to constituency association chairmen. Central Office was out of the loop. Heseltine and Hurd were doing exactly the same. Floating voters were courted by all three camps. We had lists of those who were declared supporters and those known not to be supporters, the rest were divided up for an approach by people who knew them well. Some were offered meetings with John Major, indeed some saw all three candidates.

There was, in fact, relatively little for people like me to do and I became a glorified messenger boy and chauffeur. I ferried Norman Lamont around on an almost daily basis – the Treasury Chief Secretary did not much like walking. Then one morning a shout went up. 'We need a car. Anyone got a decent British car?'

'I've got a Jaguar,' I called out.

'That'll do.'

It was the only time during the campaign I drove John Major. Our candidate had a photo opportunity in St James's Park. I picked him up with Norma and his PPS, Graham Bright, at Downing Street, drove up Whitehall to Trafalgar Square, and turned left into the Mall. Halfway down we stopped. About forty journalists and cameramen were waiting to record John and Norma's stroll across the bridge. We were very excited when we got back to base. The fact that so many had turned up suggested the tide was running in our favour.

The real work was undertaken by parliamentarians in each of the three camps talking to their supporters and to those who were undecided. Delegations would visit John Major at Number 11, but most of the work was done on the phone. Richard Ryder and William Hague were taking the lead – one, I imagine, to twist an arm and the other to kiss it better.

I enjoyed unhindered access to the Chancellor's residence during the five-day campaign. I spent many hours gossiping over the washing-up in the big rambling kitchen of 11 Downing Street with Norma Major and Barbara Oakley, John's secretary – a lady I have known since I was nineteen when she occupied an adjoining office to mine at Conservative Central Office A former candidate herself, she had dedicated her life to the Conservative Party, and has been a very able parliamentary secretary to many Conservative MPs.

One day I was running late. Norman Lamont was on a tight schedule and needed ferrying between interviews. As I was rushing out, John poked his head out of his study.

'Ian,' he asked, 'how do you think we're doing?'

'Sorry, can't speak to you now, John. I'm in a dreadful hurry.' The day was imminent when I would not dare to speak thus.

During a party leadership battle, the candidates themselves, in an effort to appear outwardly dignified and above the fray, have relatively little to do. The Machiavellian intrigues are left to the schemers and plotters in the campaign HQ and the darkest passageways of the House of Commons, where pressure is exerted and the carrot of ministerial office is dangled before an MP's eyes. John Major remained, after all, the Chancellor of the Exchequer during the campaign. His ministerial red boxes did not suddenly dry up as he pondered a higher ambition.

Each of the three camps tried to maintain a degree of secrecy about their undeclared supporters. We were constantly redrawing the lists of undeclared MPs who had not revealed their voting intentions. I kept an eye on who was coming and going from the house opposite IGA's offices, where Tristan Garel-Jones was masterminding Douglas Hurd's campaign. I imagine they were keeping an eye on us. Two days into the campaign, with people literally falling out of Alan Duncan's house, I had volunteered a couple of rooms at IGA, which were gratefully accepted as an overflow. I did not expect to receive any rent for them, but Richard Ryder rang me shortly after the contest to insist they pay. With hindsight, he was right to do so. The new Prime Minister did not want to feel in any way indebted to anyone, so I accepted a cheque for £5,000 for the space and facilities – money which had been raised from John's backers.

Norman Lamont and Peter Lilley were in the IGA office on the last Sunday morning before the vote. We were just about to leave for Gayfere Street, when we noticed Tristan Garel-Jones outside, about to give a television interview.

'Quick – back inside,' I shouted and the two senior members of HM Government ducked out of sight to wait, peering from behind curtains, until their fellow government member had disappeared. I then did a recce of the area to ensure all camera crews had left before they went scurrying down the street.

Forty-eight hours to go until the vote and I was walking down the large staircase at Number 11 with Norma Major. She was heading back to Huntingdon, when she suddenly stopped. She had remembered something of vital importance.

'John's shirts!' she cried and disappeared back up the stairs. She returned moments later with a large bundle of dirty laundry which she intended to take home to Huntingdon to wash.

I thought for a second. Here was a man already ranked number three in the government, now on the verge of becoming the leader of his country, and his wife was having to take his shirts home to wash. Number 11 Downing Street has no staff other than a woman who comes each morning to prepare breakfast. In Britain, we expect some of our leading public figures to fend for themselves. I could not imagine the same thing happening in France or the USA. Mrs Thatcher can justifiably claim to have been a politician and housewife, but I did wonder why the nation could not afford basic assistance for its leaders, who are so frequently criticised for the few comforts they enjoy.

*

It was a tense wait for the result of the ballot. There were around fifty of us at Number 11. A crate of champagne was on stand-by, win or lose. Then we heard the result: Hurd 56, Heseltine 131, Major 185. A huge cheer went up. Then, moments later, a second, when we heard that Hezza had withdrawn from the next round (Michael Heseltine had acted generously and pulled out even though Major did not have the 187 votes he required for an outright victory).

IGA was already adding clients to the books both at home and abroad. Our turnover was approaching £2 million. Despite the pressures we were all under, warm friendships had developed during the hectic days of the campaign. John Major saw the lobbying business as a further link to the views of industry. 'Ian,' he said once, 'you help me to do my job.' He recognised that listening to industrialists was an important part of a Prime Minister's role. Soon after his election, he attended a luncheon party for some of my clients at the Berkeley Hotel. John Major is always at his best when he is speaking to small groups of people. The twenty chairmen and chief executives of IGA client companies found the opportunity to talk to him, on an off-the-record basis, invaluable. I saw more of Norma. She came to lunch at the flat above IGA's Westminster offices on a couple of occasions, each time with Barbara Oakley. Once, as Norma got out of the car, a taxi driver called out to other cabbies, 'Look, there's Johnny's girl,' which I think she rather liked.

One weekend I was invited to Chequers for Sunday lunch, which was quite a grand experience. One of my newest clients was the Kuwaiti Government, who had hired me in the last few days of the Gulf War. Having been fêted in every Western television studio during the conflict, the Kuwaiti authorities were intelligent enough to recognise they would soon face hostile questions about issues such as human rights, democracy etc – something for which the Kuwaiti Embassy in London was not well prepared.

That weekend, I had Kuwaiti State Television in town to do an interview I had arranged for them with Mrs Thatcher to mark the first anniversary of the end of the war. My pal the late Peter Morrison had put some pressure on the former Prime Minister for me. She had agreed to come along to the Dorchester Hotel for the interview the following Monday morning, but had stipulated it could last no longer than ten minutes.

I was seated next to a very senior civil servant who knew Mrs Thatcher well.

'Of course, the Kuwaitis are beside themselves with excitement at the prospect of meeting Mrs Thatcher,' I was telling him. 'They've had Fortnum's bake them some little commemorative cakes.'

'She'll like that,' he nodded.

'Oh, and they want to give her some sand.'

'Sand?'

'Yes, from the desert. It's supposed to be a memento of where the British troops fought. The only problem is, they brought it over in a plastic carrier bag and it's been leaking all over the carpet of their hotel room for the past week.'

'So there's not very much left then?'

'No. I had Asprey's make a glass container and there was just enough left to fill it.'

'That was lucky. You know, you've done jolly well to get Mrs Thatcher,' he enthused.

'Yes, it is quite a coup, I suppose.'

'It must have taken for ever to arrange. I know she's very fussy about her make-up. I suppose you must have spent days choosing the right make-up team for her.'

I gulped. I could feel the colour draining from my face. It was mid-afternoon on a Sunday. I was in the middle of the Buckinghamshire countryside. I had the world's most formidable elder stateswoman arriving for a television interview with my clients at 10 the following morning. And I had forgotten to hire a make-up crew. I was heading for disaster.

'Yes,' I answered, after a pause, 'it was quite a job.'

I made my apologies soon after lunch and headed back to

London. I immediately picked up the phone in the car and arranged for Rob Pinker, the executive at IGA who worked on the Kuwaiti account, to meet me at the office. He was already phone-bashing by the time I got back. The hotel was hopeless. No beauticians or hairdressing salons were open on a Sunday night. All the schools and colleges of make-up were on answerphone mode. Eventually, someone, through a friend of a friend of a friend, hit upon a couple of girls, who said they did make-up for West End shows.

'What kind of West End shows?' I asked.

'I suggest you don't pursue that line of enquiry too deeply,' I was told.

This seemed like sound advice. It was now late in the evening. These girls were available and could be at the Dorchester for 10 am.

The following morning, Mrs Thatcher arrived half an hour early. The camera crew were still setting up. She was not amused that everything was not in place. I chatted nervously over a cup of coffee (strong and black for Mrs T) in the anteroom. We spoke about the Gulf War and she told me how shocked she was that the troops hadn't fought through to Baghdad. As for Saddam Hussein, they should have 'captured him and got him', she said, warming to her theme. This was all good stuff, I thought, for the interview.

When we were called into the makeshift studio, her make-up was just being completed and she was in full flood. She launched into a bitter condemnation of NATO's combined military command. She was still going strong when they started the cameras rolling. They had expected to film ten minutes' worth of material, but she showed little sign of slowing down after forty.

The Kuwaitis were ecstatic and left London with a very valuable tape. Sadly they left me with an expenses bill of £30,000. Over the following months, I phoned and I faxed, but was getting no sense out of anyone in Kuwait City.

I was on the verge of giving up when, quite by chance, Lady Olga Maitland said to me one day, 'I'm off to Kuwait tomorrow. Are you still working for them?' In the 1987 election, the daughter of the Earl of Lauderdale had contested Bethnal Green and Stepney for the Conservatives – it is hard to imagine a less likely candidate for this rough East End constituency.

I knew Olga well enough to ask her to chase the monies owing to my company. Determined and single-minded at times, she browbeat Kuwaiti Television into writing a cheque for the full amount, which I received within days. Very thankful, I paid her a fee of £3,000 (10 per cent of the original bill) for recovering my money. This was several months before the 1992 general election, and although Olga had been selected to fight Sutton and Cheam, she was not yet an MP. Obviously she did not, and could not, declare the payment.

Olga was elected in June. IGA's financial year ends the same month and as we were preparing our books for audit we discovered we had paid the £3,000 fee without receiving an invoice. I rang the newly elected MP at her office in the House of Commons. She apologised for the oversight and, without thinking, submitted an invoice on House of Commons notepaper. The *Guardian* later portrayed this very unfairly as a payment from Ian Greer which she had failed to register with the House of Commons' authorities. The explanation is simple: she was not a Member of Parliament when the money was paid to her – but by the time she was able to explain, it was too late. The initial allegation, however untrue or unsubstantiated, as I have found to my cost, is often all that people remember.

In February 1992, IGA celebrated its tenth anniversary. So many MPs wanted to attend our birthday party that the Government Whips' office was informed. They arranged Commons business so as to give MPs an easy ride that evening. I hired five rooms on the first floor of the National Portrait Gallery and invited over 300 guests from politics and industry. Virginia Bottomley, Lord Tebbit, Lord Wakeham, Norman Lamont, John Gummer, Lord King, Sir Colin Marshall, Michael Hoffman and Sir Geoffrey Mulcahy were amongst the many leading political figures and industrialists who arrived to the accompaniment of a small detachment of a Guards band. Mohamed Fayed, who, although still a client, was someone I had not seen for years, was not invited. He had by this time embarked on a legal challenge in the European court against the British Government over the damning DTI report on his takeover of the House of Fraser.

I knew Norma Major would come, but both Graham Bright and Barbara Oakley arrived from Downing Street and were unsure whether the Prime Minister would be able to join us. I was greatly relieved when he walked through the door. On arrival he was, like everyone else, immediately handed a glass of vintage champagne.

'You know, Ian,' he whispered to me, 'what I'm really dying for is a gin and tonic.'

There was no gin and no tonic anywhere in the building. Leaving the Prime Minister talking to Lord and Lady King, I grabbed a waiter and sent him out into Charing Cross Road, with instructions to find a pub.

Ten minutes later the PM was still awaiting a drink. In the nick of time, the waiter arrived back. They were immaculately presented on a silver tray, but were only a single glass of gin and one small bottle of tonic, which the waiter had carried from a pub several hundred yards away.

'For God's sake, is that all you've bought?' I said.

'Yes, sir.'

'Suppose he wants another one?'

'Er . . .'

I stuffed a twenty-pound note in his hand and sent him off to buy a bottle of gin.

The PM's gin and tonic episode, for what it's worth, has attained mythological status as journalists have exaggerated the story. If one believes what one reads in the paper, the drink's journey across Trafalgar Square that night required the assistance of a police escort and blue flashing lights. I doubt even the PM could have ordered that.

Shortly before the 1992 general election was called, the Chief Whip, Richard Ryder, rang me: 'Ian, can you provide someone to help Elizabeth Peacock?' he asked. 'It had better be one of your tougher guys. I'm genuinely worried for her safety.'

It was a friendly request, and one to which I was happy to respond. Elizabeth was defending a majority of only 1,362. For the duration of the campaign I stationed one of my staff in her Yorkshire constituency, Batley and Spen, to assist her. Elizabeth was re-elected with a slightly increased majority of 1,408. We were delighted with her success as she deserved to win.

The request from the Chief Whip simply demonstrates the extent to which the parties accepted IGA's assistance by 1992 – and not just the Conservatives. I sent one of my most trusted directors, Robbie MacDuff, and a senior researcher, Richard Kramer, to help the Labour frontbencher Chris Smith, along with a small donation of £250 towards his constituency fighting fund. Robbie was keen to help out the Islington South MP. They had a lot in common. Both men are Labour technocrats, they share a similar political outlook, and, unlike some architects of New Labour, both Robbie MacDuff and Chris Smith are relaxed about their sexuality. During the campaign I drove to the constituency to shake hands with the candidate and wish him luck. He did not need it. Chris Smith, who entered the election defending a majority of only 805, romped home by 10,652 votes.

Chris became a good friend to IGA over the years and it saddens me that after the collapse of my libel case in 1996 he sought to distance himself from the company. Faced by hostile reporters at that year's Labour Party conference, he told ITN, 'I have no connection at all with Mr Greer. The facts of the situation are that during the last general election campaign, Ian Greer Associates made a donation of £200 to Islington South and Finsbury Labour Party.' He said. He went on to tell the BBC that he had 'no idea' why I had made a small donation to his campaign. 'Ian Greer had asked no favours,' he said, but had I done so I would have received a 'swift rebuttal'. I am glad to hear it. I would expect nothing less from him. I felt hurt that he should imply otherwise. His interview did not mention the valuable help he had received from Robbie MacDuff and Richard Kramer during the campaign.

Chris Smith had also come to IGA's offices on several occasions to meet my clients. As recently as March 1996, while still the shadow Social Security Minister, he lunched with twenty company chairmen at the Connaught Hotel. Intelligent, eloquent and convincing, he went down extremely well. My clients, who included Powergen, British Gas and 3i, were impressed with his grasp of detail, particularly in regard to the social security implications of the Social Chapter.

Chris Smith was also happy to brief my staff at occasional half-yearly sessions that we would hold at the office with prominent politicians from all the main parties. He always gave me the impression of enjoying these events and benefiting from the free-flow of ideas that took place.

Another Labour MP, a good friend, Gwyneth Dunwoody, received £250 for her campaign in Crewe and Nantwich.

As for the Conservatives, Neil Thorne was fighting a desperate campaign in Ilford South. With a majority of just over 4,500, neither a £250 donation nor the help provided by IGA's twenty-six-year-old Max Earnshaw for the three weeks before polling day could save him his seat. Labour scraped in with a majority of 402.

Lynda Chalker, an old friend and one of the government's most hard-working ministers, headed the same way. Two hundred and fifty pounds from me was hardly equal to the task. She lost Wallasey to Labour's Angela Eagle and headed to the House of Lords. The only Conservative I supported financially in 1992 who managed to hold on to his seat was Robert Atkins in South Ribble. Again, he had only received £250. For the Liberal Democrats, Alan Beith was returned in Berwick-upon-Tweed, and he received an unsolicited donation of £250.

All candidates, irrespective of party, raise money from local businesses and trade unions within their constituency at the time of an election. It is not suggested that a candidate is under any obligation to his or her backers once they are elected – which is why I find ludicrous the suggestion that somehow I was attempting to buy access by donating £250 to the constituency association of a friend fighting a very marginal seat.

I estimate that I have raised, directly or indirectly, around £750,000 for the Conservative Party over the years – something of which I am very proud. Many of my clients sought my advice as to how they should make donations to the party machine. I suggested that they should earmark their contribution for specific marginal seats. We also arranged for one client, ADT, to donate mobile telephones to a number of Conservative candidates.

For the first time one of my staff members was fighting his own campaign. Andrew Smith was taking on the formidable Ann Clywd in the Welsh Labour stronghold of Cynon Valley. IGA donated £1,000 to his campaign and I went there in the last few days before the election to help. He lost, as expected, but increased the overall Tory vote. He is about to fight the same seat again – one of three former members of staff to run for office in 1997.

Another director, Jeremy Sweeney, went to help Graham Bright, the Prime Minister's PPS, in Luton South. Graham is someone I have known since he was national vice-chairman of the Young Conservatives in the early seventies. Graham held his seat. Also assisted with IGA staff were John Bowis, Sir John Wheeler, Tom Sackville, Ian Twinn and Colin Moynihan.

I offered my constituency member, Norman Lamont, the use of my home as a bolt-hole during the campaign. He took up the offer on one or two occasions. Rosemary, his wife, and he had lunch there on polling day.

As for me, I spent most of polling day in Colin Moynihan's Lewisham constituency. Clive was with me and all that was left to do was ferry Conservative supporters to the polling stations. By this time, I had already made a significant contribution to the former Sports Minister's re-election battle.

Colin Moynihan faced one of the toughest fights in the country, defending a Tory majority of under 5,000 in an inner London seat. A year before the election, he had devised a strategy for his own re-election which put Central Office to shame. It included a grandiose plan to raise £36,000 to fund what he called a 'full campaign team'. By the summer of 1991 this team was sending out 2,500 personally signed letters to his constituents every month.

I helped him raise money by organising one or two dinners at the Carlton Club, which were attended by sympathetic businessmen. One dinner, in June 1991, was with representatives from Kobe Steel. The gentlemen running this Japanese company were very keen to meet Margaret Thatcher – who wasn't? – and hoped she would tour one of their projects on an upcoming visit to Japan. Over dinner, Colin agreed to do what he could to help. A few days later he sent me a warm thank-you letter. He had just received a cheque for £1,000 from Kobe Steel. 'I have written to Margaret,' he explained, 'and hope that something will be able to be arranged, since I'm confident that this will not only assist Kobe, but that they are keen to do what they can to help in the build-up to the coming election.'

Sadly, despite our efforts, Colin failed to hold on to his Lewisham seat and return to the House of Commons. However, he has had more luck winning a place in the House of Lords. After his defeat he embarked on a five-year inheritance battle with his young Filipino nephews, the alleged heirs of Colin's half-brother, the third Lord Moynihan. By proving one was not the biological heir, and the other was the product of a bigamous marriage, Colin is now set to gain his father's title and take his seat in the Upper Chamber.

Despite the poor showing of the Tory candidates I supported, the Conservatives were re-elected with a comfortable majority in 1992. Yet I had no worries for my business if Labour had won, something which many had expected. I believed that the volume of legislation they would introduce would provide substantial opportunities for the lobbyist to continue to operate in the interests of his clients.

It was a gritty performance by the Prime Minister in 1992. Dragging out and climbing on to a soapbox was a sheer masterstroke. Soon after the election Alistair Cooke, the director of the Conservative Political Centre in Central Office, approached me about the possibility of publishing a collection of John Major's hustings speeches. In 1884 Lord Randolph Churchill had said, 'Trust the people. You who are ambitious, and rightly ambitious, of being guardians of the British constitution, trust the people and they will trust you.' The Prime Minister had in 1992 echoed that sentiment, making trust the touchstone of the campaign.

So the book was to be called *Trust the People*. But nobody would foot the £5,000 bill. As an admirer of the PM, I readily agreed to do it. The editor's note at the start of the book highlighted its sponsorship by Ian Greer Associates and noted how it was 'an immense pleasure for the Conservative Political Centre to be closely associated with him [Ian Greer], and his successful and expanding company'. The book was launched at an enjoyable party at Central Office shortly afterwards, which was attended by the Prime Minister and many other Cabinet Ministers.

My next challenge came when Graham Bright, the Prime Minister's PPS, solicited my help over a new portrait of the PM.

After John Major's election victory, there was a rush of attempts to capture the man in oils. The Carlton Club had commissioned an artist to paint the Prime Minister, but they were having difficulty pinning him down to dates for sittings. This was partly because Graham Bright had got there first. He had enlisted a talented artist, Peter Deighan from his own constituency of Luton South, who had already commenced work on the PM's portrait.

Graham asked me to arrange a little party to celebrate its unveiling – and to find someone to foot the bill. The National Portrait Gallery seemed the obvious venue for the occasion. We also assumed they would be delighted to add the portrait to their collection. But while the gallery was happy to accept our booking for the unveiling in May 1994, they didn't want to hang the painting. It was after all by a relatively unknown artist.

By the time I discovered this, the merchant bankers Rothschild had kindly agreed to bear the costs of the party and had already dispatched the invitations to, amongst others, Cabinet ministers and Members of Parliament. To add to my worries, the response had been poor. Although Norma Major had agreed to attend, her ever-modest husband had declined to come along to see the unveiling of his own portrait. I nervously envisaged the embarrassing scene: with half a dozen people applauding a picture for which no hook could be found.

In desperation, I went to see Norman Fowler, chairman of the party, at Central Office.

'Oh, God,' he said. 'We'll have to put a whip on it.'

'Good', I answered, much relieved.

I then moved on to my next problem, explaining that neither the National Portrait Gallery, nor indeed any other gallery, was interested in taking the picture.

'So where are you going to hang the damn thing?' he asked sympathetically.

'Well, Norman. See that space on the wall just behind you . . .'

The Tory chairman looked nervous.

'. . . at the moment it's going right there.'

Norman Fowler blanched. 'It can't possibly,' he replied weakly.

The unveiling was a great success – with an extremely good turn-out. Norma wrote the next day, 'Very many thanks to you and all your team for a really lovely party.' And from Norman Fowler: 'I thought the unveiling was a very considerable success . . . We do of course look forward to hanging the portrait at Central Office.'

It can be seen today in Smith Square, albeit not in the chairman's office, but in a corridor, next to the stairs, on the ground floor, en route to the basement.

Ex-editor of the *Guardian*, Peter Preston (*Rex Features*)

The *Guardian's* Westminster correspondent, David Hencke (*Ken Sharpe*)

Mohamed Fayed (*Rex Features*)

8

CONSPIRACY

Commenting on the resignation in December 1996 of Paymaster-General David Willetts, the third ministerial casualty in this affair, Neil Hamilton wrote in the *Telegraph*: 'I feel a heavy burden of responsibility for his misfortune as he was caught in the backwash of Mohamed Fayed's campaign to wreak revenge on me for failing to be bribed by him.'

Neil has little choice other than continually to protest his innocence at every opportunity. The allegations made against him remain unproven. He knows the British public are not cruel. When they hear of how he and Christine have suffered, of the nights the MP has spent watching his wife reduced to fits of uncontrollable sobbing, of the days spent trapped in their home besieged by photographers and reporters, he knows the public will feel sympathy. But the public also remember another six days the couple spent enjoying Mr Fayed's hospitality in Paris several years earlier. The essential arrow he fires – that he was not bribed – misses the target.

The truth is Mohamed *did* fail to bribe Neil Hamilton. After two years in the Whips' Office, Neil fought the 1992 election and was returned with a majority of 15,860. His hard work on the Conservative Backbench Trade and Industry Committee paid off. Immediately after the election, John Major made him Corporate Affairs Minister at the Department of Trade and Industry. It was a fateful decision. It is my belief that had Neil gone to Education, to Transport or to any other government department, none of this whole cash-for-questions affair would have blown up. In my view, it is all as a result of Neil's appointment to the one job in the government that was crucial to

Fayed. With Neil in post, Mohamed Fayed saw an historic opportunity. A previous Corporate Affairs Minister, Michael Howard, had set up the DTI enquiry into House of Fraser. Fayed believed the new Corporate Affairs Minister, his old friend Neil Hamilton – a man who had enjoyed his company and his hospitality, and who had fought passionately on his behalf in the House of Commons in the past – would be able to set the damning DTI report aside. Hamilton failed to deliver.

On 15 April 1992, immediately following Neil's appointment, Fayed wrote a letter of congratulation. Rather than send it to the House of Commons, where it would have been opened by Christine, who was his secretary as well as his wife, Fayed posted it to the DTI, where it was opened by a civil servant. I did not see the letter, but it caused tremendous embarrassment for the new minister. Fayed was, by this time, suing the government in the European court alleging that the powers of the inspectors under the Companies Act contravened the European Convention on Human Rights. Fayed had written to the man he was technically suing.

Private and Confidential

Dear Neil,

Well, I suppose they can't keep a good man down forever! Congratulations on your appointment. Long overdue.

As your ministerial offices are almost next door to the Army and Navy [store, owned by House of Fraser], I shall expect you to be contributing to *my* trade and industry by popping in regularly with your orders. The Wine and Spirits department offers a splendid selection of vintages much favoured by your Westminster colleagues . . . I hope that your new responsibilities will allow you the time to come into Harrods to join me for lunch some day soon. . .

The letter ended with his confident assertion that he would be successful at the European Court of Human Rights.

'That idiot Mohamed has written to me,' Hamilton told me. His closest departmental aides, apparently well aware of their new master's pro-Fayed sympathies, advised him not to reply. But ignoring friendly letters from former friends like Mohamed Fayed was hardly Neil's style. He asked me to relay a message: 'Tell him I'm not being rude, but my sympathies are too well known.' I spoke to Royston Webb, and asked him to pass on the message. I am told that a similar message was passed on via Peter Hordern.

Also awaiting the new minister's attention was a written parliamentary question on the House of Fraser affair from the Liberal Democrat Alex Carlile, who, despite later changing sides, was one of a number of MPs frustrated that the DTI enquiry had come to nothing.

The Serious Fraud Office had declined to prosecute Fayed on publication of the report, and no further action was to be taken against those professional advisers who had acted for him during the acquisition. On one of the most pressing concerns – control of the 105-year-old Harrods Bank – it had taken fifteen months for the Bank of England to act. Threadneedle Street has a statutory duty to ensure that a bank's owners are 'fit and proper', but it did not strip the Fayeds of their control of the Harrods Bank – the sole branch of which is in the store's basement – until June 1991.

The then Governor of the Bank of England, Robin Leigh-Pemberton, questioned by MPs in February, a full eleven months after publication of the DTI report, conceded it was 'most unlikely' that anyone condemned in the way that the Fayeds had been would be deemed fit to control a bank. But it took him a further four months to negotiate a settlement for the bank's 4,000 depositors.

The Harrods Bank remained wholly owned by the store, but was to be managed through a trustee, Debenture Trust Corporation. The Fayeds would continue to receive dividends. Some MPs on the Commons Trade and Industry Select Committee were irritated that Leigh-Pemberton had not gone further.

In his parliamentary question, Alex Carlile wanted to know if the President of the Board of Trade, Michael Heseltine, was satisfied with the outcome of the DTI investigation. Unlike Fayed's letter, Carlile's enquiry could not be ignored. Neil Hamilton's response, drafted by his civil servants, was completely innocuous. Following the 'carefully considered and thorough investigation', it stated, copies of the report had been submitted to the regulatory authorities and it was up to them to take action. Any government minister would have answered in the same way, but it made Hamilton, an outspoken supporter of Fayed in the past, feel uncomfortable.

His departmental aides recognised his difficulties. They suggested the whole issue of Rowland, Fayed, the House of Fraser report and the case at the European Court of Human Rights be handled by another minister, Edward Leigh. Hamilton readily agreed. In future all departmental papers on the subject were to be marked 'Not for Mr Hamilton's eyes'.

Fayed waited for a reply from Hamilton. It didn't come. When the message reached him that he was never going to receive a reply, he was furious. He regarded it as another personal insult against his honour. Once again, it demonstrated his lack of acceptance by the political Establishment. The snub festered in his mind. Hamilton was a man he had counted as a friend, a man who had been an enthusiastic supporter of his cause in the past, but who now, on gaining ministerial office for the first time, chose to ignore him. Hamilton had become a marked man.

Over the course of the next twelve months, thwarted in his attempts to influence government policy towards him, snubbed by his former friends in Westminster, and finally refused British citizenship on what he believed was the personal intervention of Michael Howard, the Home Secretary, Mohamed Fayed began to turn. Miraculously, he started to bury his differences with Tiny Rowland, culminating in an historic photo-opportunity on 22 October 1993. Photographers crowded round the two men laughing and shaking hands in Harrods' Food Hall, as a large stuffed shark called Tiny was ceremoniously lowered from the ceiling. They began meeting socially, although infrequently. Both men were entrepreneurs and social outcasts and enjoyed sharing tales of the poor treatment they had suffered at the hands of the British Establishment.

A further development was the *Guardian's* takeover of the *Observer*. The *Guardian's* editor, Peter Preston, began to develop a relationship with Fayed, despite his vicious denunciation of the man in the past. Following an approach by the Harrods boss, he and the *Guardian* editor first met on 14 July 1993. Preston claimed that this first meeting dealt mainly with Mrs Thatcher and certain Saudi donors to the Conservative Party. The allegations against Neil Hamilton, he was to say, came up 'almost in passing'. Strange, then, that Mohamed Fayed should have had a copy of Hamilton's six-year-old Ritz Hotel bill to hand. He showed this to Preston, but would not allow him to take a copy at that time. According to Preston, Fayed claimed that I had approached the Harrods boss and offered to arrange for Neil Hamilton and Tim Smith to ask parliamentary questions on his behalf. 'As far as I recollect,' Preston wrote, 'Mr Al Fayed mentioned the figure of £2,000 per question.' He took a few 'jottings' at this meeting, but can no longer locate them.

No political lobbyist worth their salt would suggest anything quite as crass as paying MPs to ask questions. What is the point? Each year 45,000 questions are tabled. There are 651 Members of Parliament. I would not have been doing my job if I was unable to find one of them to ask questions in defence of Mohamed Fayed in 1985, one of Britain's leading businessmen, an acquaintance of Mrs Thatcher and the Sultan of Brunei, the new owner of the blue-chip department store Harrods and a key figure in the preservation of sterling as a major trading currency; a man fighting a rearguard action against Tiny Rowland, who, through the left-leaning newspaper he owned, was engaging in the most vicious personal attacks on the Conservative Prime Minister, her family and Britain's friends abroad.

I wonder now whether the *Guardian* would have stood up in court and argued convincingly that, in these circumstances, it was necessary for me, an experienced political lobbyist with many friends in the Conservative Party, to pay a backbench Tory MP to ask questions. It would have been inconvenient to have acknowledged that I may have been able to persuade one of them to do it for free.

Fayed claims that I approached him directly and, at our first meeting, made this extraordinary offer to engage in high-level political corruption on his behalf. In fact, my introduction to Mohamed Fayed was made through Lord King of British Airways. Fayed claims he only afterwards checked out my bona fides with Lord King. Why then did he not mention to the BA chairman – or, indeed, to Sir Peter Hordern, his paid parliamentary adviser – the alleged remarkable assertion that 'you had to rent MPs like you rent a London taxi'? Why did Mohamed Fayed hand over so much money to MPs to further his campaign in the House of Commons, when Lord King would have told him that I had marshalled parliamentary support for his airline without having to pay Members to do so? Surely, a businessman as astute as Mohamed Fayed would have realised he was getting a very bad deal.

Apparently, according to Peter Preston's account of this first meeting with Fayed, I suggested to the Harrods boss back in October 1985 that Tim Smith would be one of the MPs who would ask questions for cash. The record shows I barely knew Tim Smith at that time. He was somebody I was bound to want to brief, as an officer of the Backbench Trade and Industry Committee, but I had no way of knowing at that time whether he would support Fayed or not in his campaign against Tiny Rowland.

As a result of these allegations against Neil Hamilton, Tim Smith and myself, which Preston had heard 'in a casual reference by Fayed', he returned to the *Guardian*'s offices and immediately put two of his most senior journalists – Westminster correspondent David Hencke and reporter John Mullin – 'virtually full-time on the Ian Greer story'.

Soon after, Neil Hamilton received a phone call at 8.30 one morning at his Battersea flat. The caller was Hencke, a journalist with whom he had lunched a number of times at the Tate Gallery restaurant. Hamilton says he enjoyed Hencke's company, his chaotic manner and sense of humour – things I never witnessed. Hencke wanted to see the MP urgently that day and could not talk on the telephone. They arranged to meet at tea-time on the Commons terrace.

When Hamilton arrived, he was surprised to discover that Hencke was not alone, but accompanied by John Mullin. According to Hamilton, Mullin did not have the same pleasant and easy manner as Hencke. For over an hour they interrogated Hamilton, who did not handle the encounter well. They operated a finely honed double-act, with Hencke the soft man and Mullin the hard interrogator. Immediately defensive, Hamilton was vague about his stay at the Paris Ritz. The journalists then confronted him with the dates and room number. They lied, saying they had a copy of the bill. Hamilton was staggered. He imagined Tiny Rowland must have prised this out of a member of the hotel staff. His trip, he explained, was a private visit and therefore did not need to be registered. Hamilton says the journalists did not put to him any allegations regarding cash for questions in this interview, nor at any other. They spoke a lot about IGA, probing Sir Michael Grylls' friendship with me – Michael had been knighted in the New Year's Honours – before entering the conspiracy-theory stratosphere: Ian Greer, they believed, was capable of dictating government policy from the Prime Minister downwards – a ludicrous suggestion.

Hencke and Mullin had met Tim Smith in similar circumstances, and put a number of allegations to him. Smith was 'agitated and nervous', they reported.

They also began telephoning IGA's clients. Prudential, Powergen, British Airways, British Gas and others all came back to me, saying that the *Guardian* had been asking questions. To some they said they were writing a piece on the 'rise and rise of Ian Greer'; to others that they were doing a survey on lobbying. When neither approach worked, they claimed they were about to uncover a scandal which would shock our clients to the core. This yielded little also. Mullin admitted later that I had received from all my clients 'glowing references . . . both the way you work and for your reputation'.

Having drawn a blank with my clients, Hencke and Mullin started phoning my staff at home. Would they talk off the record? Were they happy at IGA? How were they treated? How much did Ian Greer earn? And there were questions about my personal life. Both of them doorstepped Perry Miller, a director of IGA, one Saturday evening. Every one of my staff was wonderful and reported back to me the non-conversations they had had with these two men.

Eventually they made a direct approach for an interview. By this time I was angry, but agreed to meet them in the boardroom at IGA. Angie Bray, who had joined IGA after the 1992 election with responsibility for media relations, and my lawyer, Andrew Stone, suggested I deliver a stern lecture at the outset. The journalists were shown into the room, and seated before I appeared.

It was the first time I had met either of them. Hencke struck me as intelligent but obsessive. Mullin – younger, six feet tall, thick-set and aggressive – I dismissed as an unpleasant bully. They sat on one side of the table. Angie Bray and Andrew Stone sat with me on the other. Between us, two tape machines recorded our conversation.

Before either man could open his mouth, I began my 'I've been in the business twenty-five years' speech. I told them I had built up friendships with a number of journalists but that this was the first time I had sat down to talk to two people who had created such a hostile atmosphere before giving me an opportunity to say one word.

They were not here to do a 'hatchet job', Hencke protested. 'There seems to be a great misconception and, to be honest, I am not sure where this comes from.' Phoning my clients and my staff with impertinent questions at home, perhaps? No. 'We are here to do a piece on lobbying,' he whined. 'We're here to learn a bit about lobbying. Any suggestion that our interview will not be conducted in a polite and fair manner is wrong.'

With hindsight I now realise the purpose of this meeting. They needed to be able to say they had interviewed me and put their allegations to me, but having created a genuinely hostile atmosphere, they knew I would not be inclined to be helpful. Their agenda dictated that I should be 'Ian Greer – the corrupt political lobbyist'. My lecture at the outset played into their hands. It mattered little how I answered their questions – indeed it served their purpose better if I gave fulsome denials to their allegations. I would not be believed anyway.

I was careful about what I said to them, but I spoke warmly of my company and my dedicated staff. I explained about donations companies made via me to MPs' election fighting funds, I defended my practice of sending staff to help candidates during election campaigns, I told them about the commission payments I had made to Sir Michael Grylls (without revealing the names of the other recipients) and about my enthusiastic support for a register of lobbyists.

One of their sources had told them that I had supplied computer equipment to Lynda Chalker in the 1987 election, which was not true.

Mullin then moved on to Neil Hamilton's stay at the Paris Ritz – a guest, he said, of a former client of mine, Mohamed Fayed. They said they had spoken to Tim Smith, who had told them he had been invited to the Ritz. 'He was given two teddy bears and said he declared the two teddy bears.' As for the trip to the Paris Ritz, the MP had declined to go.

'Tim said that?' I asked incredulously. I certainly did not recall Tim Smith turning down the opportunity to stay at the Ritz. I was not sure whether to disbelieve Tim's words or Tim's words as reported by this *Guardian* journalist. I had better be careful what I say, I thought. 'Let me correct you on one thing,' I said. 'House of Fraser is still a client.' IGA was still receiving £500 per month for parliamentary monitoring.

'It is still a client?' Hencke gulped. Now it was his turn to disbelieve what he was hearing. It had not occurred to him that his secret source, Mohamed Fayed, could accuse a man of corruption while continuing to pay him a fee for professional services. But then it had not occurred to me either that Mohamed Fayed, a man with whom I had enjoyed a friendly and businesslike relationship, could be quite so deceitful.

I did not think that Mohamed would want me to talk to the *Guardian* about any of this. 'I wasn't invited,' I said, 'and I didn't make any arrangements for anyone, at any time, to go there.' This last assertion was technically true – the proposed April 1987 trip had been called off before any firm arrangements had been made.

'Tim Smith said there was the offer of going to the Ritz,' Mullin replied, 'but he actually said it had come via your missive.'

'No, under no circumstances of any kind did we make any arrangement,' I repeated emphatically, wondering what else Tim Smith had said – or what these journalists were about to claim Tim Smith had said.

It was now Hencke's turn. 'One allegation that has been made about the House of Fraser is that, in return for a parliamentary question being asked by a friendly MP, a brown envelope stuffed with fivers would be passed to the MP.'

I was stunned by the allegation. Plenty of MPs had consultancy arrangements with businesses, but the idea of their being paid in cash or on a per question basis seemed extraordinary (I still find it extraordinary). 'I've absolutely no knowledge of this . . . I find it . . .' I was incredulous that this man, an experienced political journalist (I thought), could have believed such a notion. 'For God's sake,' I exclaimed, 'I would be amazed if any Member of Parliament would allow themselves to enter into that sort of arrangement.'

'We were surprised,' answered Mullin. 'The extraordinary thing was, it came from sources who, in theory, might know about it, that's why we took it seriously. We checked in questions [parliamentary records], and it's true! We talked to Tim Smith. He put down seventeen questions!'

'I can't believe it,' I answered doubtfully, 'not Tim.'

'Yes,' Mullin continued enthusiastically. 'We then got interested in why people would put it to us that this may have happened!'

I stopped him in his tracks. 'With great respect,' I said, 'a number of people seem to have put some rather wild ideas into your head.' I reminded him of a somewhat vicious, untrue accusation they had made, some few weeks earlier during the questioning of IGA staff, when they claimed I had used inside knowledge from my political contacts to help me in share dealings. I had demonstrated then why this allegation could not possibly be true. Suddenly their confidence deserted them.

'I would not want to get into that,' Mullin replied uneasily. 'We have to take these things seriously. Er . . . you need to question . . .'

Why? I wondered. Hencke, who had been silent for some time, jumped in to help his friend. ' . . . because sometimes it clears things up,' he offered weakly.

It struck me that these men wanted to believe that the British political system was corrupt. Hencke especially believed the worst, because he wanted to. These allegations were so obviously wide of the mark. I had challenged him on one and his confidence had crumbled. Who else, though, has challenged him over the last four years, or questioned the *Guardian* agenda?

During that summer of 1993 Hencke says he spoke to between twelve and fifteen people. One of his interviewees told him that Neil Hamilton was able to obtain, through the 'good offices' of Ian Greer, free British Airways tickets for his 1987 trip to the Paris Ritz. The *Guardian*'s Westminster correspondent believed this without question. The Hamiltons, in fact, drove in their own car to Paris that summer. But Hencke had heard a sexy allegation about air tickets; it involved me; it served his purpose; therefore it must be true. But Mr Hencke and his colleagues had failed to spot a crucial detail. The bill for the Hamiltons' Ritz Hotel trip, which had been seen by Peter Preston, shows an amount for the garage parking of the Hamiltons' car. He did not stop to ask himself the question: why would they need British Airways tickets?

After over an hour, the interview came to an end. One of their photographers was lurking in reception. Could they have a picture? I stood self-consciously at one end of the boardroom table, while the shot was taken. Hencke and Mullin left IGA and went back to the *Guardian* offices to pick over the bones of the story.

Subsequently, they would make out that they had put to me the central allegation that I had given MPs cash for questions. They hadn't – as the transcript clearly demonstrates. They had little of worth. Their main source, Mohamed Fayed, wanted to remain anonymous. He was keeping the Hamiltons' bill from the Ritz Hotel tight to his chest. There was no verification from any other source regarding cash for questions. How could there be? All these cash payments, according to the Harrods boss, had been handed over at private face-to-face meetings. There was an interview with me, but all my clients had vouched for my integrity. Tim Smith had received two teddy bears.

The *Guardian* editor, Peter Preston, had a further meeting with Fayed at the end of September. He left convinced that his source would eventually go public at some point in the future. It was, in any case, worth waiting. Nobody else had the story. The longer they waited the more chance there was that people would forget that Mohamed Fayed had been exposed as a liar in the past.

In any case, at this stage of the plan, it was important to build up the reputation of Ian Greer and his lobbying company. If this little-known, but allegedly influential individual was to be later accused of corruption, it was important he was given the highest possible profile in advance.

As the party conference season got under way, we heard that the article focusing on Ian Greer was about to appear. As a sideline, Neil Hamilton expected a hatchet job over his stay at the Ritz. Other journalists at Westminster had warned him that Hencke had been boasting that the Corporate Affairs Minister would get into 'a lot of trouble'.

On 1 October, Hamilton sent a lengthy and strongly worded appeal for 'balance' to Peter Preston, with a copy to his lawyer, Peter Carter-Ruck. He repeated his assertion that his interest in House of Fraser affairs predated IGA's contract with the company; that he had got to know Mohamed Fayed reasonably well and as a 'convivial person' liked him; the Ritz trip, he repeated, was as if to a private residence and did not need to be declared; his support for Fayed ended when he joined the government –

as a minister he had voluntarily exempted himself from any decisions involving Fayed.

'It seems pretty clear,' Hamilton wrote to the *Guardian* editor, 'that Mr Hencke is trying to weave a conspiracy along the lines of: "Greer lobbies for Fayed and persuaded Hamilton to put down PQs etc. as backbencher. Hamilton then goes into government as Competition/Company Investigation Minister and uses influence to promote interest of Greer client, Fayed". . .

'You will note that I refer this matter to my solicitor and, no doubt, you receive many such statements. I would only add that although the litigation is both time-consuming and expensive for all parties, I fought a successful libel case against BBC *Panorama* some years ago – costing the BBC a total of £500,000. You may wish to check your cuttings. **I will have no hesitation in pursuing the legal route again**, which might be more necessary now because of my present Ministerial position, if your newspaper prints any of the untrue facts and insinuations that Mr Hencke appears to be planning.'

Readers must be reminded at this stage that Fayed was still a client and I had no reason to suspect him of being the source of information to the *Guardian*.

Our latest information was that the article would appear on the first day of the Conservative Party Conference, Tuesday 5 October 1993, and we headed off to Blackpool with some trepidation, worried what effect an unhelpful and possibly inaccurate article might have on our relationship with our clients. This was an important conference for us. We had already spent £5,000, not for the first time, sponsoring the conference fringe guide and had a number of company and client receptions arranged. The evening before the conference, IGA traditionally hosted a dinner for lobby correspondents at the Riverhouse Restaurant just outside the town. Andrew Smith and I left early to go back to my suite at the Pembroke Hotel. The staff still remaining in London, who were coming up the following day, were planning to pick up an early edition of the *Guardian* to fax through to us.

As I watched it churn out of the fax machine, I stared at the headline straddling the full-page article on page six: 'The Power and Prestige of Ian Greer'. Below it was a large picture of me taken in the boardroom at IGA. This was not what I was expecting. I gulped, rather embarrassed, and began to imagine the ribbing I would receive from my staff. I was even more embarrassed to discover it had been placarded all around the conference – 'The Power and Prestige of Ian Greer' – for delegates to see. At a party at the end of conference week, Andrew Smith presented me with a framed copy of the billboard.

The article was full of exaggeration: I was 'a workaholic with no family commitments' earning £275,000 a year (my salary was, in fact, almost a third of that figure). Lest I sounded dull, I was 'widely agreed to throw the best parties'. John Major's secretary, when she told me the PM would be attending IGA's tenth birthday party, was falsely reported to have said, 'If it's for you, Ian, he'll be there.' The *Guardian* reported that when the PM arrived, I dispatched a police escort with the waiter to buy him a gin and tonic. Even the photograph of my house in Kingston was an estate agent's dream. The shot had been angled in such a way as to make the short driveway appear a mile long.

'John Major and Norman Lamont are among the long-standing political friends of Ian Greer. Yet his £3m lobbying business is tied to only one Tory MP, Michael Grylls,' read the strapline. I had, apparently, 'wooed' Cedric Brown, the chief executive of British Gas, earlier that year with a 'vintage Greer operation'. I invited him to lunch at Claridge's, where the guest speaker was Employment Secretary, Gillian Shephard. 'Seated around the table were Lord King of British Airways, Adrian Cadbury of Cadbury Schweppes, and Marmaduke Hussey of the Royal Marsden Hospital,' the article said. I remember the lunch. It was not at Claridge's, it was at the Connaught Hotel. Hencke had drawn the names of my guests from a variety of different lunches I had hosted that year.

At the time the article read rather oddly and I could not quite understand why these men, who were so irritating throughout the summer, should devote a full page of their newspaper to my company alone – and barely criticise me. The closest they came was a suggestion that I had adopted an 'autocratic style' and the atmosphere in the office was 'juvenile'. With hindsight, one realises what a clever article it was. There, interwoven among all the hyperbole, are the first soft suspicions of improper influence, a focusing in on MPs' registration of gifts, an unwarranted interest in parliamentary questions and the names of people who were to become important in their allegations later.

Neil Hamilton's stay at a mysterious 'five-star hotel in Europe' had been upgraded to a week and linked directly to me: 'The differing approaches of MPs to accepting and registering gifts emerge from an episode involving one of Ian Greer's clients and two conservative MPs, Tim Smith and Neil Hamilton ... The *Guardian* for reasons of confidentiality, will not name the company, though it will happily lay out the evidence should that be necessary.'

The 'evidence' – Hamilton's bill from the Ritz – was, in fact, still in Mohamed Fayed's possession, but the article stated that the bill totalled more than £5,000. One bottle of wine alone, it said, cost more than £150. This level of detail was not on the bill, which was not itemised to this degree, but was provided by Fayed at one of his meetings with Preston. The bill had been exaggerated; it actually came to £3,602. The same bottle of wine is later reported to have cost £200.

Tim Smith, by this time a Conservative Party vice-chairman in charge of finance and candidates, had, they claimed, been invited to the same hotel after asking parliamentary questions helpful to my client. 'He turned it down, but accepted Teddy Bears for his sons – which he duly registered. Between October 28, 1987 and January 23, 1989, Mr Smith asked 17 separate questions about the company's affairs.' Hencke cleverly created the impression that the offer to Tim Smith of the hotel trip was a reward for having asked these seventeen questions. As close inspection of the dates demonstrates, the offer of the visit to Paris was made several months *before* the period when the questions were asked (see Chapter 2).

Parts of the letter Hamilton had written to Preston the previous week were quoted in his defence. Because he was staying in 'private rooms' at the hotel, the bill was no more than 'a notional transaction for internal accounting purposes'. He admits he did not register the trip, but said, 'There is more attention to the subject of registration of interests today than there was six years ago. The visit was, in effect, to a private residence in Paris and, therefore, the question of registering the interest did not, I believe, arise.'

On the morning of the article, Neil came to my hotel room in a dreadful state. He was still a young minister, only a year into the job, and was justifiably worried about the possible effect such bad publicity could have on his career. The article, however, concentrated on the Ritz affair and fell short of accusing him of any wrongdoing. He was concerned about the letter he had sent the previous week to Peter Preston. He felt that if it were published it could be misconstrued.

He picked up the phone and dialled the *Guardian*'s number. Within minutes he was speaking to Peter Preston and gained his agreement that his letter would not be published. (Preston was to renege on this promise a year later.) He then sent a fax from my room, confirming the conversation he had just had on the phone.

At lunchtime, he came with me to IGA's annual lunch at the Pembroke with over 150 ministers, MPs and clients. Amazingly, David Hencke and John Mullin gatecrashed the event. I was polite to them, but Neil got involved in an angry exchange.

I was puzzled about how the *Guardian* knew so much about Hamilton's stay at the Ritz. I rang Royston Webb, Fayed's legal adviser, who agreed to make some enquiries. A few days later he phoned me back and alleged that the leak had come from a disgruntled former senior member of IGA's staff who had spoken to the *Guardian* under guarantees of anonymity. Despite these guarantees, however, he had now been exposed to me – I suspect in an attempt to throw me off the scent and protect the real source of the allegations: Mohamed Fayed. Webb, I believe, like me, remained in the dark until the very end about his boss's involvement with the *Guardian*.

The week after the 'Power and Prestige' article, Peter Preston met with Mohamed Fayed to plan the next stage of the strategy.

The date was 14 October 1993. They held further secret meetings on 22 November, 31 January and 14 March 1994, at which they hatched a plot against Jonathan Aitken, who had stayed at the Paris Ritz for a weekend in September 1993, sending a 'cod' (fake) fax on House of Commons notepaper to the hotel asking for a copy of Aitken's bill and purporting to come from one of Aitken's assistants. Throughout these months, House of Fraser remained an IGA client, paying £500 per month for our parliamentary monitoring service.

At the end of November, the chairman of the Select Committee on Members' Interests, Geoffrey Johnson-Smith, wrote to Neil Hamilton. The committee had discussed the *Guardian* article and Hamilton's free stay at the mystery European hotel. The committee did not want to investigate the trip, he said, but expressed concern at Hamilton's implication that MPs did not pay close attention to the rules of registration before 1987.

The committee was satisfied with Hamilton's response: 'I was not saying that Members have ever treated the register in a cavalier fashion but that Members' perceptions of what might be thought registerable had altered as public attitudes had become more critical,' he told them.

Should Neil, at this point, have taken a different course of action? Rather than wait for the committee to contact him, should he have written to them, stating, 'This has been drawn to my attention, perhaps I should have registered it'? His difficulty was with the amounts involved: not £5,000, as alleged by the *Guardian*, but nonetheless a large figure. Trying to argue that the real cost to Mohamed of his stay at the Ritz was much less – 'The mark-ups were high at the Ritz' – in my view lost him public sympathy.

But for IGA, the tone of the 'Power and Prestige' article had been broadly positive. Some of our competitors took great exception to it. My staff coming up to Blackpool on the train were confronted by the angry overbearing figure of Tony Hutt, a former Conservative Central Office worker and now a lobbyist with another company. 'Bloody IGA,' he stormed, 'getting all this publicity.'

Our expansion continued. Over the next six months, the company attracted an extra half a million pounds' worth of business. Our staff numbers increased to close on fifty. We opened offices in Dublin and Edinburgh, in addition to our office in Brussels. Sir Tim Bell, Mrs Thatcher's former adviser, made a formal offer of £2 million to acquire IGA and bring it into the Lowe Bell Group. The deal would have allowed me to continue to run the company as I wished; it would have made me a full shareholder in the group and personally rich. But it would ultimately have meant giving up my independence and it would not have necessarily provided the security that I wished my staff to have. I continued to harbour the thought that one day I would be able to hand over the company to my employees. I decided to say no – I was not quite ready to take the plunge. I wish now I had.

9

THE STING

After the collapse of the communist bloc, IGA was one of many British companies which grew excited about business opportunities in Eastern Europe. We linked up in a joint venture with a recently formed group of political consultants working out of Warsaw, Budapest and Prague. We agreed to introduce them to Western companies looking to invest in the East, to whom they could offer strategic political advice. In return, our partners in Eastern Europe would introduce companies in the region looking to harness our growing expertise in dealing with Brussels.

Our partners did very well out of the arrangement. We did not. I was ferried around four Eastern European capitals, speaking to potential clients at a series of conferences. At the very first one, a representative of the Polish coal industry asked if IGA was a non-profit-making organisation and would be providing their services for free. I quickly realised that the communist ethos of state provision still prevailed. The Polish airline, Lot, tried to take us on, but they wanted to pay for our services in airline tickets. I turned them down – there are only so many times you can fly to Warsaw in a year.

It therefore came as some relief, early in March 1994, when Clive received a call from a British businessman who represented a group of Moscow-based investors with a total of £40 million to invest in the West, and the possibility of another £40 million to follow. The caller, Richard Roberts, purportedly ran a Los Angeles-based company called Ecocon Ventures. He was seeking out investment opportunities in London and Paris, was particularly interested in the British Government's privatisation programme and was preparing to hire a political lobbying firm like IGA.

Roberts had telephoned Sir Michael Grylls, offering his sympathies on the death of Grylls' father, who had passed away some days previously. Roberts said he had met the MP previously at a reception – Michael Grylls could not remember. When they spoke, Roberts sought advice on his Russian investors' desire to hire a top firm of public affairs consultants. Michael Grylls suggested he contact IGA. He was not to realise that he was being used by Central Television's *The Cook Report*, who had carefully laid a trap.

Richard Roberts, a tall, bearded, overweight man of about forty, had rented a plush Park Lane apartment which he shared with his assistant, Ben. He told Clive he wanted to meet me that very day. I was desperately tied up with other things, having just returned from a trip to Pakistan – and still recovering from a bug I'd picked up out there – but offered to send over my managing director, Jeremy Sweeney, an enthusiastic, hard-working former army officer. He took with him two IGA researchers.

'They're a bit odd,' he reported back to me on his return.

'What do you mean?'

'They appear to be rather nervous.'

I thought this seemed a somewhat hasty judgement. 'Perhaps they're nervous sort of people,' I suggested.

They were applying pressure, Jeremy warned. 'They've made it quite clear we're in a competitive situation. They're talking to other lobbyists. Oh, and they're very keen to meet you,' he added.

I went, along with Jeremy, to meet Richard Roberts the next day. The apartment block was attached to the Dorchester Hotel. Richard Roberts' assistant, Ben, a young black man in his twenties, bounced down to meet us. He had a smiling, chatty manner, and spoke excitedly about the chances of Roberts and himself living in London again as we went up in the lift. Richard Roberts was waiting for us in the apartment.

A large, buxom middle-aged woman, with peroxide blonde hair, offered us coffee. She was introduced as 'Sylvia' and spent much of the meeting in an alcove in one corner of the room, behind what looked like a typewriter.

Richard and Ben gave the impression of being a couple. Their Russian 'principals', as they kept calling them, did not much care where they invested their £40 million – London and Paris were their preferred options.

They were in a hurry to proceed with the investment and had identified, of all things, the National Insolvency Service – which the government was considering selling off – as a possible investment. Their Russian backers were, they claimed, from well-established political families in Russia and were used to dealing with politicians at the highest level. They were looking to invest 'close to government' and wanted to be sure that IGA enjoyed good access to ministers. They made it quite clear that if we did not enjoy such access, they would head elsewhere.

They wanted names – who could they meet? As it happened, the National Insolvency Service came directly within Neil Hamilton's remit at the DTI. I had little doubt he would be enthusiastic about securing £40 million of foreign investment in the UK. Jeremy Sweeney explained that he counted Graham Bright, the Prime Minister's parliamentary private secretary, as a friend, after helping his election campaign in 1992. Graham was always a good sounding board. David Amess, PPS to the Chief Secretary Michael Portillo, would also be worth briefing – his boss was in charge of realising any income from privatisation. We explained our ability to talk to all three and that we felt we would be able to arrange meetings with them. That was our job.

I broached the subject of exactly where their principals' money came from.

'They have amassed various artefacts,' Roberts half-explained. 'What we're dealing in is the product of some of these items.'

'Yes?'

'And I think if I said any more it would be wrong,' Roberts added.

The money seemed shrouded in some sort of mystery. They would have to come clean sooner or later, I thought. I did not want to cause the government any embarrassment – although I knew that ministers, civil servants, bankers and accountants would rigorously scrutinize any foreign investment. That was their job.

'I think the only point that I would like to make is we're an honest company,' I said, hoping not to offend them. I supplied the names and telephone numbers of three referees from amongst our clients: Sir Colin Marshall, chairman of British Airways; Mike Hoffman, chief executive of Thames Water; and Sir Geoffrey Mulcahy, chairman and chief executive of Kingfisher – an impressive list. 'We're happy for you to talk to any of them,' I stressed.

Roberts asked if we could arrange for parliamentary questions to be tabled. It was a strange request, as I could not see why it would be necessary. However, I did not foresee any difficulties in doing this should the need arise. There was interest from both sides of the House in the government's privatisation programme – our potential clients were holding out the prospect of substantial foreign investment in the UK. As a first step I suggested that they allow IGA to carry out some serious research. There was, after all, no guarantee that the National Insolvency Service would be privatised, or even subjected to market-testing. Even if it were, the opportunities for straightforward cash investment were limited. 'If your backers are seriously interested in investing in government agencies,' Jeremy wrote in a follow-up letter, 'IGA would need to research the market carefully to clarify exactly what opportunities may be available, the timing of the private sector's involvement, and the extent to which investors would be expected to manage the organisation once it had taken control of it. We would also prepare a detailed report on the government's plans to sell its residual shareholdings in previously privatised corporations.'

We offered to 'test the water' at meetings with Neil Hamilton, Graham Bright and David Amess. 'You would need to be prepared, however, to be as open as possible at these meetings, as MPs are likely to expect to be told the source of your funds and the names of your backers,' he wrote. At the end of that period of research they could decide whether they wished, in the interests of their backers, to pursue the possible investment any further. The whole process would take three or four weeks. We suggested a project fee of £10,000.

'Right,' Richard Roberts nodded. 'So at the end of this three or four weeks, perhaps I can persuade one or two of my principals to come from Russia, and they too could certainly then have their meet. . .'

'Yes, of course,' I interrupted. These people were certainly keen on their meetings.

They went away to mull over our proposition. A few days later, I was in my office when Liz, my secretary, came in. 'Ben's in reception,' she told me. We had no appointment arranged, but I went down to see him.

'I've got very good news for you,' he beamed. 'I've just had a call on my mobile. You've got the contract!'

I was delighted and shook his hand warmly. IGA was, by this time, putting on new business at the rate of £1 milliion per year. The £10,000 from this contract was a drop in the ocean but, together with the satisfaction of knowing we had beaten other lobbying companies, we suspected it could lead to bigger things as it fitted in with our plans for Eastern Europe.

'We must all go for a drink to celebrate,' I suggested.

'Yes, I'd love to. As a matter of fact, I'm on my own at the apartment tomorrow afternoon. Richard will be away looking at houses. Why don't you come over? I'll be alone.' He stared at me. I thought I smelt a rat.

I went back upstairs. Clive was just coming off the phone.

'Ben and Richard's Russians have come through,' I told him. 'We've won the contract. And I've had an invitation to go over and see Ben tomorrow afternoon – he made it very clear it would be just him and me. But I have no intention of going.'

Our contract with Ecocon Ventures commenced on 14 March 1994. Jeremy took control, dispatching a researcher to the DTI library, where, he had learned, a summary of a report on the Insolvency Service by Stoy Hayward, the management consultants, was lodged. It was available to the public. He also spoke to Graham Bright, who agreed to meet Richard and Ben, albeit with some reluctance. 'He stressed his time was limited,' Jeremy reported back to Richard Roberts. Jeremy was aware IGA's credibility was at stake. 'I don't want you to prejudice your ability to gain access to these people,' he added. 'Neil Hamilton will want to know who your organisation is, where they have come from, why they are interested in this area and all sorts of things.' Richard, impressed with the speed of IGA's operation, made vaguely soothing noises at further meetings, but continued to stress that his backers needed to be convinced that IGA was close to ministers and Members of Parliament.

We had completed the main body of research in just under two weeks. We had had a total of about four or five meetings with Ecocon. Richard, Ben and Sylvia were keen to see IGA's offices and came to tea one afternoon. Shortly afterwards, we received an unexpected call from Richard Roberts. He had to leave for the States almost immediately. 'I am absolutely furious about it,' he said. Worse, he was not sure if and when he would be returning. 'It means Ben and I won't be able to realise our dream of living in England as the whole project is now on hold.' His backers wanted to cancel the contract, but would pay for what they had received so far – namely IGA's summary of the Stoy Hayward report. We settled on a fee of £3,000.

Jeremy phoned me shortly afterwards. 'Ian, that woman from Ecocon has turned up in reception and she's got three thousand pounds in cash. What do I do?'

I told him to issue them with an invoice and arrange for the cash to be banked that afternoon.

It was two months later, Thursday 12 May, a bright spring morning and Clive and I were in the car driving along the King's Road towards the office. We were approaching the end of a busy week. On the Monday evening I had organised the unveiling of John Major's new portrait at the National Portrait Gallery (see page 110). The previous evening we had taken a number of clients to the Dorchester Hotel for a Labour Party fund-raising dinner. The phone in the car rang. It was Susan

Child, our head of research. She had been at the office since early morning.

'I thought you ought to know. We're all over the front page of the *Guardian*,' she said. 'We've been involved in a sting.'

My immediate reply was, 'What's a sting?'

I went cold as she read the headline: 'Tory Ministers and MPs are named in lobbying scandal. Television exposé dropped after Ian Greer – Britain's top political lobbyist – boasts of the contacts he can deliver at the heart of Whitehall and Westminster. David Hencke investigates the varied activities of a high-level player.'

David Hencke. The very name of this unpleasant man sent a shudder through my bones. We pulled up outside a newsagent's and bought a copy of the newspaper. This was the second time we had commanded a full-page in the *Guardian*, only this time it was the front.

There was that same photograph of me taken in the board-room a year earlier. Beneath it the text began: 'A television exposé of the operations of one of Britain's biggest political lob-byists – in which he makes extraordinary claims about the friends and contacts he has at the heart of Westminster and Whitehall – has been shelved on the orders of senior manage-ment.

'The Central Television programme, an edition of *The Cook Report*, revealed how the lobbyist Ian Greer, claiming direct links with John Major, was prepared to solicit ministerial help for for-mer Russian Communists to buy up a British government agency.'

For the first time he formally 'outed' me, describing me as a sixty-one-year-old bachelor whose family is his company,' who had 'set up his first consultancy business with his gay partner, John Russell, twenty-five years ago'.

I winced as I read my reported words in answer to a question put to me by Richard Roberts: 'It is very convenient to us that we know John Major ... he's a good friend and we had a lunch party for him just a few weeks ago ... at our client's luncheon and he very kindly came along.' It was many months later that we gained a full transcript of this meeting and I was able to compare David Hencke's version to what I had actually said at the Park Lane meeting with Roberts. I had been pressed on my friendship with John Major and asked if I was not too dependent on him, bearing in mind there might be a leadership challenge. 'Before I started the company I worked for the Conservative Party,' I had said, 'therefore one's breadth of contacts is pretty good, as it damn well should be. We're not tied to one man. It's very convenient that we know John Major and he's a good friend and we had a lunch party for him just a few weeks ago at our client's luncheon and he very kindly came along.'

According to the *Guardian*, I had 'admitted breaking parliamentary rules to get questions tabled for clients: "We would never go out and say we can arrange to have a question tabled, but actually we can. If we went out and said that, there's bound to be someone who would take great offence to think that a middle man could arrange such a thing, but, as it happens, yes of course we do." ' Indeed, Lobby journalists frequently arrange for parliamentary questions to be asked, although they wouldn't admit it.

Jeremy Sweeney had 'boasted' that he used to work for Graham Bright: 'He is just somebody who I can pick up the phone to and just run things past on a totally off-the-record basis,' he said. With regard to Neil Hamilton, Jeremy reportedly said: 'Ian and Andrew [Brown (*sic*), group managing director] know him exceptionally well. He is an old friend. We are always delighted both from a personal point of view but also from a professional view when they gain positions of influence.'

Months later, studying the full transcript, Jeremy was outraged to see that the *Guardian* journalist had deliberately omitted his next sentence: 'But you would never look to use them inappropriately.'

The Berlin Wall had come down five years previously, yet here, supposedly, were hordes of fur-hatted Soviet apparatchiks flying in to take control of a bit of the British state by depositing a few million pounds in Britain. The scenario painted by Mr Hencke seemed ludicrous. He had chosen to ignore the fact that bankers and civil service reports, together with other checks, would be rightly carried out on any potential investors seeking to buy a government agency.

We were puzzled by an allegation that we had obtained 'details of a confidential report from the Department of Trade and Industry on the sale of the Insolvency Service'. It appears Jeremy Sweeney's research skills were better than Mr Hencke's in this respect. The report in question, by Stoy Hayward, was still unpublished. But he had found out there was a summary of it at the DTI library, where it was available for public inspection.

The article stated *The Cook Report* had used 'Vacher's guide to Parliament to contact Sir Michael Grylls, chairman of the Conservative Trade and Industry Committee'. After Grylls had recommended IGA, we had made a formal pitch to Ecocon Ventures 'in full view of the company's questionable background'. The reference to our advising Ecocon that they would 'need to be prepared, however, to be as open as possible at these meetings [with Hamilton, Bright and Amess], as MPs are likely to expect to be told the source of your funds and the names of your backers', was conveniently lost along the way.

Victims of an elaborate entrapment operation, we all felt a great deal of indignation. Not having, as the *Guardian* obviously did, the transcripts of our meetings with Ecocon, we felt handicapped. As Clive and I arrived at the office, all the phones were ringing. It was shortly after 8 am and we were already being pursued relentlessly for interviews by radio and television. Clients were ringing up either to express their support for us, or demanding answers.

Then, at 9.15 am, John Smith died in Barts Hospital. Two massive heart attacks, one at his Barbican flat, the other in the ambulance on the way to the hospital, had struck down the Labour leader at the age of fifty-five. Although clients continued to ring, the media immediately lost interest in us – except the *Guardian*. In their rather distorted view of news priorities, a second followup story on the sting displaced John Smith's death from the lead spot the following day. No other newspaper followed the story up.

We were left with our indignation, and worries over how the story would affect our relationship with clients.

It was some days before the truth emerged. David Hencke had been released by Peter Preston in the New Year, and gone to work for Central TV, who, he was told, were doing a programme on parliamentary lobbyists in general and on Ian Greer in particular. He had been a consultant on *The Cook Report* on this programme.

The costly entrapment exercise was shelved after the team suspected a leak had occurred. The material they had gained was insufficient to warrant an edition of *The Cook Report*. Despite more than three hours of covert recording of meetings where 'Richard and Ben', had sought to entrap IGA staff, even the producer was forced to confess that nothing illegal, 'improper perhaps . . . but never anything illegal', had taken place. I imagined what they wanted were dramatic scenes of ministers being privately briefed over drinks in my flat. Indeed, David Hencke, furious at the decision not to proceed, could extract from many pages of transcripts only eight ostensibly damaging quotes. Having read the full texts, Jeremy Sweeney felt fully vindicated and 'proud that despite the rigorous and sophisticated attempts at entrapment not one single inappropriate statement or act was made, or took place, during our work with Ecocon . . . Indeed, I believe the advice we gave was excellent.' I agree.

Hencke had suggested to the programme-makers that they get to IGA via Michael Grylls, who was contacted soon after the death of his father. The producer of the programme, Clive Entwhistle, has admitted that the National Insolvency Service was selected by them in order to ensure that Neil Hamilton, the minister responsible, was brought into the sting. 'It was deliberately picked,' Entwhistle later admitted, 'as the rest of the scenario was deliberately picked.'

The Cook Report had decided the principal actors in the charade, 'Richard Roberts' and 'Ben', should pose as a gay couple. I doubt the happily married Jeremy Sweeney was much impressed – but the gay subtext, even down to the choice of Ben, a young black actor, was meant to be attractive to me. *The Cook Report*'s researcher, Sylvia Jones, sought to justify the use of a gay actor for Ben. 'We used a homosexual in the film, which we did indeed, but that was only because I wanted him [Ian Greer] to feel intimately at ease,' she told another lobbyist, unaware that on this occasion she was being secretly recorded.

After my twenty-five years of conducting business with a wide range of people, many of them the chairmen of British multinational companies, it puzzles me why the programme-makers felt they needed to hire a young gay man to make me feel 'at ease' – unless, of course, part of the elaborate trap was a sexual one. I wonder what 'Ben' would have attempted had I accepted his invitation to go to Park Lane on the Saturday afternoon when he told me he would be there alone. I have no doubt the cameras would have been running.

Bringing the cash to the office was a nice touch. It would have rounded off their film perfectly for them to have been able to say, 'The standard method of payment was cash.' I suspect they were disappointed that we issued an invoice and banked the amount in the company account. To top it all, we discovered that the Park Lane apartment, rented for £2,000 per week, was owned by none other than Mohamed Fayed.

After the cash-for-questions allegations broke in the following October, Central Television, hoping to capitalise on its expensively obtained footage, tried to resurrect the programme. Amid the hysteria of 'Tory sleaze' and the allegations against me, Sylvia Jones told the same lobbyist that although 'we have no evidence of MPs being paid cash and we have no evidence of criminality . . . we have Ian Greer operating on film – it is fascinating!'

Roger Cook wrote inviting me to do an interview. I spent days expecting to be doorstepped by him and his camera crew, and relied on the advice of Angie Bray, who made me memorise a statement, in case I was confronted unawares – another startled victim caught blinking into the cameras as Mr Cook calls him a crook.

We did not rule out an interview – but Angie advised that during her time at Central Office she would not have dreamed of allowing a minister near a studio to take part in a pre-recorded interview. She invited Clive Entwhistle, the producer, and Sylvia Jones, the researcher, to come to the office to discuss the programme. From an upstairs window, I watched them arrive and immediately realised I had come across Sylvia Jones' peroxide features before. The typewriter she had been operating in the Park Lane suite, I realised, must have been some kind of recording machine.

Angie repeatedly asked for clarification of the specific allegations to be made in the programme. She also insisted on being told who else would be appearing. She was told that we would only find that out once Ian Greer had agreed to do an interview. I thought that seemed a bit unfair.

Sylvia Jones has sought to defend the use of entrapment against us. Her main complaint seemed to be that IGA failed to check out the bona fides of Ecocon Ventures. Our clients could have been terrorists wanting access to ministers, she says, all we did was phone their Los Angeles number, where we heard a tape-recorded message on an answerphone. Yet, I imagine few lobbying or public relations companies carry out stringent checks on potential clients. Perhaps we should. But there are easier and cheaper ways for terrorists to gain access to ministers. I took Richard and Ben, who, they claimed, had been employed to put me 'at ease', at face value. They did not come across as a couple of crooks. Nowadays, I trust people less. Sylvia Jones can attempt to justify the operation in terms of public interest, but it is quite simple – she set an elaborate trap and we fell into it.

Sir Tim Bell came to see me the day after the *Guardian* broke the news of the sting. 'There but for the grace of God go a lot of us,' he kindly reassured me. 'At the end of the day we are salesmen. I thought you were extremely restrained in what you said.'

I wonder what Hencke would have wanted me to say, when asked to list my contacts in the House. 'Well actually, I'm a bit new at the lobbying game. I have been in the House a few times, but I don't know anyone'? I doubt we would have won Ecocon or any other account. In any case, it would have been untrue.

Over the summer Hencke masterminded, for Labour friends, a sustained parliamentary campaign. By July, two Early Day Motions had been put down by Labour MPs calling for the film to be shown. There was no film – only several hours of unedited footage. Another conspiracy theory emerged. Central TV had recently been acquired by the London-based company Carlton TV, who were one of our former clients. Despite our contract with them having ended the previous November, long before the sting operation commenced, Hencke alleged that we had somehow used our association with the television company to have the programme shelved – even though we did not know about it until we read it in his report. But Hencke had to justify his front-page story, which no other newspaper had followed up, and the embarrassment he had caused *The Cook Report*, who were furious that he had exposed their under-cover operation in printing the transcripts.

But Labour MPs found the episode a good stick with which to beat the Tories, and they signed critical Early Day Motions supportive of Hencke's position whilst continuing to come to our offices for lunch with IGA's clients. I got very annoyed with one Welsh Labour Member who, having just finished lunch, said to me, 'I hope you don't mind me signing that EDM. One of the Whips put it down, he asked me to sign it, I couldn't refuse. I know you're a good company really.'

I did mind. Our clients were having to read, on an almost daily basis, unsubstantiated and untrue allegations against the company in a national newspaper. Ultimately their loyalty would be tested.

In July, one of our Labour-supporting directors, Robbie MacDuff, wrote to a number of the MPs who had signed the Early Day Motions, setting out the true facts behind the sting. One MP he subsequently met, Alice Mahon, withdrew her name. But another handed Robbie's letter to David Hencke and that too became the subject of another *Guardian* article.

The atmosphere was hotting up. In the middle of all this, the *Sunday Times* alleged, on 10 July, that two Conservative MPs, Graham Riddick and David Tredinnick, both parliamentary private secretaries, had accepted cash for questions – although Riddick had subsequently returned the cheque. We now know they were the first scalps in Mohamed Fayed's unholy war against the Conservative Party. He had secretly lunched with

Andrew Neil, the *Sunday Times* editor, in January. In confidence, the Harrods boss told him that MPs would ask questions for £1,000 a time. (Preston reports that at his first meeting with Fayed six months earlier the figure had been £2,000.) The *Sunday Times* set out to prove the claim through its own elaborate sting operation, involving a reporter posing as a businessman offering financial inducements to Members of Parliament.

When I saw the claims in the *Sunday Times* I was utterly astonished. From my experience the story did not seem credible. I knew that there were greedy MPs – as there were greedy businessmen and greedy journalists – but that did not make them corrupt. As it turned out, Riddick thought he was taking on a consultancy, which he planned to declare. He felt uneasy when he discovered the consultancy consisted of asking a single question, which is why he returned the cheque.

But the *Sunday Times* article prepared the ground for the much bigger cash-for-questions scandal to be alleged in the *Guardian*. Peter Preston continued to meet Mohamed Fayed on a regular basis and they spoke on the telephone frequently. Two full-page articles about IGA had appeared: unbeknown to us, there was one more – the killer blow – to come. Preston blames Fayed's advisers for preventing Mohamed being anything other than a background source on the first two articles – 'perfectly good people doing their job. They could see nothing but difficulty if his private disgust became public. They had no faith that British society would thank the Egyptian for pulling off its scabs. They were wary of the retribution an incensed Establishment might wreak. They were probably right. He had to remain a background source. And, sometimes with ill grace, he stayed that.' And, amazingly and treacherously, until August, he remained a client of IGA.

Royston Webb, in his letter of 19 July 1994 giving notice of the ending of the contract, wrote, 'We thank you for the advice which you have given us over the years and trust that our paths will cross again in the not too distant future.'

After the exposure of the sting, it was obvious the *Guardian* were gunning for us.

Hencke used every opportunity to speak publicly about IGA. He appeared on a BBC Radio 5 Live discussion programme on lobbying and, in his first answer, announced that there was a company called Ian Greer Associates which had provided a chauffeur-driven car to John Major during the Tory leadership campaign. Thus can an assertion which in itself is close to the truth offer a hint of wickedness which then sets the tone for all that follows.

Hencke was invited to speak at the civil service college in Sunningdale. A senior civil servant in the Inland Revenue told me later that the audience had been warned beforehand that Mr Hencke would not respect Chatham House rules of confidentiality – and they should understand that, unlike the other speakers on the course, anything they said he would feel at liberty to use. According to the civil servant, Hencke spoke at length about his part in the sting operation. She goes on:

> He told us that it was well known in parliamentary circles that Ian Greer was a homosexual and that IGA was staffed almost exclusively by homosexuals [the latter claim being totally untrue]. As a result, the key element of the 'sting' operation was to choose two good-looking young men to 'front' the bogus company [Ecocon], which was representing so-called Russian interests. He said that these men were chosen on the basis that they were 'appealing' to Ian Greer. In his view this tactic had worked very well. The two men had been entertained to lunch by Ian Greer [not true] during which, according to Hencke, he [Greer] had said that he could help them and that he might be able to get them invited to certain parties – the sort of parties at which certain Cabinet ministers might be present. Hencke said this in a highly suggestive way, and the clear implication to me was that these were parties of a homosexual nature.

The civil servant, who had never met me, intervened at this point, saying if Hencke's objective was exposing corruption and manipulation, Ian Greer's sexuality was irrelevant. She took particular offence at the supposedly liberal *Guardian* describing me as a sixty-one-year-old bachelor. She continued:

> I felt this was extremely hypocritical and asked Hencke whether or not they would describe someone as a 'married man' in similar circumstances. He replied that there might possibly be occasions on which he would do this, but he conceded I had a point and that they probably would not have done so in this particular story . . . I went on to say that what I found offensive about the way in which he reported the story was that it undoubtedly encouraged the tabloid press to run their own version of it from an anti-gay perspective.

I do wish I had been there to see this able lady verbally handbag the man who had become a thorn in my side. She concludes by saying: 'Hencke appeared somewhat shaken by my intervention. It was certainly not what he was expecting to hear from his audience and it took him several minutes to regain his composure. His presentation finished shortly afterwards.'

Baroness Turner, one of our non-executive directors, became the subject of an article on 22 July 1994 under the headline, 'Lobby row inflamed by letters in the Lords'. Hencke alleged that the Labour peeress had written to all the Labour MPs who had signed the Early Day Motion about IGA to try to get them to withdraw their signatures. This had led to a 'row' and a number of MPs were 'furious'. Baroness Turner was reportedly 'unavailable for comment'.

She subsequently wrote to the *Guardian*, pointing out that the story was inaccurate. She had not circularised MPs asking them to withdraw their names. 'It would have been improper for me to do so,' she said. 'Second, as I had been in the House of Lords – mainly in the Chamber – throughout the time in question, it could scarcely be seriously maintained by an experienced parliamentary correspondent that I was not available. I had simply not been approached.'

The *Guardian* refused to publish the letter, so she complained to the Press Complaints Commission. After a protracted correspondence involving the PCC, the *Guardian* finally published the letter on 19 September, two months later.

As Parliament rose for the summer recess, Clive and I decided to visit South Africa. It was to be our first visit to that beautiful country: we had both steadfastly refused to visit South Africa prior to the breaking down of apartheid, despite invitations to do so. It came as no surprise that, although thousands of miles away, the office in London was regularly in touch, as were clients – not least the House of Fraser. One morning Andrew Smith phoned to inform me that he had been contacted by Fayed's PA, Mark Griffiths, who said that they had received, from 'very good sources', information that a DTI minister had submitted a report to the Home Office urging that the Fayed brothers' application for citizenship be rejected. Andrew told me that they suspected that Neil Hamilton was the DTI minister concerned. I was dismissive of the story as it made no sense. 'Why,' I asked, 'would the DTI get involved in any citizenship application?' It is solely a Home Office matter. I told Andrew to tell Griffiths that I thought they had their facts wrong. Within hours I was being bombarded with calls from Mark Griffiths and Royston Webb, who, convinced that their stories were right, urged me to investigate. I telephoned Neil, who was astonished. As I had expected, he had not been consulted, nor could he understand how Mohamed could think that he was involved. He assured me that if his opinion had been sought, he would have been very supportive of both Mohamed's and Ali's applications as he felt that both were overdue citizenship.

After further discussions with parliamentary friends, I realised how the confusion might have arisen. Charles Wardle, who had served as a Home Office minister, had been entrusted with the decision on the Fayeds' application for citizenship by his then boss, the Home Secretary Michael Howard (who had refused to play any part in the process). However, by this time, Wardle had been appointed as a minister to the DTI.

I telephoned Mark Griffiths and passed on my findings. Although he seemed to accept them, I did feel that he was reluctant to do so. He seemed to want to believe that Neil had played a damaging role in the citizenship affair.

On my return from South Africa, and given the *Guardian's* continuing hounding, I sought the advice of my friend Peter Morrison, Mrs Thatcher's former PPS, who suggested that I speak to Bernard Ingham, the former Number 10 press secretary, about an idea my lawyer, Andrew Stone, had had. Andrew's idea was that I should go and have a word with Peter Preston about the vendetta his reporter appeared to be waging against me. One must remember that at this point, no allegations about me passing to MPs cash for questions had been put to us.

Peter Morrison invited Bernard and me to his Pimlico flat for a drink and we spent an hour discussing the idea. On balance Bernard's advice was that I was possibly better off not confronting the *Guardian* editor. Thankfully, I took the advice. Had I gone to see Preston, I imagine the next article would have been that I knew the allegations in advance and had pleaded with – or pressured – him not to publish. That I should have sought Sir Bernard's advice demonstrates the anxiety and concern I felt that summer over David Hencke's unhealthy interest in my company. A worried journalist friend in the House spoke to the *Guardian* correspondent about his apparent obsession with Ian Greer.

'You wait for the Big One,' Hencke had muttered enigmatically. 'Just you wait for the Big One.'

10

THE 'BIG ONE'

T ea at Harrods. A dubious pleasure, particularly when Mohamed Fayed is pouring. The summons had arrived while I was having lunch. It did not take a genius to work out what it was about. That morning, 22 September 1994, I had heard a newsflash on the radio. Fayed had just lost his appeal to the European Court of Human Rights – the infamous DTI report could not be struck down. Its damning verdict – that Fayed had lied his way to the ownership of Harrods – remained.

Mohamed had lived with this indignity for over five years now, but the wound was as fresh as the day it was first inflicted. It allowed the press and his opponents to call him a liar with impunity and it blocked his ultimate goal of demonstrating his 'acceptance' in the country he had adopted as his home. Now his costly legal efforts to have the report set aside had failed. My half-hearted attempts to set aside tea at Harrods were equally fruitless. My secretary was insistent: 'Don't be daft, Ian. You know full well you'll have to go, if not today, then to-morrow. Go . . . And . . . Get . . . It . . . Over . . . With!'

My encounter with Mohamed that day on the top floor of Harrods is crucial to understanding the subsequent course of events. The way this meeting was reported in the press, and Fayed's interpretation of our conversation, have forced me here, in the only outlet available to me, to relate the encounter exactly as I recall it.

The escalator journey to the top floor of Harrods seemed interminable. As I ascended, I braced myself for the inevitable onslaught. Fayed's sometimes tortuous contract with IGA had ended only three weeks earlier. I had a horror that it might be about to recommence. I had not met Fayed for a very long time. Unbeknown to me, he had long been engaged in discussions with Peter Preson.

Mark Griffiths came to reception to meet me. He seemed nervous, and pleaded pressure of work before disappearing. I was left to wait – which was unusual. Fifteen minutes later Griffiths reappeared and showed me into Fayed's suite. He stood waiting for me.

'Mohamed,' I began. 'I'm sorry to hear about today's news.' But this was not the moment for platitudes. He barely acknowledged my remark before launching into a lengthy tirade. The theme – this 'despicable' government – was a familiar one. But he seemed to have thought very carefully about what he wanted to say and this time, determined, aggressive, menacing, his voice was thick with threat. I soon realised there would be no tea that afternoon at Harrods, only a stern lecture.

His first target was Neil Hamilton, against whom he railed bitterly for several minutes for the 'insult' he had suffered over the letter he had sent to the new minister in 1992. Hamilton, a one-time supporter of his cause in the House, and a man who had enjoyed his hospitality at the Paris Ritz and at his castle in Scotland, had been his great hope. If one Corporate Affairs Minister, Michael Howard, could start an investigation into the Fayeds, a new one, his old friend, Neil Hamilton, could set it aside. Instead, Hamilton had not even responded to his entreaty.

I did my best to defend the minister. 'He is genuinely sympathetic to your problems, Mohamed,' I stressed. There was little point. Fayed, ignoring my protestations, was sizing up his next target.

'There is no Prime Minister since Edward Heath who has not been corrupt,' he growled. His subsequent outburst against Margaret Thatcher was so emotional and irrational, I rather gained the impression I was listening to a lover scorned. He tried to convince me that the former Prime Minister had benefited financially from her son Mark's Middle-Eastern contacts. 'How else could she possibly afford the house she lives in?' he said. (This seemed preposterous, given Denis Thatcher's known wealth.) Fayed seemed to suggest he had some role in cementing these relationships. His rather wild allegations were studded with references to his own friendships in the oil-rich region and beyond. 'I had the Sultan in to save sterling and after all I did for Thatcher and her government I've been thrown to the wolves.'

He then took aim at Michael Howard and repeated at length the allegation I had heard him make before, and one in which he has tried to interest a number of journalists, that the former Corporate Affairs Minister had been bribed to the tune of £2 million by Harold Landy (a relative of Howard and a friend of Mr Tiny Rowland) to launch the DTI enquiry. The alleged bribe appears to vary depending on whom Mohamed is talking to and the family link has been over-played. A friend tells me that Mr Landy, rather surprised at the allegations, has not seen Mr Howard for twenty years. All these allegations against Mr Howard have recently been scotched by Sir Gordon Downey's report.

I had been listening to him for almost an hour. His manner was angry yet controlled, but his eyes were savage. He paused to clear his throat. I glanced nervously at Mark Griffiths, who had been present throughout. Fayed's personal assistant purposely avoided my gaze. Big Mo was building up to a grand finale.

'Ian, I want you to know,' he uttered slowly, 'that I am going to ask Brian Hitchen to act as an emissary to the Prime Minister.' Hitchen, the editor of the *Sunday Express*, one of a number of journalists friendly to Fayed, enjoyed good access to Downing Street. 'I will tell him to tell Major that his government is corrupt. I will tell him that unless he annuls the DTI report I am going to destabilise his government. If it means me selling the House of Fraser and going to live in France, where I am respected and honoured, then so be it. I want you, Ian, to give thought as to how you might be able to help and who else I should speak to.'

There was little I could say, other than what I always said to Fayed when he was in one of these moods: that I would speak to one or two friends and come back to him. I was dismissed.

'Good Lord,' I thought as I left the room. 'What have I got myself into here?' I am aware that this sounds like the Adventures of Noddy – but that is how it felt. I am aware that in writing that, I offer reviewers the chance to home in on the sentence with derision. Let them. I was at sea – and nobody in politics who denies the experience is being honest about themselves. Sometimes we would – for the sake of our pride – secretly prefer to be thought wicked rather than hopeless.

Back at the office, I picked up the phone to call Richard Ryder, the Government Chief Whip – then hesitated. I felt it must have been the heat of the moment: I knew that Fayed was prone to emotional outbursts. I did not anticipate that this was to be the prologue to two subsequent events that I did not witness – Fayed's briefing meeting with Hitchen and the ensuing contact between Hitchen and the Prime Minister.

Looking back, should I have taken Fayed's threats more seriously? It is one of the great 'what ifs' in this whole episode. Had Mohamed told me at this meeting he was already in league with the *Guardian*, I would have known where I stood. Had he mentioned payments to Neil Hamilton or Tim Smith, I would have acted. But at the time, as I pondered what I had heard that afternoon, it seemed his allegations against Margaret Thatcher were vague and unsubstantiated. The slur about Michael Howard I had heard before. If Fayed had a shred of evidence he would have already made it public. I replaced the receiver. I did not warn the Chief Whip.

Royston Webb reassured me when I went to see him at his South Street office on the Friday of the following week. He had flown back to London for a brief visit before returning to Dubai, where he was representing his boss in a court case. This was the earliest appointment I could get.

'Don't worry,' Royston said in his easy, familiar manner. 'Mohamed is just raking over the past. He was very depressed about the European Court decision. You know how emotional he can become.'

'But this is all rather serious, these things he's saying. Have you ever seen any evidence on Howard or Thatcher?' I asked.

'There's nothing that I've ever seen.' He urged me to put it out of my mind. 'Michael [Cole] and I will, once again, tell him to forget the DTI report and get on with his life.' He added that Cole, who had been excluded from my meeting with Fayed, had been furious when he heard of it the following day.

The Tory Party conference in Bournemouth gave me my first chance to speak to Neil Hamilton. As usual, IGA was hosting a lunch on the first day for clients, ministers and MPs. It was our biggest – and most successful – conference event to date, with over 200 guests.

I later met Neil Hamilton, inside the security cordon, away from the conference centre.

Neil spoke quickly. 'I had a call from Sir Robin Butler [the Cabinet Secretary] on Sunday morning. The PM's asking him to investigate allegations of corruption. Mo's said he's given me some ridiculous figure – thousands of pounds – for asking questions. Some of it through you . . .'

The words landed with a thump. This was the first time that I had heard, or even thought, that such serious allegations could be made against me.

'. . . Butler wants to see me next week.'

I was brought back to reality, if only partially.

I spent the rest of the week walking round under my own little cloud – but still I did not think that Fayed was in league with the *Guardian*. I did not know at the time that I had not been the only visitor for tea at Harrods. Peter Preston had stood in the same room just three days before me. He was there again in early October, after the European Court decision, and found Mohamed 'emotional'.

I had not invited David Hencke to our traditional eve of conference dinner with lobby journalists, nor did we invite the *Guardian*'s political editor, Michael White, as we had done in previous years. My only sighting of David Hencke that week caused problems for me later. I was leaving Peter Morrison's party, when I saw the Leader of the House, Tony Newton, heading towards me in the corridor. It was an ideal time to tell him that I had heard that Labour members of the Privilege Committee, investigating allegations against Riddick and Tredinnick, were planning a walk-out in protest at the decision to hold the hearings in private. As I was telling him this, David Hencke suddenly popped up behind him.

After the conference I returned to London. Brian Hitchen had already been in to see the Prime Minister on the evening of 29 September. The PM had instructed his private secretary to take a note of the meeting. Hitchen had reported that Fayed requested a meeting with the Prime Minister to ask that the DTI report be revised or withdrawn. Tied in to this request, Fayed was also making various allegations of corruption against four minister: Michael Howard, Jonathan Aitken, Tim Smith and Neil Hamilton.

John Major replied that it was impossible for him to see Fayed under such circumstances. If ministers were guilty of wrongdoing, he was not going to make any deal, regardless of the damage Fayed might wreak on the government. He told Hitchen to make no response to Fayed while he considered his position.

The following day, the Prime Minister asked Robin Butler to investigate. The allegations (undoubtedly those against Michael Howard) were familiar. But the Prime Minister asked Butler to investigate all of them, old or new, with the ministers concerned.

Neil Hamilton was hauled in the week following the Tory Party Conference. I saw him immediately after. The Cabinet Secretary, he explained, had handed him a piece of paper upon which were typed the three specific allegations Hitchen had told the Prime Minister that Fayed was making.

- that he had received £50,000 via Ian Greer to ask seventeen parliamentary questions on Fayed's behalf;
- that Hamilton had rung Fayed to say that he would have to 'distance' himself from the Harrods boss on account of his letter of congratulation which Fayed had 'inadvertently' sent to the DTI;
- and, finally, that he had stayed for three nights at the Paris Ritz, running up a bill of £3,500. (The Cabinet

Secretary seemed remarkably well-informed about expenditure incurred at the hotel.)

Neil said he felt as if he'd been called to the headmaster's study, only the charges were more serious. The bribe of £50,000 and the telephone call he denied outright. There was, as he stated, no evidence of either. As for the Ritz affair, he handed to the Cabinet Secretary a copy of the letter he had sent to the *Guardian* a year earlier, stressing his six-day stay was a private visit back in 1987 and all prices quoted were 'retail price equivalents'. He also handed over copies of his previous year's correspondence with Geoffrey Johnson-Smith, chairman of the Select Committee on Members' Interests.

Neil felt he had given a good account of himself but was worried that he might be 'quarantined' as a potential liability and see his ministerial prospects suffer. Sir Robin had seemed satisfied but told him he would be reporting back to the PM.

It was a busy week for Sir Robin. At my September meeting, Mohamed had failed to mention either Tim Smith, the then Northern Ireland Minister, or Jonathan Aitken, the then Chief Secretary to the Treasury.

When Tim was called before the Cabinet Secretary, he admitted he had declared his consultancy with House of Fraser late. The consultancy had ended five years previously. He offered to resign – an offer the Prime Minister agreed should come into effect later in the week, at the end of Sir Robin's enquiries.

I suspect Fayed's allegations against Jonathan Aitken were an invention. Aitken had made the fatal mistake of staying at the Paris Ritz sometime earlier. Although he was not Fayed's guest, Fayed had acquired a copy of Aitken's bill, which he was later to hand over to the *Guardian*. Fayed fantastically alleged that the Chief Secretary owned two brothels in Paris and London, that he had pimped for Arabs, and that he had received $300 million commission on a deal whilst at the Paris Ritz with Mark Thatcher and an alleged arms dealer. Mohamed further alleged that he had a tape-recording of the meeting – but he has so far failed to produce it. These allegations led to Aitken suing for libel.

Sir Robin Butler notes that there were 'patent inaccuracies' in the allegations against both Aitken and Michael Howard, all of which were denied 'explicitly, unequivocally and in writing . . . I have found nothing which would cause me to throw any doubt on the validity of those denials. Moreover, the fact that there is reason to think that these allegations too have now been made available to others who have so far chosen not to publish them suggests that they too may have found that there is a lack of evidence to establish their validity.'

Even as Sir Robin was conducting his enquiries, Fayed, frustrated by the Prime Minister's response, had already agreed at a further meeting with Peter Preston, on 16 October, a Sunday, to go public and make available relevant documents. Letters and faxes from the parliamentary campaign we had waged against Lonrho in the mid-eighties started to arrived at the *Guardian* offices that same day.

On the Monday evening, it was David Hencke's turn to see Mohamed Fayed. This was to be the first and only interview he was to get with his main source. It lasted ten minutes. And Hencke's report of the meeting is confusing and contradictory. He was told that House of Fraser had retained IGA for £50,000 a year and that Fayed received from IGA invoices of £8,000 to £10,000 per month, depending on the number of questions asked in the House by Smith and Hamilton. This allegation, along with the famous quote that I allegedly made that MPs could be hired like taxis, would subsequently be quietly dropped. For some reason, the journalist did not ask whether Hamilton and Smith had received any money from Fayed via IGA. And, despite this being the main allegation of Hencke's subsequent article, Mohamed Fayed did not volunteer any information to support it in their ten-minute meeting. All Mohamed did say was that the two MPs were paid in cash, by him, at the rate of £2,000 per question. Hencke, by this time obsessed with my culpability, was happy to believe that such payments were made via me.

On the afternoon of Wednesday 19 October I received a call from Neil at the DTI. 'Ian, thank God you're there,' he said. 'I'm coming over to see you now.'

Neil came straight up to the flat. He was in a dreadful state and sat on the sofa opposite me ashen-faced. He had received a tip-off, he said, that the *Guardian* was going to publish allegations made by Fayed the next day. I called Clive and Andrew Smith into the room. We were trying to decide what to do, when my secretary came up to the flat with a fax which had just arrived from David Hencke. It was a quarter past four in the afternoon.

Dear Mr Greer

I am approaching you by fax to make sure that my enquiry is drawn to your attention.

I am working on the story of your association with Mr Al-Fayed in the Harrods campaign against Lonrho. I have many of the documents involved in that campaign. If you would like to comment, I can be reached on 0171-239 9716 or by fax on 0171-239 9997.

Yours sincerely

David Hencke

Neil checked with his office at the House of Commons. He too had received an identical fax.

When I had been last interviewed by Hencke, in July 1993, it had taken him three months to publish the article. Optimistically I hoped, considering the rate of Mr Hencke's journalistic output, I would have until Christmas to respond. However, we were desperate to know what the specific allegations might be. We did not want to start denying things we were not accused of – which would have raised unjustified suspicions. We alerted the company's lawyer, Andrew Stone of Lewis, Silkin and Partners, who dictated a response. IGA, it said, would be interested in responding to any questions Hencke might like to put to us in writing. It asked that the newspaper contact us 'during normal office hours'.

Then began the round of circular conversations of the 'what

do we do now?' variety. I watched, helpless, as controlled pandemonium began to break out. By this time, we thought we had grown battle-hardened when it came to the *Guardian*. With some trepidation we had braced ourselves for the 'Power and Prestige' article. We had been through the sting and survived. We had faced countless articles over the summer demanding that *The Cook Report* entrapment be shown. And all the time, Hencke had muttered that the 'Big One' was still to come. We would laugh about it at the office. 'Bring on the Big One', the staff would joke. Naïvely perhaps, I had thought that as we had done nothing wrong, there could not be a 'Big One'. Well, it began to dawn on us – this was the Big One.

A worried Neil Hamilton left for the House. When he arrived in his office, there was a brief message on the answerphone from the Liberal Democrat MP Alex Carlile saying that he wished to speak to him urgently. Neil phoned him back immediately. Unlike us, Carlile (a former bitter opponent of Fayed) had been briefed on the specific allegations to be made in the *Guardian* the following day. He intended to stand up in the chamber at 10 pm to raise a point of order. Although he had recently dined with David Hencke, he claimed papers relating to the story had been sent to him in an unmarked envelope. Neil protested at the injustice of Carlile's proposed action – by raising the matter in the House, other media outlets could repeat the allegations with impunity, while he, the person whom Fayed and Carlile were attacking, had not seen any of the evidence against him. Carlile eventually agreed to let Neil see the papers and they met in the Liberal Whip's Office at about 9 pm.

What Carlile produced were photocopies of various letters Hamilton had written to ministers, and photocopies of some of the parliamentary questions Neil had tabled in support of Fayed. In heated exchanges, Neil angrily declared his innocence and denied any allegations of impropriety. 'What evidence is there in anything you have shown me that says I took money?' he protested. He could not understand how Carlile, 'a QC with a criminal practice and liberal views', could consider standing up in the House that evening, 'prejudice' Hamilton's position and seek to make 'political capital out of a character assassination'. Alex Carlile was apparently unpersuaded.

After Neil returned to his office, he received a call from Archy Kirkwood, the Liberal Chief Whip, to say that Carlile would *not* now raise the matter, but if a Labour Member did, the Liberal Democrats 'would have to come in on the back of him'. It suggests that they knew by this time of the planned intervention of Labour MP Stuart Bell, the shadow Corporate Affairs Minister.

Without further warning, later that evening Bell stood up from the Opposition benches and read from the shortly to be made public *Guardian* article, saving Alex Carlile – who was seated on a crowded Liberal Democrat frontbench – the trouble. I wrote to Bell the next day inviting him to repeat the allegation outside the House. He did not reply to my letter.

The barrister Edward Garnier, Conservative MP for Harborough, complained that Bell had 'conspired' with the *Guardian* to introduce 'defamatory material under cloak of privilege' to enable the following day's papers to repeat the allegations by reporting his point of order. And he went on, 'Is it in order for Labour frontbench spokesmen to shoot the fox of the Liberal Party, when the whole Liberal frontbench, such as it is, has stayed up all night to make the same fatuous point?'

Michael Morris, the Deputy Speaker, said he had 'assumed that honourable Members had come to debate the Criminal Justice and Public Order Bill'. Both Garnier and Morris had misunderstood the Liberal Democrats' intention. Criminal Justice could not have been further from their minds that evening. Alex Carlile, having intimated via the Liberal Chief Whip that he would not raise the matter under cloak of privilege, had, instead, put down an Early Day Motion calling for an independent enquiry. He stood up at this point and told the House about it.

Elsewhere in the building, a lonely Neil Hamilton was thinking of Christine. Earlier that day, she had driven from London to their Cheshire home to prepare for a family weekend. Her parents were coming up from Cornwall and her brother was bringing his family. Neil rang her and kept her talking for the duration of the ten o'clock news to prevent her seeing the next day's

Guardian's banner headline displayed across the screen. The story was well trailed.

Christine learned about the growing storm from a journalist on the *Express*, who phoned her after she had gone to bed. Neil's efforts at protection had left her totally unprepared. Distraught, she rang the House. She knew exactly where to find her husband – the Government Whips' Office. It was, Neil says, one of the most difficult phone calls of his life, trying to pacify a perplexed and worried wife, under the stern gaze of the Whips – who were demanding their own answers.

Back at IGA, the drama was unfolding before our eyes. I called together as many directors as I could get hold of. Angie Bray, my media director, Westminster councillor Simon Milton, Andrew Smith, Robbie MacDuff, Clive Ferreira, Jeremy Sweeney and Andrew Stone, our lawyer and a non-executive director. I spoke on the telephone to another non-executive director, Baroness Turner, Labour's frontbench spokeswoman on social security in the Lords, who was, as always, solid as a rock.

We commenced a rather haphazard board meeting in the dining room. At some point someone shouted from the sitting room, 'It's on', and we all hurried through. There is something awful about the sight of your own picture on the television news, as the presenter in dark tones repeats the word 'corruption'. For the first time, we heard broadcast the allegations which were to be carried in the following day's paper: that I had been given money to pass to Tim and Neil to ask questions in the House.

The others left Clive and me alone for a while, and headed off to the local pub. I had to warn my parents – an incredibly difficult task. Both in their nineties, they live in a village in Surrey. They had always been so proud of me, their only son, and especially of my success in business.

'But son, how can they say that if you didn't do it?' my mother asked. 'How can Mr Fayed say this, when you've always said he's a very nice man?' And, of course, the question we all ask: 'What will we tell the neighbours?'

After Clive, too, had phoned his parents, we sat on the sofa for a short while. 'You know, Clive, things will never be the same again.' I did not need to say it. Within minutes the staff returned brandishing an early edition of the *Guardian*. I caught sight of the banner headline: 'Tory MPs Were Paid to Plant Questions Says Harrods Chief'. We crowded round. In utter astonishment, I stared at the 18-point strap-line: 'Mr Greer said to me you need to rent an MP like you rent a London taxi.'

I couldn't read it from beginning to end. These were outrageous allegations – far more serious, and focusing far more on IGA, than I had ever expected. 'A Westminster lobbying company was paid tens of thousands of pounds to give to two high-flying Conservative MPs for asking parliamentary questions at £2,000 a time,' it began. My eyes would focus on different paragraphs, then the pictures, then quotes from Fayed. 'Every month we got a bill for parliamentary services and it would vary from £8,000 to £10,000, depending on the number of questions.' That's wrong, wrong, so wrong, I thought.

Reproduced on the front page was the top of the letter Andrew Smith had typed in March 1989 on House of Commons notepaper from Neil Hamilton to Douglas Hurd. The letter that was never sent. The incriminating sentence NOT TO BE RELEASED UNDER ANY CIRCUMSTANCES WITHOUT THE PERMISSION OF IAN GREER was emblazoned across the top.

By 11 o'clock we had tracked down Andy Stephenson of solicitors Peter Carter-Ruck. The solicitor assured us that a libel writ would be issued first thing the following morning. In the meantime, I faxed a statement to the Press Association. The allegations, we stated, were 'wholly and totally untrue'.

Our unhappy little gathering broke up at about 3 in the morning. I couldn't sleep, but was roused at 6.30 by the phone ringing. I got out of bed and went into the dining room. The newspaper was lying on the table. My eyes were unwillingly drawn back to the headline: 'paid to plant questions'. Six-thirty in the morning and there was a journalist on the phone, the first of many. Throughout the day, that shrill ring would puncture the air every thirty seconds. 'Tim Smith is resigning,' said the voice at the other end. I thought I detected glee.

I repeated the mantra: 'The allegations are wholly and totally

untrue. My lawyers are issuing a writ for libel this morning ...
No, I am sorry I can't comment further.' I hung up and looked
out of the window. Over a dozen reporters and TV camera crews
had already gathered on the opposite side of the street. I later
learned that some had offered money to flat-owners opposite
IGA's office so that they could train their lenses on the staff
within. The phone rang again. It was a neighbour from
Kingston. It appeared we were surrounded at home as well.

'There are reporters here, Ian,' my neighbour told me. 'I've
just been asked what it feels like to live next door to a lobbyist.'

The media had created a new political swearword.

11

THE PRICE OF
REFUSING TO COME TO
AN ARRANGEMENT

I sit here staring at a pile of press cuttings a foot high. All were generated in the two weeks immediately following the Big One. They are too numerous to quote in detail – needless to say, few say anything complimentary about me. I am described as the 'smooth-talking Mr Fixit' enjoying 'unrivalled access to MPs'. The home I live in is described as the 'Fixer's Fortress'. Much is made of the fact that I am a 'confirmed bachelor'. Two of my remarks to the bogus Richard Roberts of Ecocon Ventures – about knowing John Major and my company's ability to get parliamentary questions tabled – which had previously only interested the *Guardian*, are repeated in annotated detail every-where else.

One of the documents the *Guardian* received at the beginning of that week was Neil and Christine's bill for their stay at the Ritz. The paper very cleverly held it back until the Friday, the day after their cash-for-questions story. The *Sun* newspaper was also furnished with a copy, thus enabling a two-pronged assault in broadsheet and tabloid. 'PUTTING ON THE SLEAZE' was how the *Sun* memorably recorded it in their front-page headline. On page three, the parliamentary couple's requirements from room service were minutely itemised, even down to each indi-vidual postage stamp.

The delay in releasing the bill was a subtle piece of manipu-lation. Coming a day after Tim Smith had resigned, the effect was utterly damning. Having spent a day denying he had accepted undeclared cash for asking parliamentary questions, Neil Hamilton, the minister for business probity, was suddenly faced with a bill which proved he had accepted a £3,600 holiday from the same man – a man who was angry with him for his extravagance. This he could not deny. Even some parliamentary friends, who did not believe the MP would accept cash for questions, began to be concerned.

We were holed up in our Westminster office with the phones ringing constantly. We counted seventeen journalists camped outside on our doorstep. They would be there until midnight. My staff had to run a gauntlet of camera flashes and enquiries as they darted into the office: 'Is Ian Greer in?', 'Have you got any comment?', 'What do you think of the allegations?' After once or twice being caught on film, peering out, I decided to keep away from the windows. All day we held our urgent crisis meetings in rooms at the rear of the building, worried that long-range listening devices in the street could be recording our conversations. Meetings, briefings and client lunches had to be cancelled or hastily rearranged – as it became evident that we would not be able to do any serious work for weeks. I could see the worry on the faces of my staff – worry that they might not have a job for very long.

That morning I had tried to ring Michael Cole, Fayed's press man, to see if he could talk some sense into his boss – but he refused to take my call. Naïvely, I still thought Mohamed would issue a retraction at this late stage. But only Royston Webb, by this time back in Dubai, would speak to me.

'Royston, it's Ian.'

'Hello, Ian.'

'How are you?'

'Well, the court case over here is going brilliantly, but I think I've spent half the day on the phone with people over there in England, from Dale Campbell-Savours to God knows who. I gather Tim Smith has resigned.'

'Yes, apparently . . .'

'His involvement in receiving the money,' Royston said.

'Apparently,' I answered. 'I have no idea whether he had a

relationship or not.'

'I think it's incredible. Tim Smith never struck me as the type.'

Royston, it appeared, had been left out of the loop also. I wanted to get on tape Royston's understanding of the arrangement between Mohamed and IGA before he too, like Michael Cole, clammed up, so I rushed in breathlessly: 'Mohamed's made the astonishing claim that he paid me money and that, on the basis of how many questions the MPs asked, the money was topped up. They charged £2,000 a question and if I got Neil or whoever to ask ten questions they presumably got £20,000. Now you know and I know that's not true.'

'My only knowledge was of the fixed fee arrangement which was an annual fee agreed and paid monthly. I don't know of any variable,' the lawyer said.

'Exactly.' Mohamed and I had agreed a £25,000 annual fee at our first meeting, later reduced in 1990 to £500 per month for a parliamentary monitoring service. Royston had authorised these payments.

'The only thing you're aware of with Neil is about the hotel?' Royston asked.

'Yes. Although Mohamed made some rather bizarre statement that he allowed him to do free shopping in Harrods.'

'Gosh, I wouldn't mind that arrangement,' Webb replied.

'So you're not aware of that either?' I prodded.

'Certainly, I'm not.'

I brought him back to my alleged role in paying MPs. 'Mohamed is completely dotty. He said that the invoices from me used to vary on a monthly basis, or quarterly basis, dependent upon how many questions had been asked, which of course is wholly untrue.'

Royston confirmed he had no knowledge of that. Until this point he had been rather guarded in his conversation with me, sensing my vulnerability. Suddenly Mohamed's lawyer relaxed. I think he needed someone to sound off to. 'It's quite ridiculous,' he sighed. 'Here we are in court over here instigating proceedings against the ruler of Dubai in which one of the allegations made by the other side is that we've tampered with statements –

something we've now exposed to be absolute nonsense. But of course the document that was on every table this afternoon was the front page from the *Guardian*.'

'How terrible for you.' I could appreciate his difficulty. Royston was trying to convince a Dubai courtroom of Mohamed's integrity, at the exact moment Mohamed was vehemently telling the world that he had bribed Members of Parliament.

'It's so bloody embarrassing,' Royston cried.

'Have you been able to speak to Mohamed?'

'Oh yes. Not that he's said anything. I gather I was mentioned in the *Guardian* article, not by name, but being in receipt of various documents that were . . .' – he did not want to say the word 'incriminating' – '. . . as an adviser.'

He was referring to one paragraph of the *Guardian* article which read: 'The most detailed connection between Mr Hamilton and Mr Greer is shown in two faxes from Mr Greer to Mr Al-Fayed and his legal adviser on March 29 and April 2 1989.'

Royston was agitated. 'Now I'm going to have a serious word with Peter Preston about that, because if the inference is that I was aware of these payments, then Preston is going to print a withdrawal of that, because I regard that as professionally quite damaging. Like this afternoon, the other side clearly had the bloody thing there in court with them. Firstly, because it was embarrassing to us as the claimant in the article, but, secondly, because it was personally embarrassing to me. And they made damn well sure there was a copy of the *Guardian* right there on the table next to me!'

'You said last night, Mohamed didn't really seem to understand the damage he's done.'

'He just seems to be consistently in some obsession at the moment. I hope he'll start to take some advice. I'm terribly sorry that I have been away for this last . . . it may just be a coincidence but that's when it's happened.'

I brought him back to a remark I remembered him making the previous evening. 'You said last night that the sad, sad thing is that he had Neil and he had Tim and he had Michael Grylls and he certainly had me as enormously devoted fans. OK, less was achieved by a long chalk than he hoped and a lot of what he hoped to achieve was impossible . . .'

'What about Michael Grylls' position . . . there's no suggestions of anything else?'

'No, none at all,' I answered. 'He hasn't featured at all. But, I mean, Mohamed's finished Tim's career. And for what purpose? He's damaged Neil, perhaps irreparably, and caused him and Christine enormous hurt. He's embarrassed me terribly. I've had seventeen journalists or cameras sitting outside here since seven o'clock this morning. We finished at quarter to three. The phone rang here the whole night. I had to stay here in London, but the phone rang all night at my home as well. I can't go out of the front door here at the office because there are six or seven journalists camped outside. All because of allegations that he made about me receiving money to pay Tim and Neil which he knows are not true . . . I said to you last night, Royston, I really felt the best thing he could do was to say roughly something along the lines of "I was emotionally driven and I withdraw it".'

'Michael [Cole] had a rather florid statement prepared about injustice and all that sort of thing. So I said don't use it, Michael, because that just brings the issue, when he doesn't really want it, to the public front again.'

I asked Royston what Dale Campbell-Savours' view had been.

'I think Dale was concerned his side might go completely over the top and read too much into the article and just take everything at face value. But I could not give him any comfort on that at all. Because I'm not aware of any such arrangements doesn't mean that there were no such arrangements.'

'Mohamed's issued another statement this afternoon, which is a pretty silly statement. It's all tied up with sleaze and people in pin-striped suits . . .'

'Oh no,' he wailed. 'That's the one I thought I had killed off.'

We ended the phone call on friendly terms. Guiltily, I took the microcassette out of the recorder and handed it to Andrew Smith. Royston and I have not spoken since that call.

'Parasites in pin-striped suits' – a ready-made *Sun* headline – was the phrase presumably coined by Michael Cole and fed to the press that afternoon. 'Compared with the Tory MPs, Ministers and fixers I've had the misfortune to meet, a carpet salesman in the Cairo bazaar is a man of honour,' Mohamed's statement read. The press loved it – especially because the statement went on to hint at further 'revelations' to come. Michael Cole, who, a month earlier, had felt frustrated, was now in his element. From the top floor of Harrods, the BBC's former court correspondent served up a daily diet of sensational off- and on-the-record briefings to journalists. 'In a classic PR operation, Mr Cole appeared to give slightly different titbits to each paper,' noted the *Daily Mail*.

That morning, I also rang a number of clients such as Sir Geoffrey Mulcahy, chairman of Kingfisher, Sir Colin Marshall, chairman of British Airways, Mike Hoffman, chief executive of Thames Water, Nigel Whitaker, director of corporate affairs at Kingfisher, and Ed Wallis, chief executive of Powergen, together with good and wonderfully supportive friends such as Valerie and Derek Thrower and David Clarke, a former Tory candidate. They were all outraged by the allegations, never for one moment doubting my innocence. To others, I sent the following fax:

> I have seen the *Guardian* article and read, in particular, the allegations that I have obtained money from clients to pay Members of Parliament to place parliamentary questions.
>
> I advised the *Guardian* yesterday that the allegations are wholly and totally untrue, which they are. After a series of articles about this company which we have treated with the contempt we felt they deserved, our patience has finally expired and we will be issuing a writ today.

We copied it to Conservative Central Office and the four other big lobbying companies who had founded, with us, the Association of Professional Political Consultants, our fledgeling industry watchdog. Angie Bray once more came into her own, taking charge of the press. She arranged for me to do one or two television interviews. I angrily told Channel 4 news audiences, 'I know of no Member of Parliament who would take money to ask questions. It would be a corrupt act.'

Clive, Andrew Stone and I put on a brave face at lunchtime and booked a table at Green's Restaurant in nearby St James's. Victor, my driver, went to fetch the car while the three of us waited in the hallway with Angie. On the other side of the front door reporters and photographers, sensing something was about to happen, jostled one another for space. Angie gave us our orders: 'Wait until we hear the car pull up outside,' she said. 'I open the door. You walk straight over to it and get in. Smile and don't be deflected by questions.'

The car weaved its way through the crowd and stopped outside. Angie flung open the front door. The cameras started flashing and the questions began. We followed closely behind Angie, as she elbowed her way through the crowd, like a butch mother hen with her chicks.

Most of the questions were pretty silly. 'How do you feel, Mr Greer?', 'Have you anything to say about Mr Fayed's allegations?', 'Are you issuing a writ?' One I thought was harmless: 'Where are you going?' a reporter shouted. 'I'm going to have lunch, a good lunch,' I called back, as I clambered inside the car. It made the evening news, as did the footage of my accidentally trapping Andrew Stone's leg in the car door. Eventually we sped off, but with one female journalist, notebook in hand, chasing the car down the road shouting, 'But has the writ actually been delivered?'

We arrived back at the office after lunch – more cameras – in time to watch Prime Minister's Questions. After my recent meeting with Fayed, I was probably less shocked than the House of Commons by Major's revelation. He told the House that allegations of ministerial impropriety had been brought to his attention privately three weeks previously. 'It was clear that the allegations reported to me originated, although did not come directly from, Mr Al Fayed. I made it absolutely clear at that time that I was not prepared to come to any arrangements with Mr Al Fayed.' He added that he had ordered Sir Robin Butler, the

Cabinet Secretary, to undertake an independent and full investigation.

The new Labour leader, Tony Blair, still in his first week at the dispatch box, fluffed his question to the Prime Minister. Rather than homing in on why it had taken three weeks to investigate the allegations and the precise nature of the desired 'arrangement', Blair laboured over his carefully prepared shopping list of reforms for what he described as a 'tainted' government: new rules on membership of quangos, restrictions on ministers leaving office to join the boards of privatised companies, and for the cash-for-questions enquiry against Graham Riddick and David Tredinnick to 'now be broadened, made deeper, held in public and made fully independent, so that the confidence of the British people in their government can begin to be restored'.

At the next Prime Minister's Questions, having faced five days of sleaze allegations, a panicky John Major would deliver to the Labour leader virtually everything he asked for – and more.

To me this was all barmy. The Tory benches were gasping at the Prime Minister's hint at blackmail. But knowing Mohamed, I still saw it as just another of his lunacies which had got out of hand.

Knowing exactly when the allegations would emerge, Michael Cole had been preparing his press strategy for two weeks, part of which involved inviting Tiny Rowland to lunch at Harrods the very day the allegations were first made. Cole then planned to spend the afternoon peddling the popular line that the two businessmen had been comparing notes from their bitter battle in the eighties.

Paul Eastham in the *Mail* swallowed the spin whole: 'Some observers believe the motive is that they paid for favours which were not delivered.' 'Rowland – no Establishment lover – is beginning to vouchsafe who got paid for what,' added Peter Preston.

Tiny Rowland resented this interpretation of the lunch. Mohamed had spent much of the meal trying to get the Lonrho boss to admit to bribing Michael Howard. He did not succeed. Rowland was furious when Cole revealed that their 'sensational' conversation had been secretly recorded. Mohamed threatened to release the tape which he claimed provided 'circumstantial evidence' of a Lonrho bribe. Rowland was forced to issue a denial: 'Lonrho have never paid a penny to any minister or member of the government. We have never tried to bribe anyone in government, but if Fayed has got a tape which he wants to play, then he should do so at once – unedited.' Fayed chose not to. An edited transcript which did emerge a week later was a damp squib. There was no bribe – not even 'circumstantial evidence'.

The following day, Friday, Michael Cole released Mohamed's business diaries, showing that he met Tim Smith nineteen times and Neil Hamilton twenty-one times between Friday 16 January 1987 and Tuesday 21 November 1989. Also released was a typical monthly bill from IGA to House of Fraser for 'Parliamentary and Public Affairs services'. It totalled £2,395.85 including VAT. Given the circumstances, it was made to appear very sinister – and so it was printed in newspapers the next day. The allegations that the invoices varied from £8,000 to £10,000 per month were not printed – the reason being that the invoices did not exist. Journalists were also fed an elaborate account of my meeting with Fayed on 22 September – the Tea at Harrods episode. Some, like Tom Bower in the *Daily Telegraph*, reprinted it uncritically and without checking the material facts with me. According to him, I had called for the meeting after the Strasbourg case had gone against Mohamed, fearing that the Harrods chief was about to expose alleged payments to MPs. I then 'begged discretion' and urged him not to embarrass any politician. Fayed's anger had 'exploded', and he had threatened to expose the methods deployed in fighting his parliamentary battles during the eighties. I had left urging Fayed not to 'harm all those who helped us. Don't cause trouble.' It is this kind of allegation – so long unanswered – which has forced me to write this book.

Mohamed's alleged £250,000 donation to the Conservative

Party suddenly became a bundle of cash which the Harrods boss had handed personally to Lord McAlpine. Conservative Central Office were required to follow their long-standing policy of refusing to confirm the source of their donations. It was all made to look very shifty.

There is no doubting Michael Cole did a fantastic job – although he failed to nail Fayed's chief prey: Michael Howard, the Home Secretary.

The *Daily Mail* cautioned against the biggest rumour emanating from the top floor of Harrods – and one that Fayed had unsuccessfully attempted to get Tiny Rowland to confirm over their tape-recorded lunch – that a senior minister had accepted a £500,000 bribe. Noting Fayed had an 'axe to grind', the paper said, 'Mr Al-Fayed should put up or shut up. Enough of scurrilous innuendoes. Let him present his facts, if he has any. It is time the issue was given a thorough airing. In the clear light of day.'

The *Daily Mirror* treated the story differently, running a huge front-page headline next to a picture of Fayed saying, 'I'LL NAME TORY MINISTER WHO TOOK £500,000 BRIBE.' The paper also featured a new logo it had designed – a rosette for the 'Official Sleaze Party' made out of five-pound notes with the slogan 'I'm Tory – Buy Me'.

Rumours of the alleged big bribe to a Tory minister swept Westminster. The amount seemed to vary from £500,000 to £1.5 million. Mohamed had told me £2 million when we had met on that fateful day after the European Court ruling. Crucially, the main source of the allegation, Francesca Pollard – the woman who had claimed, back in 1989, that she had been defrauded by Harold Landy – had admitted in a signed statement as far back as June 1991 that she had been paid by Mohamed Fayed to spread false information. But this did not quell the enthusiasm of some journalists. One, David Owen, the political correspondent of the *Financial Times*, in his rush to be the first to get a denial, found himself served with a writ for slander from Michael Howard.

Newspapers began running stories on the alleged big bribe,

whilst also alleging that Michael Howard had been one of the ministers investigated by the Cabinet Secretary – but without connecting the two stories. Many Labour MPs chose to play party politics. Doug Hoyle, who was boycotting the Privileges Committee in protest at its private hearings over Riddick and Tredinnick, told the *Daily Mirror*, 'The public demands that the investigation should be in the open and not behind closed doors. If there is something about Michael Howard, he should come before the enquiry too.' Dale Campbell-Savours, once he had finished talking to Fayed's legal adviser in Dubai, told the press he was writing to the Prime Minister about Michael Howard. 'Very serious allegations' were circulating, he said, and he wanted an assurance 'that no conflict of interest had arisen' because of Howard's family link to Landy.

As for Fayed's passport application, the Home Secretary was forced to issue an unprecedented statement explaining that, despite the matter being referred to him on three occasions, he had insisted that his junior minister Charles Wardle make the decision.

Meanwhile, back at the House, Tim Smith's description of his immediate resignation from the Northern Ireland Office as a 'painful personal decision' made 'in the interests of the government and Prime Minister' diverted attention away from him, but focused pressure on Neil Hamilton.

After hearing the allegations repeated on the floor of the House on the Wednesday night, Neil had retreated to the Dolphin Square flat of the Government Whip, Derek Conway. He knew his own flat in Battersea would be besieged by this time. Conway and Hamilton sat up talking until about 3 am. On the Thursday morning, the two men left early for Westminster, where Neil cancelled all his DTI engagements for the day. He then set off for the Cabinet Office, where a grim-faced Richard Ryder and Sir Robin Butler were waiting for him.

'You are going to face the most intense media pressure,' they warned him. The hint was obvious. Neil held his ground. He was asked to write out a statement for the Prime Minister. If he was planning to issue libel proceedings, he was told, he must do so quickly as the Prime Minister would need to announce that at Question Time that afternoon.

The Chief Whip and Cabinet Secretary left at about 10.25 am to attend the Cabinet meeting at Number 10. Neil was placed in a Cabinet Office ante-room to make some phone calls. He said he felt that he had been 'sent there to "do the decent thing" and half-expected to find the pearl-handled revolver in the desk drawer'. He did not open the desk drawer, but within an hour had resolved to fight on, and instructed Carter-Ruck to issue a writ. He left a message to that effect with Sir Robin's private secretary. His main concern was to get to Cheshire to be with Christine. He set off for Heathrow airport to catch the lunchtime flight to Manchester. Just as his ministerial car was pulling into Terminal 1, he received a call from an agitated Richard Ryder, who was angry that Hamilton had not stayed to tell him what was going on. Hamilton told him his priority was to be with his wife.

A neighbour picked him up from Manchester airport. With around fifty journalists and photographers blocking the drive which led to his house, he had to be delivered via a rough track at the back. He hugged his tearful wife, and then checked that all the shutters were down to keep out the prying long-range lenses. Christine's family arrived, as planned, for the weekend, but the police had to be called to ensure they would get through the crush of waiting pressmen.

The couple awoke on Friday morning to a new storm. Their bill from the Ritz was all over the morning papers. Stupidly, Downing Street sources had briefed the lobby the night before, mistakenly telling them that the visit had already been cleared by the Members' Interests Committee. It had not. The committee chairman, Geoffrey Johnson-Smith, to whom Neil had written, had merely sought clarification of Hamilton's comments to the *Guardian* about MPs not taking very much notice of the register in 1987. Hamilton had shown the Cabinet Secretary his correspondence with the *Guardian* and the committee chairman, but somehow, *en route* to the lobby, the message had got muddled.

Labour members of the committee gleefully pointed out Downing Street's mistake. One told the *Sun*, anonymously, 'Downing Street is guilty of lying or gross negligence'. Alex Carlile, careful not to be pipped to the post again, raced to be the first person to put down a formal complaint against Hamilton, forcing a full investigation by the committee. As the day progressed, rather unfairly some voices would suggest that Hamilton had attempted to mislead the Cabinet Secretary.

To this day, nobody has questioned why Fayed exhibited such disproportionate anger over Hamilton's £3,600 stay at the Paris Ritz when, if he is to be believed, he was already allegedly making regular and much larger cash payments totalling 'tens of thousands' of pounds to the man – much of it supposedly via me.

It wasn't a time for cold rational questions. That Friday, 21 October 1994, the Tatton MP had a constituency engagement to perform, opening a new school: Wilmslow High. Christine, despite being shattered and confused, accompanied her husband. As the couple left their home, Neil told reporters, 'I have the full support of the Prime Minister and that is demonstrated by my being a member of his administration, and that's the end of the matter.'

Once inside the school, he was told that Michael Heseltine, his ministerial boss at the DTI, wanted to speak to him urgently on the telephone. He was ushered into the headmaster's study and took the call, not an easy one, surrounded by several people. One of the many questions Heseltine asked him was, 'Have you ever had a financial relationship with Greer?' Hamilton answered, 'No.' The MP then forgot about it. Heseltine compiled a minute of their telephone conversation and filed it away.

Hamilton had other concerns on his mind. The pupils at Wilmslow High had baked him some large ginger biscuits. As he left the building, the press surged towards him. A journalist shouted, 'Is that a Ritz cracker?' Foolishly, Neil held one aloft and quipped, 'I shall be registering this biscuit in the Register of Members' Interests.' It was a typical Neil witticism. He had provided the next day's headlines and the most memorable television footage and newspaper photograph from that period. The *Sun* called his performance 'cocky'. The *Mirror* asked, 'Is he taking the biscuit? No, he's taking the p**s.'

Over at the IGA offices, we received another fax from David Hencke at the *Guardian* on the Friday. 'Mohamed has told us that you met him on September 22 1994 to discuss the situation following the European Court ruling,' the fax stated. 'We believe that you passed on this information to the government. This led to Sir Robin Butler's enquiry. Is this correct?' It appeared that Fayed had now told the *Guardian* that I was the intermediary between himself and Downing Street. Worse, Hencke seemed to believe it. In his fax, he went on to say that he had seen me 'lobbying' Tony Newton at the Conservative Party Conference and 'you were also seen meeting John Major's former PPS, Graham Bright, at the Commons just before the reshuffle. Is this connected with the enquiry? Mr Newton tells us you did not lobby him as chairman of the Privileges Committee.'

Hencke had turned spy, it seemed. I envisaged a future full of faxes from David Hencke, demanding to know the purpose of my every movement. I had not been 'lobbying' Tony Newton in Bournemouth, but tipping him off about the proposed Labour walk-out from the Privileges Committee.

Hencke also wanted to know if Hamilton was aware that I had used his name in a letter to Ecocon Ventures the previous March, when we had said it might be possible to set up meetings with him, David Amess and Graham Bright. I sent him back a fax stating: no, no and no.

His article was really a rehash of his front-page piece about the sting the previous May. David Amess was quoted as saying he was 'staggered' by the disclosure of his name to Ecocon Ventures. 'It is one thing for lobbyists to bandy about MPs' names in conversation but quite another to write them down in a letter promising a meeting.' He later apologised to me for this. His research assistant, he said, had issued the statement without fully checking it with him first: 'Of course, I know if you wanted me to meet someone, Ian, I would see them as I trust you not to waste my time.'

Clive and I had been trapped in the Westminster flat above the offices for days. By the Friday evening, having barely slept for two days, we were desperate to get back home to Kingston. Rain pelted the windows. It had grown dark outside, as we packed up our things. Suddenly Angie barged into the flat.

'What are you two doing?' she asked.

'We're going home,' I replied weakly.

'Don't be daft,' she barked. 'You can't possibly go home.'

Clive and I looked at one another.

'You *know* they're looking for a picture of the two of you together,' she went on. 'Just forget it. You're not going home.'

I took a deep breath. 'OK, we'll stay in a hotel here.'

'You can't possibly stay in a hotel,' she barked back. 'You've got to get out of London.'

We had no weekend clothes. It was a filthy, rainy night in late October. And we were surrounded. Andrew, our housekeeper, had been hiding inside the Kingston house all day. A gaggle of photographers were still hanging around the gate. We arranged to meet him in Putney, where he would hand us a packed case. Clive left to fetch the car from the garage. I agreed to leave a few minutes later and take a taxi to meet him in Sloane Square.

A ragtag of rain-sodden, disgruntled reporters, on the second day of their doorstep vigil, lunged forward as soon as I opened the door. I dived into the taxi and they watched me disappear into the gloom alone. I met Clive in Sloane Square and we set off for our rendezvous with our housekeeper in Putney. It seemed such a performance. He handed us a case and we headed westwards with no idea of where we were going. We were both mentally and physically exhausted. Clive attempted to read the map, which began to fall apart. Then the interior light in the car went out and I navigated from memory. We began phoning hotels from the car. Most were fully booked, but eventually we found accommodation at the Bear in Woodstock, Oxfordshire – an upmarket country inn with timber beams and roaring fires.

We rang Andrew Smith to let him know we had managed to get in somewhere. It was, perhaps, a mistake. We simply transferred the traumas from Westminster to the Oxfordshire countryside, relieved only in that we had escaped the media. By the time we reached our room the phone was ringing. It was Neil with the latest update on the horrors he and Christine were suffering. It was too late to dine in the restaurant. We ordered sandwiches and collapsed.

The skies cleared overnight and Saturday dawned a fabulous autumn day. The trees had never looked so sensational. But all we did over the entire weekend was talk about the crisis which had engulfed us. Saturday's papers were grim. My picture was in most of them and my face had been on the previous night's news. The *FT* featured me in their 'Man in the News' column. I imagined, I hope wrongly, that everyone in the hotel had by this time recognised me and was secretly muttering under their breath. Early on the Sunday morning I got the newspapers. Back in the room, we read them in silence. The heavy hand of Michael Cole was at work. Each paper prominently repeated the allegation that I had paid Hamilton on behalf of Fayed. Many followed this up with an absurd call for a ban on the activities of professional lobbyists. 'Welcome to the House of Sleaze' was how the *Sunday Times* put it. The Prime Minister was accused of weak leadership for not responding more quickly to the three-week-old allegations. Readers were reminded that already twelve of his ministers or PPSs had been forced to resign after allegations of sexual or financial impropriety. David Mellor, Michael Mates and Tim Yeo had been dragged, they claimed, from office. Now, the press concluded, it was Neil Hamilton's turn to fall on his sword. Only the *Mail on Sunday* poured equal opprobrium on the activities of Mohamed Fayed, pointing out that 'at least in Britain, it is just as big a sin to attempt to corrupt as to be corrupted'.

We gave up and drove back to London. During the course of the evening I had a long and emotional telephone conversation with Andrew Smith. I told him to start looking for another job as I did not think the company could survive such damaging publicity much longer. Tearfully, he said he wanted to stick by me.

Those Labour MPs who did not know the company now decided we were *personae non gratae*. Angela Eagle, the chairwoman of Labour's Employment Committee, summed up the mood when she refused to meet representatives of DHL International for a lunchtime briefing session. 'In view of the recent revelations,' she told them, 'I now make it my practice not to allow myself to be associated with anything connected to Ian Greer Associates and must therefore decline your kind invitation.' Despite letters like that, DHL International remained loyal. Other Labour MPs who knew the company, like Doug Hoyle, remained supportive, but not publicly.

The majority of Tory MPs were fine. Very few distanced themselves. Richard Ryder, the Chief Whip, had always been someone I would go to see every few months. It had become a useful exercise. I would voice some of the concerns my clients had about the performance of the government. He would listen courteously, giving very little away. Now, perhaps understandably, those invitations to Number 12 dried up. A freelance photographing Ian Greer walking into Downing Street would have been another opportunity for the media and the Labour Party to exploit. There was also some reticence on my part – I did not want to embarrass friends in Parliament.

Reactions in the business world were more brutal. The big eight accountancy firms, led by Price Waterhouse, who were paying IGA £120,000 per year, immediately cancelled their contract. British Steel Tinplate, worth £60,000 a year, followed suit. 3i, the investment bank, put me through intense questioning for an hour. I had to battle to win back the board's confidence and only just saved the contract. The Royal Brompton Hospital jumped ship.

Marmaduke Hussey wrote from the Royal Marsden saying, 'We all very much hope and believe you will emerge with ease and success from this current imbroglio. Nevertheless, I am sure you will appreciate that I must, for the record, ask from you a categorical assurance in writing that none of the questions asked in Parliament about the Royal Marsden were prompted by payment of a fee. No doubt all these accusations are totally without foundation, but the hospital has clearly to be in a position to state the facts if asked.' Thames Water asked for similar confirmation. Having to repeat the denials again and again became humiliating.

The story ran internationally. We lost the chance of a new contract with the Government of Malaysia. New business dried up. I had to shed four members of staff almost immediately. A company with profits nearing half a million pounds, which I could have sold for two million a year earlier, had become, overnight, virtually worthless and heading towards a loss for the first time.

But the cruellest loss of all was the cancellation of a contract which IGA had undertaken at no charge. For several years, we had been providing a free service to the development charity ActionAid – lobbying on their behalf at both Westminster and Brussels. Notwithstanding the legal efforts we had undertaken to try to clear our name, the charity's head of communications, Dominic Byrne, wrote to me cancelling the agreement 'with immediate effect'. 'As a charity,' he explained, 'we do need to be particularly careful about our public image and the probity of any companies with whom we have a relationship. In view of the questions raised in the media and in Parliament we have little choice but to cease relations.'

What was happening in London was being mirrored in Brussels. Patrick Ferreira, IGA's managing director in Europe, who had been with the company for eight years, found himself facing an appalling situation. Many Labour MEPs followed the lead given by their colleagues at Westminster and did everything they could to embarrass Patrick and his team in the conduct of the work they were doing on behalf of the company's clients. Lack of knowledge of the controversy – what was true or untrue – mattered little: it was mean politics. An even greater problem that Patrick and his team faced was the unpleasantness of competitors, many of whom took obvious pleasure in malicious gossip for what they hoped would be commercial gain. Patrick and IGA Europe fought valiantly, and their professionalism, dedication and commitment to clients paid off. It was, however, in many ways a worse situation for the team in Brussels, who suffered the same media exposure that we did in London, but were not able to play as great a role in decision-taking.

It was only through the intense loyalty of my staff that we did survive for another two years. I do not believe any other lobbying company could have gone on for so long. But, at the end of the day, there are only so many direct hits you can take.

I have learned that after the initial set of allegations are dealt with, the press (and not just the tabloids) begin digging for other dirt. One rumour we had to contend with was that IGA was really some kind of front organisation for the Serbian Government. It was put to us that we had been raising money for the Balkan state, passing it through the company's books before dispatching it, undoubtedly in violation of international law, to the Serbian Government. Allegations such as this, which sound preposterous, take time and energy to disprove. There were many which were equally baffling and are equally unfounded.

We hoped attention was subsiding about a week after the initial set of allegations. We had returned to our home in Kingston when we received a late-night knock on the door.

'You are Mr Greer, aren't you?' the reporter asked, identifying himself as being from one of the Sunday tabloids.

'I am sorry,' I said. 'We've issued a statement today. You'll have to read that.'

'No. It's not about that. My editor . . .' he gulped nervously. 'My editor would like to know who you sleep with in this house.'

I was staggered by his question. He was grossly embarrassed to have to ask it. I think we were both relieved when I abruptly terminated the interview.

As neighbours grew tired of being asked for incriminating tales of goings-on in deepest, darkest Kingston upon Thames, journalists turned their attention to Humphrey, our chocolate-brown standard poodle.

'Is this Humphrey Greer?' one asked Andrew, the housekeeper, who was taking the dog for his morning constitutional in the park.

'I've never thought of him as that. I suppose he is,' Andrew answered, rather stunned.

'We are told that he's very badly behaved in the park,' the hack remarked.

'That's hardly surprising,' said Andrew. 'He's only ten months old.'

'I understand,' the hack went on, 'he's named after Sir Humphrey from *Yes, Minister*?' From that moment, Humphrey has always enjoyed his title.

Reader, you may be growing weary of all this by now. I have bombarded you with many allegations. You will, I hope, be able to imagine how we were feeling. But the worst was yet to come.

There were more sinister forces at work at that time – compelling us, eventually, to hire a security company to protect us. On the first day of the press fury, credit reference checks were run on all IGA's directors, including myself. To this day, we do not know who carried them out. Details of our credit card statements and bank account were obtained by an unknown third party. I was stunned to learn that there are companies who will provide this service for a £50 fee. My credit card statements gave the names of restaurants where I regularly dined. Over the course of the next few weeks, these restaurants received mysterious phone calls from individuals, claiming to be my lunch guest, wanting to confirm whether or not they had the right address. The plan, I suspect, was for them to find out where I was eating and then try to book an adjoining table. We later learned that Aspreys the jewellers, where I have an account, had been probed. Peter Jones telephoned to say they were very worried that someone had been making enquiries about the company's account. If information had leaked, they promised, it was not from them. Neil Hamilton's Inland Revenue tax officer contacted him to say that somebody had attempted to gain access to his tax records.

But the ultimate Big Brother experience came in the form of a British Telecom van which was parked opposite the office. It had been there from Monday 24 October. By the Thursday we were becoming suspicious – not least because it had curtains in the back. We telephoned BT and read out the registration number. 'That's not one of ours, mate. We sold it at the beginning of the year.' We immediately called the police, but before they arrived, the van had driven off. Further checks revealed that the van had been bought by a private investigator.

Support for Neil ebbed rapidly away. The Sunday political pro- grammes on TV gave ample scope for ministers and back- benchers alike to give voice to their concerns. Citizen's Charter Minister, David Hunt, put up to defend the government and, in theory therefore, its minister, Neil Hamilton, made a hash of his BBC appearance. 'At the end of the day,' he said, 'it is up to each individual to explain the circumstances in which they came to accept hospitality of any sort. My view is that ministers and backbenchers must never allow themselves to get into any posi- tion where anyone outside could level an accusation against them that they weren't adhering to the highest possible stan- dards in public life.' His lack of support for a serving minister was seized on by the press. For this, David Hunt, always an unlikely government troubleshooter in my view, was severely criticised by many in the party.

Other MPs sensed an opportunity. Edwina Currie, an old sparring partner of Neil over Europe and a well-known rent-a- quote personality, said on *Breakfast with Frost* that Hamilton would do the government 'a lot of damage' by remaining at the DTI. 'A lot of us would feel more comfortable,' she said, 'if we could support Neil from the backbenches.' Alan Clark, too, urged Neil to leave the government temporarily. 'I'm surprised John Major hasn't told Neil to go. He would be perfectly within his rights.' The Scottish Tory maverick Sir Nicholas Fairbairn went further: 'It is a matter of honour. He has brought disgrace on the government. Taking money for asking parliamentary questions seems to me to be a criminal offence because it is bribery. Though he is innocent until proven guilty, simply tak- ing a week's free holiday at the Ritz in Paris with his wife is quite sufficient to say he is not fit to be an MP.' Marcus Fox, whose support as chairman of the 1922 Committee was crucial, was reported by the press to be highly critical of Neil in private. This was malicious. Marcus was a good friend of Neil Hamilton – they lived in the same block of flats in Battersea – and he remained very supportive.

Neil, buffeted by the cacophony of conflicting voices, was facing a no-win situation. He knew if he resigned at this stage, four days after the initial allegations had emerged, it would seem as if he was accepting the truth of Fayed's claim that he had received bribes. If he hung on, he knew he would be accused of embarrassing the government.

And still the press wallowed. 'A Nation At Sleaze With Itself' was how Richard Littlejohn put it the next day in the *Sun*, complaining that the government was 'being engulfed by its filth'. And that was one of the more supportive pieces, which described Hamilton as a 'bright, witty and capable' minister whose departure would be a loss to the government.

Hamilton's closest friend and ally, Gerald Howarth, came to his aid. The forty-seven-year-old former MP had been Margaret Thatcher's acting PPS after she left Downing Street. He was known as 'the terrier'. He lost his seat in 1992, although he is standing again in Aldershot in 1997. He fought alongside Neil during his successful libel case against *Panorama* in 1986. They had both faced the accusation that they belonged to 'Maggie's Militant Tendency'. Their loyalty to one another is legendary. At one point during their battle with the BBC, Neil was offered a settlement. He turned it down. 'If the offer does not include Gerald,' he told the corporation's lawyers, 'then forget it.' Neil knew that Gerald would always be by his side.

Amid the clamour and excitement, Neil flew down to London. Howarth arrived at his Battersea flat and the two men set about compiling a three-page defence of the MP's behaviour which they released to his constituency press late on Monday evening. The finished text included one unfortunate line: 'There is no reason whatsoever why a Minister of the Crown should not remain in office whilst undertaking libel proceedings. Indeed, the Prime Minister did just that – and quite rightly so.' His local papers passed it immediately to the nationals, with the inevitable result.

A junior minister, fighting allegations of freeloading, bribery and corruption had compared himself to the Prime Minister, who had successfully sued a satirical magazine for libel.

Those who were quick to criticise Neil for what was obviously an indiscretion had little comprehension of the pressure and suffering caused to Neil and Christine. Many on the Tory backbenches cared little. It was politics at its most unpleasant.

By Tuesday morning, as he resumed his ministerial duties, members of the press and television were having to be restrained by police in Bexhill, East Sussex, where he was due to make a speech to a local business partnership scheme. The minister was bundled into the De la Warr pavilion, and chased up the stairs by journalists and boom microphones. Every journalist was yelling the same question – 'When are you going to resign?' His press secretary advised him not to take questions at the end of his speech as they were unlikely to be on the subject of business partnerships. He set off in his ministerial car for his second engagement: the annual lunch of the Sussex Chamber of Commerce at the Gatwick Ramada Hotel at Horley. *En route*, he received a call from 10 Downing Street. He was to cancel lunch and return immediately to Whitehall.

He was required to attend a meeting at the Cabinet Office between 1 pm and 1.30 pm. When he arrived, he was told to take the connecting corridor to the office of the Chief Whip at 12 Downing Street. There he found waiting for him Richard Ryder, the Cabinet Secretary, Sir Robin Butler, and the President of the Board of Trade, Michael Heseltine.

They told him that new allegations had emerged. Sir Robin read the first charge: that the MP had five years previously failed to declare a consultancy with Mobil Oil. 'No I didn't,' Neil protested. 'Look it up.' The Register of Members' Interests was consulted. They had been looking in the wrong year. Hamilton pointed to the record of his consultancy with the oil company. 'Ah,' replied an embarrassed Cabinet Secretary. 'You will forgive me. I must go to lunch.'

Richard Ryder then read the second charge. Hamilton had once been a director of a company called Plateau Mining, and that company was to be the subject of an investigative television programme later that week. Plateau Mining, he was told, was part of a Serious Fraud Office investigation.

'Yes, I was a director,' Hamilton said, 'but only for six months. I resigned immediately I became a Whip in 1990. There was certainly no impropriety when I was there.' He added that he was appointed to the board immediately after the flotation of the company – a flotation managed by the very respectable City stockbrokers James Capel & Co. Any suggestion that Hamilton was involved with illegality was preposterous.

'Ah,' the Chief Whip conceded. 'You will forgive me. I must go to lunch.'

Hamilton was left facing Michael Heseltine across the desk. They were silent for a few seconds.

'I think you ought to resign,' muttered the President of the Board of Trade.

Hamilton knew he had reached the end. He returned to the House of Commons to draft his resignation letter. Elsewhere in the building, he heard the Prime Minister stand up to announce that, although Sir Robin Butler had found no evidence to support the *Guardian*'s allegations against Hamilton, 'other unconnected allegations which were not the subject of his investigations have been made against my honourable friend. I must consider whether the combined impact of these allegations disables my honourable friend from carrying out his responsibilities as Minister for Corporate Affairs. I believe they do, and my honourable friend agrees and has resigned from the government.' The Prime Minister went on to say that the other two ministers identified by Fayed had been cleared by the Cabinet Secretary. He refused to name them.

Hamilton had been swept aside by the new broom with which the Prime Minister wanted to clean up the House of Commons. He told MPs he had asked Lord Nolan 'to examine current concerns about standards of conduct of all holders of public office, including arrangements relating to financial and commercial activities, and make recommendations as to any changes in present arrangements which might be required to ensure the highest standards of propriety in public life.' It was a knee-jerk reaction to a very serious and complicated situation. The Nolan Committee was heralded as a panacea for all supposed parliamentary ills. The Prime Minister should have realised that its proposals, once published, would be irresistible. But they turned out to be more far-reaching than Major had ever intended – a complete sea-change, in fact, in MPs' relationships with the world of business and a major step towards the era of the professional politician. I doubt Margaret Thatcher would have responded to the crisis in the same way. Had she appointed Lord Nolan, she would have foreseen what recommendations he might make and known how far she would be prepared to see Parliament change.

The Prime Minister had one piece of good news for us. Sir Peter Tapsell, in an obviously pre-prepared exchange, asked him 'whether the Director of Public Prosecutions will examine whether Mr Al Fayed should be prosecuted for attempted blackmail'. The PM confirmed that a note of his meeting with Fayed's informant had been passed to the Director of Public Prosecutions.

We were all delighted that Mohamed was going to be investigated by the DPP. I picked up the phone to commiserate with Hamilton, who, although he had just lost his job, was cheered that the focus had been temporarily shifted to his accuser. Naïvely we both looked forward to a rigorous police enquiry – which we felt would clear us.

Not surprisingly, Fayed reacted angrily to the Prime Minister's announcement. Michael Cole issued a lengthy statement on Harrods notepaper, which bears the insignia of four royal warrants. 'No one had or has authority to speak on my behalf,' it stated. 'However, I did wish to speak to the Prime Minister. I wanted him to be aware of the great sense of injustice my brothers and I feel at the decision to institute an investigation of my acquisition of House of Fraser in 1987, more than two years after the event.' He then threatened to sue Sir Peter Tapsell if he repeated his suggestions of blackmail outside the House of Commons.

Major's words only served to heighten speculation as to the

identity of the mysterious 'informant'. I was aware from the *Guardian* fax that Mohamed had suggested the informant was me – a claim denied by Downing Street. He now adopted a new position:

> I had a meeting with Mr Ian Greer of IGA at 5.30 pm on 22 September in my office at Harrods. Knowing of my concerns, Mr Greer said he would arrange a meeting with the Prime Minister and offered to do so. I rejected his offer. I did not consider him the right person to make an approach on my behalf . . . If the Prime Minister was approached by someone other than Mr Greer, their discussions would be known only to them and I could not be expected to comment upon them.

A reporter faxed his statement to our office for a response. Angie and I immediately set to work on one – which we faxed back within minutes.

> I hope that the conversation I had with Mr Fayed on 22nd September, at the meeting he requested, was fully recorded and that he will be able to release the recording so that it can be clearly demonstrated that his version of the discussion is complete fiction. I would like to make it quite clear that at no stage of the meeting did I offer to arrange a meeting with Mr Fayed and the Prime Minister or anyone else for that matter.
>
> Mr Fayed's version of events becomes more confused by the day. It was only a few days earlier that he suggested that I was the intermediary between himself and 10 Downing Street. This has subsequently been denied by Downing Street sources. He now appears to be suggesting that he rejected the offer he claims I made.
>
> I can only say, while denying vehemently this latest allegations, that I remain totally mystified as to why Mr Fayed continues to try and implicate me in this way.

Two days later we learned from a Commons reply that the DPP had passed the file to Scotland Yard for investigation. I waited to be called to give a statement. Apart from the Prime Minister and Fayed himself, there were really only two people for the detectives to interview: Brian Hitchen, who would have been revealed as the 'informant' by the Prime Minister's note, and myself. I waited. Nothing happened.

After making a few telephone calls, we identified the chief inspector at Scotland Yard who was in charge of the enquiry. I called him personally. He knew exactly who I was as soon as I said my name. 'I imagine you will want to come and see me,' was how I left it.

'Thank you very much, Mr Greer,' were his last words.

I went to see Graham Bright at the House of Commons and handed him a synopsis of the meeting I had had with Fayed on 22 September and the allegations made by him. I also persuaded Neil to hand Michael Howard a copy, although Neil told me that the Home Secretary would be too busy to pay much attention to it.

I heard nothing more until a month later when I read press reports that the Crown Prosecution Service would not be mounting criminal proceedings. Mohamed felt 'fully vindicated' and demanded a public apology from the Prime Minister in the House of Commons. He did not get it.

Irrespective of whether the DPP and the Metropolitan Police reached the correct conclusion, I was unimpressed by their investigation. I had not been interviewed. It appears the police spent their time studying the lengthy transcript of a tape-recorded conversation between Hitchen and Fayed, which took place on 27 September. This was five days after my meeting with Fayed and two days before Hitchen's visit to Number 10. The conversation, the police concluded, did not prove the commission of any criminal act.

The police said they had to take out a court order to obtain the recording of the meeting on the 27th. At the outset Fayed repeats his various allegations against government ministers before saying to Hitchen, 'I'd just like you to tell me how you want to do it, what you want.'

'Well, I'll go to John Major,' Hitchen says, 'and I'll tell him that I believe that he needs to listen to something of national importance, because things are happening here that clearly shouldn't be happening. And then I think that the two of you have got to meet like that, the pair of you.'

'Yes,' says Fayed, 'I am ready to sit with him, show him the same documents, say, here it is. Somebody done all this for the country. Right . . .'

Shortly afterwards Hitchen asks, 'What will you settle for?'

Fayed: 'Just withdraw the report. That's all. I want my dignity back. Because I can't just live with shit hanging round my neck.'

Hitchen then asks, 'Suppose John Major . . . won't withdraw the, er, or won't say he'll look at it again. Suppose he refuses to withdraw the report, or starts another report, or refuses to start another report. What then?'

'Then I will go to the courts or I will go to the Labour Party.'

'Or to me,' Hitchen replies. One assumes the editor of the *Sunday Express* was unaware that Fayed had been holding meetings with the editor of the *Guardian* for the past eighteen months.

'Yeah,' Fayed responds. 'Or you. Fine. But if you're ready to put it on the front page.'

'Sure.'

Fayed is angry over the slow progress of his application for British nationality. Hitchen describes the delays as 'unbelievable'.

'They'll have to move, clearly, won't they? They will *have* to move,' the editor says. 'We'll embarrass them into moving.'

'Whenever you talk to Major again . . . to ask him actually.'

Hitchen insists, 'I will talk to Major, I will.'

'Say this guy has been shitted upon.'

'Sure.'

In January 1995 the *Guardian*, who were depending on Fayed's testimony in court to defend their libel action against Neil and myself, quoted the above conversation at length under the headline: 'Tape of Harrods Owner Does Not Bear Out Blackmail Claims'.

*

The Prime Minister watched helplessly as the wave of sleaze allegations caught a great raft of his party in its wake and his plans to launch a new peace initiative in Northern Ireland were effectively wrecked. The media were in full cry and sleaze was the predominant story. The allegations, whether true or false, did not matter as long as they sold newspapers. On Monday 24 October 1994, the mild-mannered backbench Tory MP Michael Colvin was dragged into the affair when he admitted acting as an undeclared consultant to a lobbying firm, Strategy Network International. On Tuesday, after the Prime Minister's announcement about Nolan, Michael Howard admitted he had been quizzed by Sir Robin Butler. On Wednesday the fiasco over Chief Secretary Jonathan Aitken's bill for a stay at the Ritz Hotel in Paris commenced. On Thursday, the party's vice-chairman, Dame Angela Rumbold, resigned her directorship of Decision Makers, the firm which had lobbied on behalf of Ebbsfleet for the Channel Tunnel station.

Hamilton and Smith were not the only ones to lose their jobs over the Fayed allegations. They were also to bring about the downfall of Peter Preston, the *Guardian*'s editor of twenty years. Immediately following the allegations against the two ministers, he revealed that a third, the Chief Secretary Jonathan Aitken, had stayed at the Paris Ritz. Preston had been tipped off by Fayed, but to protect his chief source's anonymity and to protect staff at the hotel, Preston had authorised the 'cod' fax requesting a copy of the bill, written on House of Commons notepaper and purporting to have come from a member of Aitken's parliamentary office.

By the time the story of Aitken's stay at the Ritz hit the front pages of the *Guardian*, the Cabinet Secretary had already investigated the matter and cleared the Chief Secretary. In the course of the investigation he had learned of the 'cod' fax. Preston came clean on 28 October and was subsequently hauled before an outraged House of Commons Committee.

He immediately resigned from the Press Complaints Commission. His 1,500-word letter of resignation included the ingenious suggestion that 'nobody was and nobody could in any material way have been deceived by the fax, which is the only reason I allowed it to be sent'. Nobody, obviously, did not include MPs or the newspaper-buying public. 'It was to protect a member of staff at the hotel,' he went on. 'The fax was sent to our source. The source immediately faxed the bill back. The fax was placed in files so that the source at the Ritz, if there was any question of where the *Guardian* bill came from, could claim to have been deceived.'

Preston's days were numbered. In December he faced further criticism when he 'regretted' the departure of Richard Gott, a senior *Guardian* executive, despite the revelation that he had been a KGB contact for many years. The following month Preston bowed out. After twenty years in the driving seat, he had soured his final hours with two stupid mistakes.

David Hencke, on the other hand, who had accepted one man's word at a ten-minute meeting and who had not objectively examined the allegations that had been made to him, was, surprisingly, to win the *What The Papers Say* Journalist of the Year Award. The job of presenting him with his prize at the Savoy Hotel fell to the unfortunate Stephen Dorrell. The irony was not lost on the hacks in the audience, who grinned smugly as the National Heritage Secretary handed over the award to a journalist who had cost two of his ministerial colleagues their jobs, and left a third in serious trouble. Afterwards, tackled by Neil Hamilton on his spectacular own-goal, an embarrassed Dorrell apologised. 'I'm sorry,' he said, 'I had no idea that he had won until he got up there on stage. What could I do?' It is breathtaking to think that in such a tense political atmosphere his private office had left him so badly briefed.

The concern that other lobbying companies felt over Nolan was tempered by their enthusiasm to poach IGA's business. Apart from one or two exceptions, we received very little support from other lobbyists, who realised the potential to grab new clients from the smouldering wreckage of IGA. Many began briefing the press against us.

The newly formed Association of Professional Political

Consultants, our fledgeling industry watchdog, failed in its first big test. A month before the story broke, we had adopted a new code of conduct, which had committed us:

> save for entertainment and token business mementos, not to offer, give or cause a client to give any financial incentive or other incentives to a representative or employee of Parliament or to any public servant or person acting on their account; or to receive any incentive (whether from a client, supplier or would-be supplier to the company or elsewhere) that could be construed in any way as a bribe or solicitation of favour.

At the next meeting of the association, the then managing director of one rival company argued that I should resign my membership until the libel case was over – a move I fought hard to resist and won.

It was not until the beginning of December, with press attention finally abating, that the *Guardian* set out its defence of the allegations against Neil Hamilton and me. It was an abrupt initiation into the curious world of libel law. I was stunned to read that the allegations they set out in their defence were different from those that had been so damaging in the original article. The 'tens of thousands' allegedly paid to IGA to give to Hamilton and Smith (the opening paragraph of the *Guardian*'s 20 October story) had disappeared. They were now alleging that at 'face-to-face' meetings Mohamed handed Neil Hamilton cash and Harrods gift vouchers totalling £28,000. The only payments they identified to IGA, apart from the agreed £25,000 fee were the two cheques for the 1987 election campaign and the cheque to cover additional work upon publication of the DTI report.

Labour members serving on the Members' Interests Committee got excited when Mohamed's solicitors wrote saying the Harrods chief was 'in possession of relevant evidence' about cash payments to Neil Hamilton and would be happy to give oral evidence 'in public'. Their excitement was short-lived. The only evidence the Harrods boss delivered was diary entries showing meetings he had held with Neil Hamilton.

As for alleged payments via IGA, Fayed's solicitors could only identify the three cheques apart from our regular fee. They wrote to Geoffrey Johnson-Smith at the beginning of December: 'Mr Al Fayed agreed a consultancy fee of £25,000 per annum plus VAT [with IGA] in November 1985. Such consultancy fees were, we understand, paid up to 1990. In addition, we are instructed that Mr Al Fayed made additional payments of £12,000 and £6,000 in May 1987 and £13,333 plus VAT in 1990. These payments were also made to IGA, though Mr Al Fayed tells us that he was told by Mr Greer that they were to place him in funds so as to make payments to, amongst others, Neil Hamilton for the work that was being undertaken.'

There was no suggestion of cash payments to me. And for two years, there remained no suggestion of cash payments to me. Only as pressure mounted in the last few days before the collapse of the trial did that allegation emerge. And then it was that I had received varying amounts of cash to pass on to MPs. Now, judging by a book recently published on the affair, I understand Fayed is saying that he and I agreed at our first meeting in Park Lane an especially 'low' fee of £25,000 for IGA and an additional £20,000 'slush fund' to be paid quarterly in cash for me to pass on to MPs.

His story has changed three times. One might ask why, if he had been paying me cash (as opposed to anyone else) – either various amounts or at the fixed rate of £20,000 per annum – he had failed to mention this to the *Guardian* or his own lawyers at the outset, he had failed to mention this to his own in-house legal adviser, Royston Webb, and he had failed to tell Geoffrey Johnson-Smith and the Select Committee back in December 1994.

But, as I was about to learn to my cost, legal fact and legal fiction are relative concepts. The *Guardian* would not defend themselves based on whether I was innocent or guilty of the main charge of paying MPs to table parliamentary questions. Instead, they would prepare to fight the case on the alleged corrupt private and professional life of Ian Greer.

12

A TWO-YEAR LEGAL MELODRAMA

I had been biding my time about approaching Tim Smith. I was still smarting over his resignation letter which, whilst confirming he had received money from Fayed, failed to mention it had not come via me. I went as an observer to the Public Accounts Committee, on which he now sat, and waited. As he left the room, I timed my own exit so that we collided in the corridor outside.

'Why the hell did you not say that you didn't receive money from me?' I asked rather brusquely.

Poor Tim was somewhat taken aback. 'I'm sorry. I wrote the letter in enormous haste,' he spluttered. 'I was under great pressure. I should have said that, yes. I'm sorry.'

I felt sympathy for him. This whole episode had been ghastly for him too and, of course, I accepted his apology wholeheartedly.

As for the case, we were buoyed up. We thought we were going to win. Mohamed could not produce any evidence of his claims, other than diary entries of meetings with Neil Hamilton. As for the 'tens of thousands of pounds' allegedly paid to me to pass on to Neil and Tim Smith, he produced photocopies of three cheques: the two for the 1987 general election, which totalled £18,000, and the third for £13,333 plus VAT, totalling £15,332.95, the project fee for work undertaken by IGA on publication of the DTI report in 1990.

We ransacked the files and found that the donations to the candidates' fighting funds in 1987 matched to the very penny the amounts I had received from Fayed and DHL International. Hamilton and Smith had received none of this money. There was even a letter to Ali Fayed confirming that the money was meant for the election.

As for the third cheque, we scrutinised our parliamentary activity on the House of Fraser account. Fayed's dates simply did not match up. The payment was made in February 1990: eight months after Hamilton had ceased supporting Fayed in Parliament, nine months after Tim Smith's last involvement and years after Michael Grylls' and Andrew Bowden's involvement. Why, we asked ourselves, did Fayed hand me a cheque for more that £15,000 to pay Hamilton in 1990, when he already had a far more industrious supporter, Dale Campbell-Savours, in the House of Commons, who, by Fayed's own account, which I believe, was providing support at no cost?

Libel cases grind slowly along. Our optimism about the eventual outcome was tempered by worries for my company, around which the whiff of corruption hung in the air. From being the most successful and profitable lobbying firm in Westminster, IGA began making losses at the rate of £20,000 a month. Most clients remained rock-solid supporters. But up to £1 milion of annual business was what we called 'project work', where clients would appoint us for the duration of the passage of a particular piece of legislation. Until we cleared our name, we stood little chance of winning any of these contracts. When bidding for new business, our rivals could be heard to mutter, 'Ah, IGA. Such a good company at one time. It's so sad what's happened to them. They're completely finished, you know.'

In Parliament Dale Campbell-Savours mounted a one-man crusade against us. In February 1995 he tabled parliamentary questions asking every single government department in turn what correspondence ministers had received from 'Messrs Ian Greer Associates in the past month'. We were the only lobbying company targeted in this way. It was a vindictive and petty act on his part – a sharp kick in the stomach when we were already down.

We began haemorrhaging staff. Four people had been made

redundant immediately after the article. Now, Angie Bray, who had fought so hard against press attacks and the machinations of *The Cook Report*, suddenly announced she was leaving too, along with director Simon Milton and John Fraser, head of research. The three left to set up the London office of an American rival – a company which, ironically, had sought to buy IGA out a few years earlier. Sadly I waved all three off in February, relieved only for the sake of the company's cash-flow.

Our first pre-trial hearings in the High Court were not scheduled until the end of April. There were two points to be argued. One was 'privilege' – a highly technical legal matter which I never really understood – the other was 'consolidation'. At the time, both Neil and I had taken separate libel actions against the *Guardian*, and the newspaper was anxious to consolidate both actions – something we were resisting. Much as I sympathised with Neil, I wanted IGA's case to stand or fall on its own merits.

'You are likely to lose on the issue of privilege and win in keeping the actions separate,' Andy Stephenson, our bright, if scruffy, solicitor from Carter-Ruck explained. My own presence was not required at this stage, so I took the opportunity to get away for a few days' walking in the Highlands. Clive and I were on the train – looking forward to our trip and trying to calm an over-excited Humphrey, who was causing us some difficulties – when the call came through on the mobile phone from Andrew Smith: 'We've won privilege and lost consolidation.'

It was the exact opposite of what we had been told to expect, which left us dismayed. Consolidation was quicker and cheaper for the court. We had both been libelled in the same article by the same people. While it made logical sense to consolidate the case, it came as an unexpected blow. We were now forced to fight alongside Hamilton, something we did not want to do. But then the laws of libel are not logical. As we were slowly to learn, cases in England are fought not on the truth or falsehood of allegations made against an individual, but on what other skeletons can be dragged from their closets to discredit them in the witness box.

A few weeks later we met for the first time with our counsel, the very impressive Lord Williams of Mostyn, who also happened to be a Labour frontbench spokesman. The fifty-four-year-old QC set about questioning Neil and myself on those areas where we were thought to be most vulnerable. For me it was the commission payments I had made during the eighties to three MPs for the introduction of new business. I explained that the Select Committee had already examined the matter and had said that there was nothing wrong in such payments being made to MPs and agreed that there was confusion as to how such payments should be declared. Lord Williams, who, I think, was initially rather suspicious of my motives, was, I believe, persuaded that I had not acted dishonourably. When he had finished, I asked him what he felt my chances were.

'Mr Greer,' he answered, 'I don't give chances. You have three things against you: you are well spoken, you are well dressed and you are gay. As far as your case is concerned I have no worries.'

Lord Williams then turned his attention to Neil, questioning him on his stay at the Ritz and the fact that he had failed to declare it. Then there were two commission payments he had received from me and his failure to declare these – not just to the House of Commons authorities, but to the Inland Revenue. Neil said that with regard to the latter, he had sought his accountant's advice and had been advised that one-off payments did not need to be declared to the tax man. Counsel's bruising interrogation of the MP reduced Christine Hamilton to tears, and Neil left the Inner Temple a little shell-shocked.

I went away wondering if it was too late to learn a Liverpudlian accent before the summer!

The vehemence of Neil's denials over undeclared cash payments from Fayed convinced us of his innocence – but the MP's defence, as the *Guardian* well knew, was hobbled by his perceived bad judgement over the Ritz and his fatuous justification over the mark-up on a bottle of wine.

We began the painstaking task of analysing Hamilton's role in the ten-year-old Harrods campaign and started by compiling a detailed chronology of the alleged payments and work undertaken by the MP.

7 November 1985	2 written parliamentary questions [Lonrho & *Observer*]
24 February 1987	2 WPQs [replies to letters]
11 March 1987	EDM 724
13 May 1987	Meeting [at DTI with Paul Channon, accompanied by Hordern, Grylls and Smith]
2 June 1987	**Alleged payment £2,500 cash**
18 June 1987	**Alleged payment £2,500 cash**
8 July 1987	**Alleged payment £2,500 cash**
29 July 1987	Meeting [at DTI with Lord Young, accompanied by Hordern and Smith]
8–14 September	**Ritz visit**
21 November 1987	Letter to Lord Young
28 January 1988	Letter to Lord Young and Mohamed Fayed
18 February 1988	**Alleged payment £2,500 cash**
7 June 1988	2 WPQs [DTI enquiry progress and cost]
12 July 1988	EDM 1358 [Rowland propaganda barrage]
19 July 1988	**Alleged payment £2,500 cash**
29 July 1988	Letter to Lord Young
4 October 1988	**Alleged payment £2,500 cash**
6 December 1988	Letter to David Waddington
15 December 1988	**Alleged payment £3,000 gift vouchers**
25 January 1989	**Alleged payment £2,500 cash**
15 February 1989	Oral parliamentary question [on David Leigh and Westland]
16 February 1989	**Alleged payment £1,000 gift vouchers**
20 February 1989	**Alleged payment £1,000 gift vouchers**
12 March 1989	Letter to Mohamed Fayed
21 March 1989	Letters to Douglas Hurd [not sent] and George Younger
6–12 April 1989	4 WPQs [Lonrho arms sales and Marwan]

7 April 1989	Letter to the DTI [on Lonrho and Libya]
18 April 1989	Signature to EDM 758 by Dale Campbell-Savours
2 May 1989	Signature to EDM 801 by Dale Campbell-Savours
3 May 1989	EDM 809 [on Lonrho and Gaddafi]
15 May 1989	Signature to EDM 857 by Tim Smith
20 June 1989	Signature to EDM 992 by Dale Campbell-Savours
20 June 1989	Signature to EDM 993 by Dale Campbell-Savours
27 July 1989	**Alleged payment** £2,500 cash
21 November 1989	**Alleged payment** £3,000 gift vouchers

Hamilton had been an enthusiastic Fayed supporter over the years, although not as active as others. When we studied the list carefully it became clear that the allegations failed to make any sense. There were long periods when he was supposedly receiving considerable amounts of money whilst providing no apparent parliamentary support. There were other times when he was writing letters or signing Early Day Motions without supposedly being paid. We tested a possible scenario whereby payments could have been made 'in advance'. We then imagined a scenario whereby they might have been 'in arrears'. Either way, at least half of them would have been handed over for no conceivable benefit. Hamilton's alleged receipt of £28,000 began to appear a very poor investment for Mohamed, a shrewd businessman. On top of all this Fayed was alleging that additional payments were made via me. Fayed further alleged that he had provided free shopping at Harrods and gift vouchers, but did not produce evidence to substantiate his claim.

In May the *Guardian* demanded copies of Neil Hamilton's bank statements and tax returns for the period June 1987 to January 1990. Neil had to hand them over – although he found the process understandably humiliating – under a legal concept known as 'discovery' where each side can demand personal and sensitive documentation from the other. If abused, the process can become a sort of fishing expedition where a newspaper, lacking any real evidence to support a libel, can dig deeper and deeper through an individual's age-old personal and financial records in the hope that they will find something which cannot be easily explained. If you want to imagine how Neil felt at that time, find one of your bank statements from eight years ago and then try to explain every credit or debit shown.

Our solicitors were surprised by the *Guardian*'s unusual focus on Neil's bank accounts. Banks are not the only place where cash is deposited. Although they wanted 'other financial records' as well, they made no specific reference to building society pass books, credit card statements or other personal financial records. Neil's bank statements showed a substantial rise of just under £26,000 in his deposit account during the period when six of the alleged payments were made, which they explained as a loan from Christine's mother for their house. Although innocent, it was further 'baggage' for the MP to explain away in the box.

Our solicitor began to wonder if the *Guardian* were so keen to get hold of Hamilton's bank statements because they already knew what was in them: Fayed, at the time, was alleging that he had handed over £28,000.

Hamilton desperately wanted the matter settled in the High Court – not by a parliamentary committee. He needed to feel his accusers would undergo tough cross-examination. Feelings on the Tory benches were running high after the treatment of Riddick and Tredinnick by the Privileges Committee, where the quality of questioning left much to be desired, and various members of the committee appeared ill-prepared and demonstrated little understanding of their brief.

This was a dreadful period for the Tories. Months of sleaze allegations had seen the party languish in the polls. The media presented every Tory MP as 'on the make'. Although there were concerns over Neil, with many of his parliamentary colleagues feeling he had been treated very shabbily over his dismissal from the government, there were greater concerns over Nolan. No one knew quite how far the Law Lord's enquiry might go and to what extent their business interests would be affected.

Alex Carlile rushed to report Fayed's allegations – that Neil had accepted undeclared payments and undeclared hospitality at the Ritz – to the Select Committee on Members' Interests. Its chairman, the affable Geoffrey Johnson-Smith, was seen by many to be extremely weak.

Johnson-Smith was faced with a dilemma, because the payments allegation was already the subject of Hamilton's high-profile libel action. The committee could not investigate the matter before the case came to court as their verdict might influence a later one by a jury. But Johnson-Smith also recognised the mood of Opposition MPs and the press, who would accuse him of sweeping the issue under the carpet for party advantage.

The committee chairman consulted colleagues, including the junior Whip, David Willetts, who wrote a memorandum for the Whips' Office which favoured the committee restricting itself to those matters which were not *sub judice*, adding Johnson-Smith 'wants our advice'. The Willetts memorandum was to bring about his own resignation from the government two years later, but even some Labour members of the committee privately accepted the logic of Johnson-Smith's conclusions: Parliament could not be seen to pre-judge a matter before the courts.

Arguments between the Tory and Opposition members of the committee delayed its lengthy investigation of the Ritz affair. Neil's relief was palpable when the Whip Andrew Mitchell joined the team in February, less because he was a Whip and more because he had a reputation for being tough. He would put a bit of backbone into the Tory contingent, Neil thought. Mitchell fought hard to restrict oral evidence to private sessions of the committee – and won. Opposition MPs howled, but the last thing Neil or I wanted as we came up to trial was a daily repetition in the newspapers of some of Fayed's wilder accusations. We knew there would be enough of this when the case started. Mitchell was later to claim that he was not acting in any way as a Whip – he was serving the committee solely in his capacity as a Conservative MP.

Hamilton robustly defended his stay at the Ritz – but once more brought in the, in my opinion, fatuous argument over the cost of a bottle of wine – which did him no good at all. 'I do remember,' he wrote to the chairman, 'that there was a 500 per cent mark-up on the retail price of ordinary non-vintage champagne. A bottle which would have cost £11 in an off-licence was £50 on the Ritz wine list.'

The Labour Members did not wait for the verdict. They walked out before the committee published its report in June 1995. The MP, they concluded, was 'imprudent' not to register his stay at the Ritz, but they proposed no further action. Predictably, the press called it a whitewash. Labour's Angela Eagle called it the 'death knell' of the committee, which Nolan subsequently decided to lay to rest.

We turned our attention to the courts and the coming battle on the Strand. To our utter horror, after months of legal preparation, the *Guardian* tried to wriggle out of defending the case. To do this their lawyers called upon a 300-year-old statute. Article IX of the Bill of Rights, 1689, states: 'The freedome of speech and debates or proceedings in Parlyament ought not to be impeached or questioned in any court or place out of Parlyament.' As judges were, and still are, appointed by the monarch, the clause had originally been inserted to prevent royal interference, through the courts, in the work of Parliament. It gives MPs and peers the unique privilege of being able to libel individuals in the chamber without their victims being able to pursue them through the courts. But, as we were to learn, this parliamentary privilege cuts both ways. Had the allegations been over his sex-life, his outside commercial interests or his political leanings, Neil Hamilton would have been perfectly entitled to sue the *Guardian*. But because the Fayed allegations concerned his conduct in Parliament, an action for libel fought through the courts was ruled out by the Bill of Rights.

Apart from Mohamed Fayed, all the chief players in this drama attended court to hear the decision of Mr Justice May. A grinning David Hencke, along with the *Guardian* lawyers, attended the hearing. Christine Hamilton sat next to Neil, who was accompanied by the loyal Gerald Howarth. I sat fidgeting between Clive and Andrew Smith to hear the judge's decision. We lost. He ruled in the *Guardian*'s favour. The proceedings were stayed. But the judge's unease was evident from his remarks in court. Looking across at our forlorn faces, he acknowledged that the decision 'may be perceived as a profound denial of justice . . . and even a licence to publish material about parliamentary proceedings which, if it is untrue, may go unremedied'.

Hencke was jubilant and relieved. Andrew Smith and I left close to tears. To all intents and purposes, we felt we had reached the end of the line. Lord Williams gently advised us that there was little point in pursuing an appeal. Mr Justice May had quoted enough legal precedents to support his decision and, only a week before, another MP, Rupert Allason, had seen his libel case against the *Today* newspaper halted, with the judge there telling him that 'as a Member, he must take the ill consequences together with the good consequences'.

After the decision to stay the case there was enormous sympathy for Neil and me. 'The *Guardian* should be thoroughly ashamed of themselves,' people said to us. Looking back, once more with the cruel benefit of hindsight, I see this would have been the moment to bail out and sell the company for whatever I could get. The injustice, it was felt, was, perhaps, greater for me. Parliamentary privilege was Hamilton's to exercise. Little good would it do him, but he could feasibly use the floor of the chamber to denounce his accusers.

For a few days the press entertained the fanciful notion that we could fight the action through Parliament, which is itself a court. But, we discovered, Parliament had not used its penal powers to fine anyone since 1666 or imprison since 1880. And it was doubtful whether either of these powers could be revived with Britain a signatory to the European Convention on Human Rights.

Carter-Ruck tried petitioning the House of Commons for leave to allow Neil Hamilton, Andrew Smith and myself to give evidence in court. On a handwritten, parchment scroll (see pages 206–7), Andy Stephenson prayed 'that the leave of your Honourable House may be given to all the following witnesses to give evidence of incidents in the House of Commons in the said proceedings in the High Court of Justice'. The petition itself had cost several hundred pounds, but it very quickly became clear that the Speaker, Betty Boothroyd, would not accept it. She was advised: 'Parliament cannot, except by subsequent legislation, grant leave to ignore the provisions and effect of a statute.'

We were left with nothing except legal bills in excess of £150,000 each. In desperation, Christine wrote to the Prime Minister at the end of July asking for a meeting. Over the summer she waited for a reply.

Meanwhile, it was time for the cash-for-questions affair to hit another place. The man who had unsuccessfully fought Fayed's attempt to have Strasbourg overturn the DTI report, the Liberal Democrat peer Lord Lester of Herne Hill, stunned a House of Lords committee in January when he submitted, in writing, a claim that four peers had taken substantial amounts of cash to table questions to ministers. The leading human rights lawyer told the Lords sub-committee on Declaration and Registration of Interests in January that he believed the practice was widespread in the upper chamber. But Lord Lester was unable to supply the names of the four. His source, whom he described as a commercial client, had been 'reluctant' to give him any further information and had not passed on the names. His remarks drew widespread press coverage and were immediately criticised by fellow peers. The Independent peer Lord Marsh, the former chairman of British Rail, noting that Lord Lester had offered no evidence to support his claims, added that the 'information has apparently been obtained from someone whom the peer concerned is not able to name because he is paid by him'.

The following week, having effectively been blackballed by fellow peers, Lester stood up in the chamber and, in stony silence, revealed that the disclosure of his comments to the committee had caused him 'great personal distress . . . I profoundly regret the embarrassment my note and its public disclosure have caused to this House and another place.' He apologised for 'risking blemishing' the House's name – but refused to retract his

To: THE HONOURABLE THE COMMONS *of the* UNITED KINGDOM *of* GREAT BRITAIN *and* NORTHERN IRELAND *in Parliament assembled*

THE HUMBLE PETITION *of* ANDREW JAMES STEPHENSON *of Peter Carter-Ruck and Partners Solicitors for Neil Hamilton M.P., Ian Greer and Ian Greer Associates Limited :-*
SHEWETH :

(i)   *That there are entered in the Jury List of actions for trial in the Queen's Bench Division of the High Court of Justice actions entitled*

Neil Hamilton

v

David Hencke (1)
Peter Preston (2)
Guardian Newspapers Ltd (3)

Action No 1994-H-No 1664

Ian Greer (1)
Ian Greer Associates Ltd (2)

v

David Hencke (1)
Peter Preston (2)
Guardian Newspapers Ltd (3)

Action No 1994-G-No 1776

(ii)   That the issues in question in the said proceedings concern

(a)   The allegation that Neil Hamilton MP asked parliamentary questions and tabled parliamentary motions for reward, in the form of payments by Mohammed Al-Fayed and/or House of Fraser, whether direct or through Ian Greer and/or Ian Greer Associates Limited, and in the form of hospitality at the Ritz Hotel in Paris; and

(b)   The rules relating to the Register of Members Interests.

(iii)   That for the foregoing reason the evidence of certain Members of Parliament and others touching upon such proceedings in the House of Commons is relevant to the issues in question in the said proceedings in the High Court of Justice.

Wherefore your Petitioner prays that the leave of your Honourable House may be given to all the following witnesses to give evidence of incidents in the House of Commons in the said proceedings in the High Court of Justice namely:

Neil Hamilton (Member of Parliament for Tatton)
Ian Greer (Chairman, Ian Greer Associates Ltd)
Andrew Smith (Group Managing Director, Ian Greer Associates Ltd)

And your Petitioner as in duty bound will ever pray, etc

Andrew James Stephenson
Peter Carter-Ruck and Partners
75 Shoe Lane
London
EC4A 3BQ

allegations. Many had believed Lord Lester's source was Mohamed Fayed – his comments coincided with a Fayed letter in the *Spectator* which had described Lord Lester as 'wise and fair-minded, as befits a counsel of mine'. But Mohamed Fayed went on the record to deny he was the source – which took many by surprise.

In March the Fayed brothers finally received a long-awaited response to their application for British citizenship – outright rejection with no reasons given. A furious Fayed then set about fighting the decision in the courts. His Downing Street emissary, Brian Hitchen, trailed the move in the *Sunday Express*:

> Mohamed Al Fayed is more British than most of the people you and I will ever meet.
>
> Unlike the riff-raff upon whom we bestow British passports willy-nilly, Mr Fayed pays his way ... Though he wouldn't thank me for saying so, there are children alive today thanks to his unsung generosity in giving millions to our hospitals and medical research. So let's cut out the envy and malice and give Mohamed Fayed the thing he would treasure most: British citzenship. He has earned it several times over.

Mohamed was experiencing mixed fortunes in the courts. We had watched with interest the outcome of the Christoph Betterman libel trial. Fayed had accused Betterman, the forty-eight-year-old former deputy chairman of Harrods, of fraud and embezzlement of millions of dollars from Fayed companies. The allegations led to Betterman's prosecution in Dubai on criminal charges, of which he was subsequently acquitted. In February 1995 Fayed was forced to admit in the High Court that the allegations were lies. He was obliged to pay Betterman a six-figure sum in libel damages and costs amounting to an estimated £1,000,000, and to make a public apology.

The Conservative MP David Evans highlighted the case in an Early Day Motion on 20 February 1996, asking why Alex Carlile remained so 'enthusiastic an apologist for Fayed'. Indeed,

Carlile's switch to the Harrods chief rivals that of Dale Campbell-Savours. When the DTI report was published, Carlile described Fayed, at the time a Tory supporter, as a 'perjurer'. Five years later, with Mohamed thinking of donating to the Liberal Democratic Party, Alex Carlile was championing his application for citizenship and noting in Early Day Motions that 'the Conservative Party has developed an irrational and pathological hatred bordering on a vendetta against the Al Fayed brothers'.

Fayed lost another court case, once again in Dubai. Royston Webb had flown Britain's most expensive QC, Anthony Grabiner, to the emirate to fight a £40 million action against the ruling Maktoum family. Mohamed had boasted that when he arrived in Dubai in the sixties the inhabitants 'lived in mud houses and slept in tents'. But by the nineties, the oil-rich state enjoyed one of the world's highest per capita incomes and its rulers had less need of Fayed's international business skills to lever money and services out of London. In 1993 they cancelled the management contract for the thirty-nine-storey World Trade Center, which was held by one of Fayed's companies, ostensibly due to run until 2000. After winning the subsequent court case, the Maktoums, once the biggest customers at the Paris Ritz, were reported to have moved their custom 200 yards west to the Hotel Crillon.

It was nearly a year since Neil Hamilton had been accused of taking cash for questions. In his Cheshire constituency, his prospective Labour opponent, the railway worker John Kelly, was making it clear he intended to fight the election on sleaze. Neil's attempt to clear his name in the courts had been quashed on an ancient legal technicality. Things were looking pretty awful. A man who had lived for politics felt 'neutralised as a political force'. In March, when he was reappointed vice-chairman of the Conservative Trade and Industry Committee, Hamilton observed grimly, 'I am back where I started five years ago.' For Neil, the sleepless nights were lessening, but Christine, who lost a stone in weight in the three weeks after the *Guardian's* claims, was still regularly reduced to fits of uncontrollable sobbing.

The summer was coming to an end and the couple had received no reply, not even a holding letter, in response to their request for a meeting with the PM. They called upon the assistance of the new Chief Whip, Alistair Goodlad, who represented the neighbouring constituency of Eddisbury. His enquiries revealed their letter had been 'misplaced' and a meeting was hurriedly arranged at Downing Street in the short recess before the Queen's Speech.

The encounter in the PM's study was warm and friendly. They met the Prime Minister; his PPS, John Ward; the Attorney-General, Sir Nicholas Lyell; and the Leader of the House, Tony Newton. The PM listened sympathetically as Neil recounted the almost impossible position they found themselves in. The Attorney-General, who was well briefed on the *Guardian*'s legal manoeuvres to prevent the case coming to court, was asked if he could suggest any way forward. He advised that, by coincidence, government legislation for the forthcoming session included a bill on defamation. It might be possible, he suggested, to include an amendment to the bill which would enable Members to be released from the restrictions of parliamentary privilege. A good idea, it was agreed, and Neil and Christine left Downing Street happier than they had been for some time.

The Defamation Bill, based on Law Commission recommendations, was an uncontroversial piece of government legislation which sought to create a fast-track court procedure giving judges the power to resolve less serious libel and slander cases without the expense of a full trial. It also sought to create a statutory defence for distributors and printers who unwittingly communicated a libel. The bill, with cross-party support, was to be introduced in the Lords, by the Lord Chancellor, in February.

The government Whips' Office in the Lords set about secretly recruiting a sympathetic peer to introduce the amendment agreed at the Downing Street meeting. An approach was made to the cross-bencher Lord Hoffman, a Law Lord with impeccable credentials, who appreciated Hamilton's plight. In consultation with the government's parliamentary draftsmen, a wording was agreed:

Where the conduct of a person in or in relation to proceedings in Parliament is in issue in defamation proceedings,
he may waive for the purposes of those proceedings, so far
as concerns him, the protection of any enactment or rule of
law which prevents proceedings in Parliament being
impeached or questioned in any court or place out of
Parliament . . . the waiver by one person of that protection
does not affect its operation in relation to another person
who has not waived it.

The government wanted to avoid the charge of being seen to
promote a significant constitutional change purely for the benefit of one of their own backbenchers. Both Lord Hailsham in the
Lords and Tony Newton in the Commons stressed the government's neutrality on Lord Hoffman's amendment: it was a matter for Parliament to decide. But despite being granted a free
vote, behind the scenes Tory peers were expected to lend their
support, with the Whips themselves pressured by Hamilton and
his supporters all the way.

IGA went into full-scale lobbying mode. I wrote to a number
of Conservative peers whom I knew well. Lord Finsberg, a prin-
cipled and loyal friend whom I had known for over thirty years,
acted as my link to the government Whips' Office in the Lords
and agreed to speak to the amendment and lobby other peers on
my behalf. Baroness Thatcher ostentatiously turned up in the
chamber for the debate and was joined by Lord Parkinson in the
'content' lobby. More big names, such as Lord Tebbit, voiced
their support in advance.

From the opposition benches, Baroness Turner was totally
supportive, although the Labour Whips' Office informed her
that in the debate she could only speak from the backbenches
and would not be allowed to vote.

For those unimpressed by the sight of the former PM and
Cabinet ministers supporting the amendment, Lord Hoffman
persuaded many senior judges and peers from all sides with the
clarity of his argument: although it was undoubtedly in the public interest to guarantee freedom of speech in Parliament, he

said, there was no public interest in allowing newspapers free licence to make defamatory statements about what honourable Members got up to in the course of their parliamentary duties.

On 7 May 1996 Lord Hoffman's amendment to the Defamation Bill passed the House of Lords by 157 to 57. The amendment became part of the bill.

We now turned our attention to the Commons, mounting a huge lobbying operation with Neil in close contact with the Whips. We wrote to every single Tory MP, as well as lots of our friends on the Labour benches. The Conservative MPs Ian Twinn and Michael Brown rallied support on the government side.

On the morning of the debate, 24 June 1996, MPs read in the House magazine an article by Neil. He argued for a restoration of the balance of power:

The current situation is irrational, anomalous and absurd ... Newspaper editors have vastly more power to influence the public than most MPs or even Ministers. 'As flies to wanton boys, are we to the gods; they kill us for their sport.' They can devastate our lives and destroy our capacity to carry out the functions for which we were elected.

Libel actions are not fun for the defamed MP. They are hugely expensive, time-consuming and often very wounding as the libels will be repeated during the trial. Editors play with their proprietors' money not their own. The libel may have screamed from front-page headlines but the apology often nestles at the bottom of an inside page.

Urging MPs from both sides of the House to support him he wrote:

To deny MPs alone the right to use the power to sue for libel turns the Bill of Rights into a Charter for Wrongs.

Compared to the quality of the contributions in the House of Lords, the Commons debate degenerated into something of a farce. Tony Newton, the Leader of the House, restated the government's neutrality: 'We believe it is a parliamentary matter and that each individual Member of Parliament should exercise his or her judgement.' A number of new amendments were tabled – some of which would have struck out Lord Hoffman's clause. Sir Terence Higgins made the fatuous suggestion that the matter be looked into by a committee of both Houses of Parliament – which would have kicked the idea into touch – although this had already been rejected by the Lords. Labour's spokesman, Paul Boateng, got muddled over which amendment would do what. MPs then arriving in the chamber complained of confusion as to what was going on. This prompted other Members, who had sat through the debate, to ask whether it was in order for Members to arrive late in the chamber, then stand up and complain they did not know what was going on. No sooner had the Speaker calmed everybody down than the seven o'clock bell rang and the House had to move on to other business.

To our great relief, when the vote was ultimately taken, later that evening, Hoffman's clause remained within the bill, which was passed by the Commons by 264 votes to 201. On 4 July 1995 it received Royal Assent.

Neil Hamilton immediately took advantage of his new right to waive parliamentary privilege and we kick-started our libel action. As Lord Williams was unable to act for us because of his involvement with another case, on the advice of Carter-Ruck we instructed new counsel in the form of the Ulster-born QC and former parliamentarian Richard Ferguson. At our first meeting, neither Neil nor I was impressed by him. Whilst pleasant and bluff, we did not think that he compared favourably to Lord Williams. Indeed, after the first meeting with him, Neil, Andrew Stephenson, Andrew Smith and myself talked about the possibility of instructing someone else. We requested that Andrew Stephenson convey this to Mr Ferguson via our junior counsel, Victoria Sharp.

Once more the *Guardian* tried to wriggle out of defending the case. In court on 16 August 1996, their lawyers argued that because Tim Smith had not waived parliamentary privilege, the *Guardian* would be prevented from putting vital information before the court. But this time they lost and we were given a date for the expected four-week trial. Not September, as we had hoped; we were given Tuesday 1 October. We consulted our diaries. This was the week of the Labour Party Conference in Blackpool, and exactly a week before the Conservatives were due to meet in Bournemouth.

As we walked down the steps of the High Court, Christine, clearly delighted, began to regale us with an enthusiastic account of her and Neil's forthcoming trip to a wedding in Turkey. 'We're going to stay with some Turkish friends,' she explained. 'They're terribly rich. They've said we can stay two nights, but I'm sure we'll be able to stay longer if we want to. It will be a champagne occasion.' I looked at Clive. Were this couple ever going to learn?

With the trial date fixed, we were making final preparations and were eager to put this episode in our lives behind us. Although confident, it was naturally an anxious period. We did, however, have a social occasion that we were much looking forward to: the marriage of Sir Michael and Lady Grylls' daughter Lara to James Fawcett. The charming and ebullient Lara was someone Clive and I knew well, and we were delighted to accept the invitation. We learned that Christine and Neil Hamilton had been invited – which was hardly surprising, as Christine had been Michael's secretary for many years and he was very fond of her. Far more surprising was the fact that the Gryllses had also invited Mohamed Fayed and his wife. On learning that the parties to the libel action could all find themselves drinking champagne together on the lawns of the Gryllses' home in Dorset a few weeks before the trial, I telephoned Michael to express my alarm. 'Have you invited a detachment of the cavalry to keep us all apart?' I asked. Michael explained that he wanted all his friends to be present at his only daughter's wedding and had therefore included the Fayeds, who had been social friends of his for many years. We went to the wedding, but the Fayeds were not present.

Also in September, *Private Eye* reported that the 'unutterably witty' Neil Hamilton had delighted dinner guests after a conference on international corruption and crime at Jesus College,

Cambridge, with the remark, 'In 14 years of being a member of parliament I have never found a trough big enough for my snout.' I waited for him to rush to deny the remark . . . I am still waiting.

Contrary to some rumours, there was no pressure placed on Neil by the government or the Party to delay the action. He did not receive a single call on the subject from anyone. The government had, after all, just changed the law to allow the case to go ahead. We were confident we were going to win: a 90 per cent chance, our solicitors told us. A victory for Neil in the courts, would be a tonic for the government so close to an election, and perhaps draw a line under sleaze. Although the date for the trial was uncomfortable, the reaction of Sheila Gunn, the head of press at Conservative Central Office, was typical: 'God, must it be then?' she said when I rang to warn her.

'I'm afraid so.'

'Then we'll have to live with it,' she said. 'Of course I understand.'

I was back on the phone to Sheila Gunn within a few days, after I learned of another event scheduled for 1 October: Norma Major had agreed to sign copies of her bestselling book on Chequers in, of all places, Harrods. In stunned silence, Sheila Gunn heard the news. Mohamed Fayed was well known for his enthusiasm at being photographed with politicians and celebrities – although Margaret Thatcher had put her foot down and refused point blank to pose with Fayed for the cameras at her own Harrods book-signing. We considered the next day's headlines, should Norma Major, on the opening day of the trial, be trapped in the camera flash with the man who had accused her husband's government of corruption beaming away beside her.

'I understand the invitations may have already gone out,' I explained to Sheila Gunn. 'Is there anything you can do?'

'You just watch me,' was her response.

Within hours, much to Norma Major's annoyance, a public signing of her new book, *Chequers: The House and Its History*, at the Harrods bookshop was hastily cancelled. I doubt she will thank me for this.

Above, left to right: Sir Michael Neubert, Rt Hon Virginia Bottomley, Rt Hon John Major, myself and Rt Hon Sir Peter Lloyd. *Below*: Lord and Lady Tebbit with Mrs John Major. At IGA's tenth anniversary party (*Barry Swaebe*)

13

A CONFLICT OF
INTEREST

Would Fayed attend court? This was the question that occupied our minds as the trial approached. Would this larger-than-life character, prone to fits of rage and exaggeration, not to mention the subject of a damaging DTI report, submit himself to the perils of cross-examination in the witness box? Whether he turned up at the High Court or not, we felt, worked to our advantage. Without him, the *Guardian*'s allegations were completely unsubstantiated. If the Harrods boss did turn up, with flashy cars and an entourage of advisers in tow, we considered his temper and colourful use of the English language would be unlikely to leave the jury, or judge, much impressed.

The *Guardian* embarked on a strategy of causing maximum political embarrassment to the government. The Defamation Act came into effect on 5 September 1996. The same day, they subpoenaed the Prime Minister, the Deputy Prime Minister, Michael Heseltine, the Cabinet Secretary, Sir Robin Butler, and the former Chief Whip, Richard Ryder. In public, Alan Rusbridger, the *Guardian*'s editor, defended the subpoenas: 'Mr Hamilton claims that our article forced him out of office. We say that he didn't resign for five days, and that the Prime Minister himself said it was due to other unconnected allegations. So we need to cross-examine the Prime Minister and ask him what those were.' It was a fatuous argument: everyone knew exactly what the allegations were and Neil Hamilton had given a full account of the circumstances behind his resignation in his pre-trial witness statement. Rusbridger would have lost little sleep over ruining the Conservative Party Conference in Bournemouth. His hacks salivated at the prospect of John Major, who would be the first-ever serving Prime Minister to give evidence in a libel trial, defending the minister he had sacked, when his presence was required in Bournemouth to rally the troops at the last conference before the election.

As for my own appearance in the witness box, I did not relish it. With the party so low in the polls and with 'sleaze' the common currency of the day, to stand there as a Tory-identified lobbyist was not an enviable prospect. Every one of my actions, I could defend. Commission payments to MPs did not perturb me. The jury, I hoped, would understand that I was a businessman and that this was common practice in business. As for the small donations to MPs' fighting funds, it never occurred to me that they would be treated in the way that they were. But I did worry that some members of the jury might be prejudiced because of my sexuality.

There was a great deal at stake. The court had approved a special damages hearing to commence immediately after the libel trial to assess what compensation my company could reasonably claim for loss of earnings if we were to win. It was feasible that the jury could decide that Neil Hamilton and myself were such worthless characters, the *Guardian* need pay us only a penny each. But I could then go on and claim some compensation for the company.

The management consultants Stoy Hayward were commissioned to arrive at a reasonable amount to claim, comprising all the contracts we had lost and all the new contracts we might reasonably have been expected to win. Their swift report landed on the desk of Nigel Tait, a partner at Carter-Ruck, in September. He immediately dispatched a copy to the *Guardian*'s legal team, and was on the phone to them as it arrived.

'Yes, we've got it here. It's just arrived . . . I can't see a figure anywhere,' said the voice at the other end of the phone.

'Turn to page thirty-one,' said Nigel, 'you'll see it there.' There was total silence on the line. 'Are you still there?' the lawyer asked three times, as the *Guardian*'s man tried to absorb the figure Stoy Hayward had calculated: £10 million.

For the newspaper, we had upped the stakes dramatically. They knew their case was weak. Fayed had been very specific about the dates of his meetings with Hamilton and the amounts of cash he had allegedly handed over. He was also careful in stating that there were never any witnesses to these meetings. But for at least one encounter, Neil had a cast-iron alibi. An author friend of his, Tim O'Sullivan, had wanted to write a history of the Paris Ritz. Neil effected an introduction to its proprietor, taking his friend to meet Fayed at Harrods on 20 February 1989. At this meeting Fayed had confidently claimed (and still does) that he handed the MP £1,000 worth of gift vouchers. O'Sullivan, who was with both men throughout, saw nothing of the sort.

More worrying for the *Guardian* team were the three cheques which Fayed alleged were to place me in funds to pay Neil Hamilton and Tim Smith. I had already proved that this was not the case. Suddenly this bit of evidence was worth £10 million.

The paper's editorial staff hoped to fight on. But those in charge of the purse strings were not convinced that they would win. I understand that the paper's owners, the Scott Trust, met in September 1996 and decided, by the barest of margins, to carry on – realising that the only way to avoid a humiliating climbdown, which would damage the paper's editorial credibility, was to go on the offensive. They had to throw more resources at the problem. The well-known left-wing QC, Geoffrey Robertson, was recruited. On top of paying his enormous legal bills, they gave him an investigative team from the editorial desk to help try to uncover anything new and incriminating about Hamilton and me. Fayed, in particular, was told that the paper was in serious trouble and was just about to get a bill for £10 million. Was there not anything else, they pleaded, that he could remember? The result was remarkable.

For two years Fayed had maintained that the only money he had given me outside of our contract were the three cheques, which, he claimed, were for me to pass to MPs. Now, just days before the start of our trial, Fayed claimed that there had been cash, too. Fayed put his own Washington-based lawyer on to the case. Three members of staff were found who were prepared to testify that they had seen him put money in envelopes, allegedly for me. There was even a scribbled note, produced from a phone pad at 60 Park Lane, stating that Ian Greer had telephoned demanding 'his' cash. Parts of these statements have now been published. I recognise very little, and there is much which contradicts Fayed's earlier story. The authenticity of the telephone message has not been tested; nobody knows who wrote it – not even his secretaries.

But the new allegations from Park Lane were nothing compared to what the *Guardian*'s team found when they went fishing in Whitehall. From the Cabinet Office they demanded several boxes of papers relating to Hamilton's final days in office. Then they turned their attention to IGA. They already had every single piece of correspondence relating to the House of Fraser account. But they knew that these did not support their claims.

'They want our accounts,' groaned Andrew Smith one day about two weeks before the trial.

'Give them the lot,' was my reaction. 'They won't find anything.' We were growing exasperated. Whereas it seemed that we had to hand over absolutely every scrap of paper detailing everything about the company's activities and finances, we were demanding nothing from the other side. 'Why don't we go for Fayed's bank statements?' I pleaded in desperation to Carter-Ruck. I was told that it would be 'counter-productive'.

Our accounts were sent over to the *Guardian* team – along with the financial working papers for these years. Within days they were coming back with silly questions: 'There are some rather high figures for decorating – are you sure you spent that on IGA? Could you not have paid for the redecoration of Neil Hamilton's house in Cheshire?' No.

Then we made a tactical mistake. Our solicitors, advising us that we would be unlikely to receive £10 million in special damages, informed the *Guardian*'s lawyers that I was prepared to refer the claim to arbitration if the newspaper admitted their mistake and agreed to pay up to £2.5 million. It gave them the impression that we were weakening – which we weren't – and encouraged them to redouble their efforts.

It was Tuesday, exactly a week before the trial was due to start, when we first heard that they had come across something for which we could not find an immediate explanation. Andy Stephenson of Carter-Ruck telephoned Andrew Smith: 'They've been on about working papers and quite a few payments to Michael Grylls, MP. Can you explain them?' I was busy doing a million and one things elsewhere. No, Andrew Smith could not explain them. He knew only of the three commission payments I had told the Select Committee about back in 1990.

Sir Michael Grylls was away. For two days, the *Guardian*'s team faxed over detailed questions about payments – some marked as 'commission', others as 'fees' – that the accounts showed I had made to Michael Grylls. We could not see the relevance of this line of questioning: Fayed had claimed that he had never paid Michael Grylls and, in fact, that Michael had always behaved properly.

Two days later I found myself in a morning meeting in our counsel's chambers with my entire legal team. As I walked into the room, I looked at junior counsel, Victoria Sharp. She turned away. I realised for the first time that they were very worried.

For once in my life I did not have an answer. The *Guardian* had discovered at least six payments to Michael Grylls. 'I'm not saying that you've done anything wrong, Ian,' leading counsel Richard Ferguson explained. 'But this is very serious. Although it has nothing to do with cash for questions, it will damage your credibility. If you said three to the Select Committee and it's more than three, they will seek to make mincemeat out of you in the box. To have given wrong information to a Select Committee is serious.'

'Yes, I know that!' I snapped back. I began to feel an awful dawning realisation of the mess I was suddenly finding myself in. I turned to Andrew Smith – the young man who had fought in my corner for two years. He too appeared – understandably – shell-shocked.

I was floundering.

'I accept that it has nothing to do with cash for questions,' said Andy Stephenson, 'but unless you do have an explanation you are going to be destroyed in the box. They will take two days going through the accounts and your credibility will be damaged.'

'I provided the information that I had been given by a member of my staff when I gave evidence before the Select Committee,' I said. 'I didn't check it. It could, I suppose, have been more than three.'

'How many were there?' asked my solicitor.

'I've no idea. I would need time to work it out,' I replied.

Now, looking back, with a cool head and under less pressure, I am able to account for what had actually taken place. The *Guardian*'s lawyers found six payments described as 'commission' to Michael Grylls, totalling £32,000 and paid between March 1987 and September 1989, and an annual payment marked 'fees' for £10,000 – this was a fee for Michael's work on the Unitary Tax Campaign, which he had declared. Michael was not a director of or consultant to IGA. However, unintentionally, I had left Andrew Smith in the dark about this. Andrew had been a junior member of staff when the payments to Grylls were first made, and I had not told him about them. It was my fault, not his. As far as commission payments were concerned, I had, apparently, made six, not three. My staff had told me three and I had said three. I was careless in not having checked the figures personally. It was a genuine mistake. The fact was that I could have said twenty-three to the Select Committee and it would not have made any difference. I was now to pay the price for my carelessness. The *Guardian* lawyers would use this mistake to crucify me, I was told. My chances of winning my action in court had suddenly gone from 90 per cent to zero.

I stared at the three legal faces staring back at me. 'You should drop the case,' was their verdict.

'I need time to think,' was my reply. I cursed the Members of Parliament who had failed to take advice from the clerk to the Members' Interests Register as to what declarations were necessary and how they should declare them. If they had done so, I would not have appeared before the Select Committee in 1990. I had made the mistake of saying there were three payments to

Grylls, rather than six: had these been declared, there would have been no problem with proceeding with the trial. Under further pressure I reluctantly and sadly agreed to drop the action. On reflection, I believe that I received bad advice that morning.

'For God's sake! I didn't realise Greer had skeletons in his closet!' an angry Neil Hamilton boomed down the telephone to Andrew Smith that evening. Andrew, facing his own doubts about Greer's skeletons, could do little to calm him. 'If this whole thing collapses,' Neil went on, 'I expect Greer to pick up the bill! Tell him that!' He hung up.

I awoke early on Friday morning, blinking into the light. Was the drama of yesterday just a nightmare? No, it had happened. Was I going to give up? Did that sound like me? Slowly, as the morning progressed, I began to knock a little sense into myself. I found an ally. 'It's just not logically possible for your chances to go from 90 per cent to zero,' argued Andrew Stone. 'Fight on!'

Unaware that I was beginning to get my act together, Neil Hamilton set off for his own final briefing with the lawyers. For several minutes Ferguson, Sharp and Stephenson listened patiently to his raging about Greer's unexpected 'bombshell' of the day before.

'You ought to read this,' Richard Ferguson interrupted, bringing out a piece of paper. 'It's just arrived.'

Hamilton stared in horror at the sheet of paper. It was a subpoenaed minute from the Cabinet Office. Written by Michael Heseltine, it recorded the telephone conversation between the two men two years earlier at the time of his visit to the Wilmslow school. Had he had a financial relationship with Greer? Heseltine had asked. No, Hamilton had answered. The charitably minded would argue that Heseltine had asked the wrong question. Had Hamilton been asked if he had ever received any money from Greer, presumably he would have answered 'yes'.

And then something extraordinary happened. It was three o'clock on Friday afternoon. Our £10 million libel trial was due to begin on the following Tuesday. At this point, the entire legal team stood up and walked out of the room, leaving the numerous case files on the table in front of Neil Hamilton. They called this a 'conflict of interest' – although I have never received a satisfactory explanation of what this was.

We were thrown into total confusion. Ferguson sounded out possible terms with the *Guardian* – although I had not specifically discussed this with him. Andrew Stone set about trying to find new solicitors.

On Saturday morning, I woke up feeling bullish – not only will I fight on, I will do it on my own. By the time I arrived at the flat, Andrew Stone (somewhat dubious as to my chances of defending myself competently) had found solicitor Mark Stephens – the astute, larger-than-life, streetwise fighter from Stephens Innocent. Over two hours, he reassured me. 'I'm not terribly sure why you're so worried about the Grylls payments,' he said. As for Hamilton, Stephens wanted me to 'stick the knife in'.

We agreed to go over and meet Hamilton's new lawyers in the City that afternoon. We were, by this time, fully expecting Neil to throw in the towel. The Heseltine minute was in my view a killer blow. Added to Neil's non-declaration of commission payments to either the House of Commons authorities or the Inland Revenue, along with the Ritz jolly (and the second trip which we were to learn about much later), he was now carrying so much baggage he could barely mount the steps of the High Court. The *Guardian* lawyers would have a field day. If I was to go ahead, I had to break the shackles which bound us together.

Hamilton's new solicitor was the extraordinary, morning-coated, suede-shoed, bow-tied figure of Rupert Grey. A man with an almost Edwardian air, Grey was the complete opposite of Mark Stephens – and the two did not warm to each other. We sat, nine of us, around a large conference table: Neil and Christine, the ever-loyal Gerald Howarth and Rupert Grey on one side; Clive, Andrew Stone, Andrew Smith, Mark Stephens and myself on the other.

'You have got a major problem,' I told Neil. 'You have got to drop out.' I was not prepared to fight on shackled to him. Neil, though, had other ideas. The MP who had lobbied the government to change the law to allow him to bring the case was planning to portray himself as the hard-done-by innocent. He would not budge.

The question was: could we go on independently? We considered the costs. Already, Hamilton and I owed something in the region of £200,000 each. Now Carter-Ruck had walked away, we would each need to invest a further £100,000 instructing separate counsel and separate solicitors. While we hoped to recoup this from the trial, our chances of winning the case had rapidly diminished. If the other side's bills were similar and we lost, we could have been facing a total bill well in excess of £1 million.

We spent hours locked in that room, and agreed to discontinue the libel action, with each party bearing its own costs. Later that afternoon, the final amended defence arrived from the *Guardian*'s solicitors. It was the last straw. We knew they were piling on the pressure. For the first time – three days before the trial was due to start – I heard that Mohamed was claiming that I had received cash, in addition to cheques, to pass on to MPs. The claim was false, but it was another mountain to climb.

We began discussing terms.

At around six o'clock, Andrew Stone turned to me: 'What will the clients think if you pull out now, Ian? Won't it be taken as an admission? Could the business survive that?'

'I think some of them will be very relieved,' I answered. Many of my clients had reservations about my embarking on a lengthy court battle. Naïvely, I thought we could walk away – the original allegations would still stand, unproven, but apart from a hefty legal bill, we would not be any worse off. I never imagined the lunacy that was to follow and that the *Guardian* would release every detail from the papers they were meant to return – that fiction would become fact, that my defence would be used to attack me and that absolutely anything they said would be believed.

I was given one chance. The following afternoon, Sunday, Clive and I were sitting reading in the study of our Kingston home, both feeling totally washed out. It was our last day before the world would find out. We knew our lawyers were haggling over terms. The newspaper was demanding a contribution to its

costs – it was not enough to win, they had to be seen to humili-
ate. Mark Stephens was acting for me. Notwithstanding his
firm's previous conflict of interest, the eighty-two-year-old Peter
Carter-Ruck was also in the frame, acting on joint instructions to
negotiate an even settlement.

The phone rang. It was Mark Stephens. The *Guardian*, he said,
were prepared to go easy on me if I 'dished the dirt' on
Hamilton. They also wanted, he added, 'a couple of bodies' for
the Tory Party Conference the following week. 'They feel you
must know stories about ministers or backbenchers,' he went on.
'They'll even pay you what they get from Hamilton, and would
also be prepared to serialise your memoirs, should you write
them.'

The *Guardian* was throwing me a poisoned life-raft, shouting,
'Here, clamber aboard with us.'

I told my solicitor to refuse the offer. I left the room and sat
quietly upstairs alone for a while. I felt a strange sense of elation.
I had not given them their 'bodies', but I had also been proved
right about the kind of people I was up against – people prepared to ruin reputations in secret deals. And, believing their
own propaganda, they thought I'd be easily bought. The man
David Hencke had accused of being a party to bribery was the
same man that the *Guardian* had failed to bribe.

On the Monday, Neil Hamilton and I agreed to pay £15,000 in
total towards the *Guardian*'s costs. I was worried for my staff at
the Labour Party Conference in Blackpool, who were completely
unaware of the drama unfolding at home because we were
under instructions of strict confidentiality. The *Guardian* had
stipulated that if one word got out about the planned discontin-
uance, then the settlement terms would be off – they wanted to
be the first to break the story. Andrew Smith briefed my directors
on a conference call on the Monday afternoon, but this could not
begin to prepare them for the suffering and humiliation of the
next four days.

Within hours, fuelled by several hundred journalists,
the news began to filter through the hotel bars that the case had
collapsed.

Over the course of the next week, the *Guardian* began publishing material going to the heart of our case. The two commission payments to Hamilton came out within twenty-four hours, but were outrageously portrayed as 'evidence' of cash for questions. A day later, the *Guardian* effectively abandoned their assertion that the cheques for £18,000 from Mohamed Fayed were passed on by me to Neil Hamilton and Tim Smith. My case was to have been that this money was used to assist various constituency associations in the 1987 election. The *Guardian* portrayed this as 'evidence' of a further twenty-four MPs ensnared in the cash-for-questions affair. I never expected this information to become public and be portrayed in the way it has been. It was to kill my company.

In Blackpool, my staff had an appalling time. Their job was to assist their clients, often representing them on their conference exhibition stand. But their presence became embarrassing when Labour politicians would approach and whisper, 'You've not got IGA on there, have you?'

There was little point in my doing interviews – as my experience with ITN demonstrated. I was repeatedly pressed on whether Fayed had given me cash to pass on to MPs to ask questions. This I categorically denied, finally delivering the soundbite: 'This man [Fayed] passed me no money at any time. I categorically deny it. It would have been a corrupt act and I'm not a corrupt person and my company isn't corrupt.' But by the time I watched myself on *News at Ten*, Fayed was changing tack again through his spokesman, Michael Cole, and was admitting that the cheques that Fayed had given to me had, as I had always maintained, been for candidates' election funds. But, rather than ITN asking to reinterview me about this change of tack, they used their original soundbite. The carefully edited and scripted report portrayed me as a liar. I reproduce the transcript in full. It demonstrates the perils of the pre-recorded television interview.

Presenter Trevor MacDonald: The row over parliamentary sleaze spread beyond the former Trade Minister Neil Hamilton today, to embroil more than twenty MPs. They were all given money for their election campaigns by the lobbyist Ian Greer. He insisted today there were no strings attached, but in an astonishing intervention, the Harrods boss Mohamed Al Fayed said that he had given money to Mr Greer after Mr Greer told him 'you could hire MPs like taxis'. Adrian Britten reports.

Reporter Adrian Britten: The lobbyist Ian Greer was setting out his case in the studios of Westminster today, as the latest revelations added another twist to the furore over political funding. Had he taken money from Mohamed Al Fayed to help fund the election campaigns of twenty-four MPs?

Ian Greer: This man passed me no money at any time. I categorically deny it. It would have been a currupt act and I am not a corrupt person and my company isn't corrupt.

Adrian Britten: Yet through his spokesman, the Harrods boss tonight issued a defiant rebuttal, saying Mr Greer had asked for money, claiming you could hire MPs the same way as you hire a taxi.

Michael Cole: Mr Greer approached Mr Al Fayed and said he needed money for some of the MPs who were going to be fighting the 1986/7 general election. Mr Al Fayed agreed to give him money. He gave him two cheques, one for £12,000, one for £6,000 drawn on his personal account.

As the hysteria grew in public, my world disintegrated in private too. Clive stood by me loyally throughout, but I lost the person who, over fifteen years, I had come to regard as a son. Andrew Smith went out for lunch on the Thursday and never returned. Later in the afternoon he left a message with my housekeeper: 'Tell Ian I've quit,' he said. I have not seen him since. Andrew is a candidate, again, for the Tories in the 1997 election, and I understand he does not want his political career 'tainted' by further association with me. That's difficult to take. Having worked so hard on the case, he was desperate to point out that he didn't know about the extra payments to Michael Grylls. He is right. He should have known me well enough to realise that I would never have suggested otherwise.

Perhaps the saddest part of all this is the hurt caused to my parents and staff. Directors such as Jeremy Sweeney, Patrick Ferreira, Perry Miller and Susan Child, and my secretary, Liz Swindin, stood by me. Fayed and the *Guardian* have destroyed my company, which, over time, can be rebuilt; they have damaged people's careers, but, given time, they might recover. However, they have also succeeded in destroying what I considered to be my family, that is to say my staff. Those wounds will never heal.

Occasionally, through the bleakness of disaster, the example of a single individual keeps you going. During that dreadful week, it was the courage of Muriel Turner, an Opposition spokeswoman in the Lords. The Labour Baroness's association with IGA was well known. Indeed, her name appeared on our company notepaper. When she joined the IGA board, she had informed the Labour Chief Whip, in writing, and made a full declaration in the Lords' Register.

As the trial was being discontinued, we spoke on the telephone. Baroness Turner was already in Blackpool. I expected her to be asked by the press about her association with IGA. It happened on the Thursday afternoon, just outside the conference hall, when she was approached by a camera crew from ITN. Its reporters had already caused Chris Smith to squirm as he distanced himself from any association with the company. They might have expected a similar response from Baroness Turner. They underestimated the lady.

She refused to follow the newly established orthodoxy. Ian Greer was a friend, she said, and she believed him to be honourable. Within hours, she rang me from her hotel room. Her voice at the other end of the line was near to tears.

'Ian,' she said, 'I'm going to tell you something I never thought I would have to say. I've been fired from the frontbench.' After the ITN interview, when she got back to her room, she had been telephoned by Ivor Richard, a former minister and

Labour's Deputy Chief Whip in the Lords. Having just heard her comments on ITN, he ordered her not to leave her hotel room. 'Don't step foot outside. Have them send your dinner up to your room,' he commanded. Some time later she was telephoned with the news that she had been dismissed. Assurances that she had been given a few hours earlier as to how her dismissal would be handled were subsequently broken. But, despite her sickening treatment, Baroness Turner was anxious not to criticise the Labour leader. 'I don't think Tony knows how it's being handled,' she told me.

Its handling was to become worse. There was no point in anyone from IGA, the new pariah, staying in Blackpool. The staff could do nothing but embarrass the clients. Desperate measures were called for. I ordered an emergency board meeting for the following afternoon. Baroness Turner agreed to catch the early morning train from Blackpool, travelling down with IGA director Robbie MacDuff, in time for the meeting.

She informed her Labour colleagues. I assume it was one of them who tipped off the press. 'The disgraced Baroness has been forced to leave the conference under cover of darkness' was the gloss placed on her pre-dawn departure. At Euston, she stepped off the train and walked into a pack of waiting reporters and camera crews. Another dozen jostled her as she arrived at our offices. For some viewers, the treatment meted out to this sixty-nine-year-old lady, who had faithfully served the Labour movement for years and who had lost her husband only a year earlier, may have seemed cruel. But it illustrated a point: New Labour spin doctors were prepared to embarrass anyone if it would provide a soundbite or headline – 'Labour Tough On Sleaze'. I would rather have the Old Labour Party, which had principles, than New Labour, I thought.

The previous night, Clive and I had talked late into the evening. Ultimately I had to make a decision. IGA was my company. We had asked for our clients' loyalty for over two years; I had asked the same of my staff. I received it from both. I began to feel very strongly that enough was enough – there was a serious danger that this loyalty would be exhausted. While I was innocent of the allegations, I felt I should step aside.

'There's no point my continuing with the company,' I explained to my staff seated around the table in the flat above our offices that afternoon. The mood was sombre and apprehensive. 'One of the reasons I have not sold the company before now is because it has always been my intention to hand it over to you. Events have overtaken me. As you can see, I am forced to do this earlier than expected. But it can still be saved. Take my 100 per cent shareholding. Share it between you. Change the company's name. I will walk away and take nothing but my pension.'

This was another misjudgement on my part. I left them to discuss my proposition, never for one moment believing they would turn it down. Perhaps if Andrew had still been around, he could have held them together. The majority panicked, and those who were prepared to tough it out realised the impossibility of their task. The board needed to stick together if the company was to survive. Rather than salvage what they could, many jumped ship. Mortgages and other financial considerations played a part in their decision. They were not prepared to take the risk.

Ian Greer Associates Ltd, IGA (Europe) Ltd and IGA International Ltd, the one-time multi-million-pound enterprise employing almost fifty people, the most successful, the most professional and the most effective public affairs company in Europe, went into voluntary liquidation just before Christmas 1996.

My ninety-two-year-old mother called, anxious about us both. 'You are,' she assured me, 'very much in our prayers. You must know that God is on your side.' Later, talking about her call, Clive and I laughed as we reflected on what could possibly have happened had God been working against us!

At times like these you learn a lot about people, and I have tried, wherever possible, to remember those who have been most loyal and kind. But even more, you learn something about yourself. If someone had said to me two years ago, 'You are going to go through the most appalling suffering, an obsession will grip your every waking moment, you will suffer sleepless nights, your ninety-year-old parents will be distressed to an almost unimaginable degree, your friends will be pursued, you will be spied upon, you will suffer lies and abuse,' I would, perhaps, have responded, 'No. I cannot cope with that.' Well, I've learned that you can cope and you can come through it.

14

REFLECTIONS

At sixty-four, I resist the temptation to look back at what has been, without doubt, a very full life. It is more exciting to look forward. Despite the destruction of my business, and the pain caused to my family and friends, the experiences and the friends gained over the last three years must provide the launch pad for the next stage in the great adventure.

The role of the lobbyist has changed dramatically from the day IGA was born back in 1982. Today, the chief executive is not content to leave politics to the politicians. He or she recognises that the constant flow of legislation emanating from Westminster or Brussels will ultimately affect their firm and its future; better they ensure that legislation is carefully analysed – not only by Whitehall, Westminster, Brussels and Strasbourg, but by them, too. Whichever party wins power in the 1997 election, there is one thing of which we can be sure: there will be more laws. 'Rolling back the state', 'cutting red tape', 'getting government off your back' are all easy slogans. They are rarely realised. Lobbyists will still be needed in the future, but their role will change as they offer strategic advice from the sidelines, rather than playing a leading role upfront.

As for the politicians? I recall a warm afternoon in the summer of 1995. Lady Olga Maitland and I were having tea in her office at the House of Commons. We had been arguing for over a quarter of an hour.

'It's true you know, they won't let you speak,' I insisted.

'But I've just come back. I'm one of the few people in this place who knows what's going on over there.'

The MP for Sutton and Cheam had just returned from Pakistan, which was experiencing a period of unrest. Her trip had been at the invitation of the Government in Islamabad. By chance, a Commons debate on foreign affairs was scheduled for the following week. She wanted to speak in the debate.

'I don't want to lobby, for heaven's sake. I just want to talk about Pakistan,' she explained again. We had been over this point.

'Phone Sir Gordon Downey, if you don't believe me.'

Olga didn't believe me. She picked up the phone to the new Parliamentary Commissioner for Standards, who had recently been appointed as part of Lord Nolan's Westminster shake-up. Within minutes, Sir Gordon was patiently listening to a high-speed travelogue of the Sutton MP's recent visit to the subcontinent, including her meeting with the then Prime Minister, Benazir Bhutto, her social affairs adviser and various non-governmental organisations, along with the issues that she had been briefed about and why she wanted to speak in the debate. 'I will be able to give the most up-to-date picture on the situation in Pakistan,' she said in conclusion. 'So can I speak?'

There were a few moments of silence. Through the open window, I listened to the buzz of the traffic circling Parliament Square.

'Oh, really. I didn't realise that. Thank you,' she said, replacing the receiver. Turning to me, she said, 'You're right.'

Welcome to the post-Nolan world of British politics, where MPs declare jars of honey, Tony Blair remembers to register a night with his family at the West End musical *Oliver!*, and Paddy Ashdown records the gift of a rug. Where MPs who know something about a subject are debarred from speaking, if they have been the guest of an overseas government. (Curiously, however, if the British taxpayer has footed the expenditure involved in a visit abroad, they are then free to speak.) Where Members are no longer regarded as honourable – not even by one another – and must give evidence on oath to their own Select Committees.

Welcome to the Westminster of the professional politician. Will he serve his constituents any better than his predecessor? I doubt it. The rigidly controlled system in America has not produced better policies or better government – or indeed fewer allegations of corruption.

Lord Nolan concluded in May 1995 that confusion, not corruption, was eroding standards of conduct in public life. So he
put a virtual end to MPs' outside earnings – a move which bred
resentment on the backbenches. Members of Parliament
received a small pay rise, which still left them underpaid. In my
opinion, they should have had their salaries doubled and at the
same time the number of constituencies should have been sub-
stantially reduced, thus leaving the taxpayer no worse off. I
would have given MPs an efficient staff and, risking considerable unpopularity, abolished the secretarial allowance which
allows an MP to hire his or her spouse.

Even before the emergence of Nolan, too many candidates
seeking political office had little or no experience of the real
world. They were former special advisers, they were parliamentary researchers, they were the bright young things of Smith
Square and Walworth Road – men and women who had never
known the battles of the boardroom or the shop floor, who had
never started their own business and struggled day and night to
see it rise. Few had ever faced a serious threat of unemployment.
Some were even lobbyists.

The battles they knew were those fought across the dispatch
box. These young bloods on the hustings in 1992, and again in
1997, are drawn from the trades and professions across the country to represent their peers at Westminster. They were already
there – party staff who temporarily left the metropolis to voyage
in search of a safe seat somewhere in the country.

I have never subscribed to the view that Members of
Parliament should be consultants or directors of lobbying companies – over the last three years IGA's rivals have quietly shed
the paid MPs they retained in these capacities – but if we forbid
this new crop of MPs the chance to develop outside interests,
there is no opportunity for them to gain any experience of the
real world. Let them supplement their income if they want to.
Let them experience something other than the hype of
Westminster.

And let them get back to the job they were elected for.
Members of Parliament are not social security officers. They are

not there to sort out the drains. They are this country's legislators. Yes, the constituency hospital closure and the road bypass should rightly occupy their time and their postbags. These are local concerns decided at the national level. But over half the constituents attending an MP's weekend surgery would do better visiting their town halls and raising their concerns with their local rather than their national politicians. If we expect our MPs to compete with local councillors, then we are demeaning their role. Meanwhile, bad laws are being passed.

Having spent my life among politicians, I do not know of any who are corrupt. There are those who are bright and those who are less so. Some behave both improperly and foolishly. There are many who are selfish and arrogant and some the opposite – caring and compassionate – as in any walk of life.

Two and a half years ago the foreign owner of a medium-sized British company alleged that certain MPs and a certain lobbying firm he had once hired were guilty of corruption. He unleashed a media frenzy. His allegations received front-page attention and led every news bulletin for days. Ministers resigned. Scores of journalists and dozens of lawyers worked full-time on the story for months, looking for more examples of corruption. The image of the Mother of all Parliaments was greatly damaged. They knew that during its lifetime that same firm of lobbyists had been hired by over 300 other British companies. They had the opportunity to ask those other companies if any suggestion had ever been made to pay MPs to undertake parliamentary work. They asked former employees. They searched the company's records. They sought any example of corruption – just one which relied on more than one man's word.

Scores of journalists and dozens of lawyers failed in their search. They found nothing to suggest corruption involving the 300 other companies which had been clients of IGA.

Mr Fayed has come to Britain and, by alleging widespread corruption, greatly damaged the British Parliament, which in my view was rightly recognised internationally as a model of Parliamentary democracy, whose Members had a reputation for honesty and integrity. His assault on our political institutions has added to the constant media attacks on the Royal Family and the Church. Cynicism, especially among the young, has been the result. But we damage our institutions at our peril. Although far from perfect, they are unlikely to be replaced by anything better.

During the research for this book, I found a file reminding me of a parliamentary battle IGA had fought, and won, in the early nineties for an organisation called the TV Listings Campaign. This was a consortium of newspapers and magazines seeking to end the monopoly enjoyed by the *Radio Times* and *TV Times* over advance information about television programmes. A member of the consortium, and therefore a client of IGA, was the *Guardian* newspaper. It seems ironic, now, that Mr Preston should have paid IGA to lobby on his behalf, given the high-handed tone he later adopted about lobbyists. It is even more ironic to think that the *Guardian* could have been paying IGA at the same time as Mr Fayed was later to claim that he had been making payments to IGA to pass to Members of Parliament.

I once wanted to be a reporter. I now don't think I would have lasted very long. Over the last few years, the battle has been to increase circulation figures at any cost. Committees of editors and journalists handed out gongs like 'Newspaper of the Year' and 'Journalist of the Year' to other editors and journalists, or to themselves, but throughout the whole Fayed affair the British media have done little to enhance their own reputation. Last autumn, my aged parents were staying with me for the weekend when Simon Heffer, the self-opinionated and subjective Saturday columnist for the *Daily Mail*, chose to write in his column, despite never having met me, that he thought I was a 'pimp and a tart'. 'Why is he calling you that, dear?', my ninety-two-year-old mother asked. I had no answer for her.

If my account of this whole affair sounds bitter, if it is too much like special pleading, or a cry for your sympathy, then I have failed. I have sought only to tell the other side of the story – the part that was edited out of reports in your morning newspapers. I walked into most encounters with my eyes open. I did not expect favours from journalists. But, I suppose, I did not anticipate lies. Often as I read the accounts of my actions I would exclaim over and over again, 'But what about . . .?' Some vital bit of information, undoubtedly known to the reporter, would have been left out – not a redeeming feature but a clue to the wider context which would have put things into perspective. What newspaper has told you that 45,000 parliamentary questions are asked every year?

The interpretation put on my actions by journalists who had their own agendas, who were never interested in finding out mine, seemed oddly at variance with what I used to believe was an honourable tradition of objective reporting. The selective quotation of my words – as in the *Guardian's* reporting of the sting or my appearance on *News at Ten* – left me angry and defenceless.

Two senior journalists from a well-known newspaper (not the *Daily Telegraph*) came to see me recently to discuss plans to serialise this book. It was the first time I had met them and their manner suggested that they had believed everything that had been written about me. Sitting opposite me, they seemed rather nervous, trapped in a small room at the top of the 'Fixer's Fortress' with no visible means of escape.

I was handed a piece of paper with a list of 'essential questions which must be answered in full'. The first was, 'What arrangements were in place for Ian Greer to talk to the Prime Minister on a daily basis?' Another read, 'What outstanding arrangements does Ian Greer have with ministers and MPs to pay them money when they leave office or Parliament for services rendered?' These were amongst twenty or so absurd questions to which I was expected to produce answers. The questions were not difficult to answer, but in doing so, it was clear that the journalists were not going to get the material that they confidently expected. The six-figure contract offer, which had already been made, was put on hold, demonstrating once again that there is virtually no interest in the simple truth, only in sensationalism, particularly if it damages and causes hurt.

This book has been an attempt to provide the wider context, to fill in the gaps, to give the words before and after the selective quotes you may have read. I have also given you the mistakes